I0605114

GUEST PRIVILEGES

GUEST PRIVILEGES

QUEER LIVES AND FINDING HOME IN THE MIDDLE EAST

GAAR ADAMS

2580 Craig Rd.
Ann Arbor, MI 48103
www.dzancbooks.org

Library of Congress Cataloging-in-Publication Data Available upon Request

ISBN 9781938603303
First US edition: September 2025
Cover design by Steven Seighman
Cover photographs courtesy of arabianEye FZ LLC/Alamy

Interior design by Michelle Dotter

Printed in the United States of America

10 9 8 7 6 5 4 3 2 1

To John D'Souza and the memory of Betty D'Souza, who embarked on a perilous journey across the globe a half century ago for the sake of a home, a family, a life still to be made.

And to Deb and Duncan, for understanding that I had to embark on one, too.

TABLE OF CONTENTS

"If you're lucky in your life, a place, or two, will be offered to you. That place won't be where you were born or grew up. It will be at some distance, and it will never be yours—you'll always be a visitor or guest. ... People treat each other better here, all of them, at all levels, and maybe there aren't even any levels, all the old ways we use to divide and rank one another."

Paul Lisicky, *Later: My Life at the Edge of the World*

"It's almost impossible to make a life here, or have lived here, without being haunted by the historical encounters between one's own community and the region itself."

Momtaza Mehri, *Dispatches from the Black Gulf*

"We have never been queer, yet queerness exists for us as an ideality that can be distilled from the past and used to imagine a future. The future is queerness's domain. Queerness is a structuring and educating mode of desiring that allows us to see and feel beyond the quagmire of the present. The here and now is a prison house."

José Esteban Muñoz, *Cruising Utopia*

INTRODUCTION: A RING

(Dubai, United Arab Emirates: Prashant and Mohammed)

Before dusk could settle over the vacant lot, I climbed a pile of cinder blocks to watch two taxi drivers wrestle bare-chested in the sand. The shorter one, standing a full head beneath the furrowed brow of his challenger, punched his thighs in pre-match theatrics while plumes of dust rose from the makeshift ring like ill omens portending his swift defeat. But when the fighters locked arms to grapple, the scrawny man pulled loose, swinging a heel into the crook of his larger opponent's knees, pitching him to the ground. As beads of sweat coursed down their torsos, the smaller wrestler grabbed the fallen man's kaupina loincloth, using it for traction to climb atop his hulking frame, triumphant. In under a minute, the bout had finished. But this unexpected victory felt like an aftershock to the initial surprise of the event itself: two South Asian cabbies, nearly naked, sparring in a barren Dubai sandlot. In a place where simply donning shorts could run afoul of the city's notoriously strict penal codes, I felt like I was witnessing not just a feat of athletics but a challenge to an entire sociopolitical order. Although it would take much longer to understand that the subversion I experienced that evening was also personal.

I was not the only spectator that day. The victor bounded out of the ring, and a stout, bearded man pulled him into a firm embrace, wiping away the sand that caked his brow. Clutching each other's shoulders, the men grazed foreheads and grinned through a muted exchange before a throng of fans hoisted the wrestler upon their shoulders. In the far corner of the ring, the next pair of wrestlers stripped out of their shalwar kameez, rubbing their biceps for warmth as they waited for the rabble to subside. Only a small tract of reclaimed land separated the sandlot from the open water, and fresh January winds blew in steadily off the Gulf. I jotted a quick line in my notebook about making sure to mention this winter chill. It was one of those things I often heard people back home in Midwest America invariably getting wrong, spouting some variation of "*Oh, but isn't it always hot over there in the desert?*" When I moved to the United Arab Emirates in 2010, I tried to dismiss questions like this as innocuous, but I was just beginning to recognize the outsized role they played in how I was taught to understand not just the region but my relationship to it as well.

I drove 150 kilometers from my home in Abu Dhabi to the sandlot earlier that afternoon for the same reason I often hopped into my car back then: to research an article. It was 2014, my fifth year living on the Arabian Peninsula, and I was filing arts and culture pieces for a variety of American magazines and international media outlets. The personal maelstrom of packing up my life and shipping it to the Middle East for the first time coincided almost to the hour with a larger seismic shift: President Barack Obama's January 20, 2009, inaugural address in which he took the remarkable step of singling out the Muslim world by name, calling for "a new way forward based on mutual interest and mutual respect."

Living in the Middle East in the early days of a new American presidential administration, the mood felt almost buoyant, as though the region had emerged from the Bush foreign policy era as one might from an extended hurricane: unfurling from a defensive crouch to open up the shutters, survey the damage, and let in the light. But over the ensuing half-decade, I watched as American rhetoric on the region failed to match the ideals of Obama's speech. The same year I began research for this wrestling article, *Newsweek*—at the time, one of the most storied magazines in US publishing—ran a cover photo on the Arab Spring that featured two bearded men, fists clenched, with the headline "Muslim Rage" in bold, capital letters. The incendiary cover seemed to encapsulate the dual lenses through which the American media presented the region: otherization and danger.

I first pitched my editor this article about pehlwani, a traditional form of South Asian wrestling, in the spirit of offering a critical response to this worldview. In addition to the heterogeneity of the sport's origins—the sixteenth-century Mughals who conquered northern India melded their Sufi-infused Persian koshti pahlavani wrestling with the region's Hindu-inflected mallayuddha form—pehlwani wrestling also enjoyed popularity across a wide swath of culturally varied Indian states, Pakistani provinces, and Bangladeshi districts. I imagined penning an article that illuminated how Dubai, the diverse capital of an Islamic country, uniquely brought together die-hard wrestling fans regardless of passport color, socioeconomic status, or religion. My hope was that if I could illustrate this reality to even a few readers, I might be able to provide a counterbalance to the onslaught of inflammatory headlines and cover stories around me.

In the face of so many misconceptions, my initial impulse was to fortify this pehlwani article with extensive historical research. I dove into the facts: treading through minutia including the physical mechanics of single-leg takedowns and the linguistic particularities of Urdu wrestling vocabulary. But when it finally came time to sit and write the article, instead of striking the keys on my laptop, I found myself continually hitting play on my audio recorder. Again and again, I would return to the interviews I conducted, poring over hours of conversations with wrestlers and spectators both banal and consequential on topics ranging from laundry to love, jobs to heartbreak, lifelong dreams attained to those yet unfulfilled. It was a troubling pattern I noticed intensifying with each new story I pitched: an inability to begin writing coupled with a looming sense that the completely unrelated material stored on my recording device was somehow more salient to my articles than any of my other research. And so it was that, in those days, I would sit and stare at a blinking cursor for hours, caught between a deadline, a word count, and a nagging dread that I could not at all explain to readers the reality of such a misunderstood place without starting the story somewhere else entirely: a beginning rooted not in historical narrative, but buried somewhere on my recorder in the depths of these stories.

"Isn't it harder for them there?" an editor working on the pehlwani article asked me when I first pitched the story. It was another one of those pervasive questions I would hear about migration to the Gulf region, home to the largest population of migrants per capita on the planet. But as much as it was a question, it was also a presupposition—one I wanted to prod with my own questions: Who is "them"? To where is "there" being compared? And what are the metrics for calculating the difficulty of making a life in a foreign landscape: one's ability to stay safe, demand capital, raise a heteronormative family, achieve a modicum of personal fulfillment?

I realized only later that these questions about the perils of migration to the Gulf had an undeniably similar shape to the ones surrounding my own journey to this landscape where queerness was illegal. But uncovering the answer of what draws people to live and work in places where they risk imprisonment, deportation, torture, and death took me on a fraught, decade-long journey of dislocation across the notorious Gulf states to conduct interviews with a kaleidoscope of queer people and migrants: flamboyant Iranian figure skaters, Filipino manicurists throwing secret drag parties, a ragtag group of international parkour athletes who call the Gulf their own despite no hope of citizenship. It would become a journey not just in unlearning my own preconceptions of the misunderstood region and the notion of home, but in reckoning with our very ideas of sexuality, gender, migration, and belonging itself.

▽▽▽

I arrived at the sandlot early on a Friday afternoon as men waited for pehlwani to begin. At that hour, the vast expanse still served as a cricket pitch—a confluence of several pitches, really, with dozens of games butting up against each other. At the nucleus of each one, batsmen darted between wickets, dodging bits of rebar that poked out of the sand. But it was the action along the outskirts that transfixed me most: players from entirely separate matches skirting past one another with such ease that it almost called into question whether the exacting lines of a regulation cricket pitch were really necessary at all.

Boundaries of nationality and occupation blurred just as fluidly. One cricket team consisted of six Pakistani docksmen who unloaded cargo with gantry cranes from nearby Port Rashid, four Indian merchants who sold jewelry in the gold souk a few blocks away, and a few Bangladeshi construction workers who traveled by illegal shared taxis from their workers' accommodation on the southern edge of the city. Pehlwani may have drawn this particular breadth of players together, but Deira, the buzzy commercial neighborhood encircling the sandlot, had served as Dubai's diverse heart since the city's first rapid period of growth in the nineteenth century, well before it entered the global consciousness as an oil boomtown.

That was another misguided notion I often heard about Dubai: the idea that the city existed solely as some kind of modern sand-to-skyscraper urban miracle. In reality, just beyond the cricket pitches sat the mouth of Dubai Creek, a shallow tidal channel that first welcomed diverse foreigners hundreds of years ago. Generations of tradesmen from cities and towns across the Indian subcontinent hopped off dhows and other merchant vessels here. The players in the lot that afternoon dug their toes into the same sand as the migrant workers who shaped the first nascent iteration of a cosmopolitan city centuries earlier.

For most of the men who gathered to watch pehlwani, Friday marked their only day of rest. The jovial effervescence in the air when I first set foot in the lot—players shouting, laughter ricocheting from one cricket match to another—only intensified as the afternoon wore on, as though the waning sunlight were a damp cloth to be wrung, squeezed of every last drop. More men streamed into the lot; some joining the cricket melee still decked out in their finest Friday attire: meticulously tailored achkan jackets, bright red mojari sandals, and intricately embroidered sindi caps. The matches continued to swell in both size and number until it seemed not one more player could wedge himself into the sand; then, just as the sun dipped beneath the nearest row of squat buildings, a man trundled forth with a wheelbarrow, sprinkling the sand with water in an oval formation. As he fashioned a wrestling ring, the cricketers parted wordlessly and formed a roughshod circle, completing their weekly transformation from sportsmen to eager spectators.

I watched two matches play out, then, just as a barrel-chested Maharashtrian wrestler vanquished his Pashtun challenger in a tight leg-lock during the evening's third match, the maghrib call to prayer rippled across the lot. The pehlwani concluded as abruptly as it had commenced. The crowd disbanded; a few men ambled toward the nearest mosque, others headed for the tandoori restaurants in the next block. But as the last of the Bangladeshi construction workers dashed across the road to catch a bus back across town, I saw two figures still lingering along the edge of the ring: the scrappy, unexpected winner of the first bout and his stocky friend who had so warmly embraced him in celebration.

The friend kneeled down, gingerly stretching the wrestler's left leg to horizontal while kneading his calves. With broad shoulders, a gray-flecked beard, and a slight paunch visible even beneath his breezy kameez, it looked like he probably had been an athlete himself once, perhaps many years ago. As a dusky half-light descended, it took a quick shout of welcome from the wrestler before I realized that his extended arm was not stretching but beckoning me toward them with a hearty wave.

Their voices trailed off on my approach, and when they abruptly stood as I tried to take a seat next to them, I was sure I had misread their welcome. But the wrestler nodded to the dim light cast by the fish market across the lot, offered a warm smile, and ushered me forward. As they led me across the sand toward the silhouettes of milling shoppers, neither man said a word. I remembered their hushed conversation at the end of the match and resisted my impulse to fill the void with my own voice. Preserving the silence suddenly felt inexplicably vital, as though any conversation might be swept up by the gathering breeze, our words carried too far off into the murky night.

▽▽▽

Harsh fluorescents dangled from the vaulted roof, banishing darkness to the market's open-air perimeter. With evening already settling in, the building hummed not with customers but with the din of fishmongers cleaning up from a day of brisk trade. Most had already stripped out of their blue-trimmed uniforms, slinging water by the pailful at little hills of ice stained copper from the blood of the day's catch. I caught the melody of "Namukku Pokam," an old Keralan song, and turned to listen to a man in a sweat-ringed undershirt warble the tune as he hosed down his tiled countertop. *Let's go, let's go*, he sang in Malayalam, as though his pleas might coax the last of his debris toward the drain.

Streams of Urdu, Hindi, and Bengali also flowed down the wide cement aisles. Amidst this torrent of languages, my two companions finally spoke. The wrestler introduced himself as Mohammed. In the sudden, jarring brightness of the market, I realized that he was in fact not scrawny at all. He towered over each fishmonger we wandered past even as they stood tall to catch our attention, abandoning the fastidious scrubbing of their workstations in hopes of landing one last sale for the day. The other man, Prashant, offered me a firm handshake while twirling his thick mustache with his free hand. When he explained that he was Mohammed's coach, I caught the wrestler shooting me a quick, wry smile.

Prashant examined each fish meticulously, leaning down to appraise the scales on piles of wilting mackerel and hamour like fine embroidery. When the first merchant declared his price, Prashant unleashed a diatribe about the exorbitant cost, scolded him for the quality of his fish, and threw his hands to the sky in exasperation, walking on to the next vendor just out of earshot. I watched in amusement as he rebuked the next six vendors with the same flair. He finally stopped in front of a burly man with a rounded face, placing his arm around the man's back and lowering his voice to a conspiratorial whisper. When the man handed over three firm Nile perch, Prashant pulled him into a tight hug. As he walked away from the vendor, I asked Mohammed if the two of them had been haggling.

"No, no—he is our friend," Mohammed laughed. "Every week, Prashant tells him the prices from all the other men, and then he gives us any fish we want." Looking back now, perhaps it was at that very moment, with Prashant grinning broadly and swinging his plastic bag bursting with fish, that I should have noted his particular kind of acumen—of reading people, of assessing situations—that I did not yet possess.

While Mohammed took our food to an Egyptian grill at the other end of the market, Prashant led me to a small kiosk, paid for three Coca-Colas, and walked outside into the darkness. We sat, resting our backs against the peeling blue paint of a market pillar, and gazed out toward the inky sea.

"Mohammed is," he paused, seeming to consider his next words carefully, "my very good wrestler." Prashant smiled not at me but out toward the water, his eyes glinting with the same wiliness as when he bade farewell to his fishmonger friend. I let the many questions jockeying for position in my mind settle and the quiet wash over us.

Several moments passed before he spoke again. When he did, I was surprised to hear him start his story not at what I considered a logical beginning—in his homeland, the place I had heard so many people reminisce about in these quiet, wistful moments, thousands of miles from friends and family—but in Dubai, this city that was not his.

"My father came here in 1976," Prashant said, turning his back to the sea and pointing toward where Dubai International Airport lay nestled in a quiet residential neighborhood a few miles eastward. He raised his eyebrows as he emphasized the year, searching my face for recognition. His father's arrival would have made him part of the first major wave of Indian migrant workers to the UAE after the country's founding just three years earlier. Later, I would need to ask Prashant where his father arrived from, and though he finally said the name of an industrial town in Punjab, he mentioned it like it was an aside, casting the name out with a swift, dismissive wave of his hand like the carriage return on a typewriter.

His father drove lorries for two years, Prashant explained, sending most of his wages back to India until his wife died, forcing him to return and care for his children. Between swigs of Coke, he recalled his father often speaking ruefully about how his time in Dubai was cruelly cut short.

"'I was only beginning,' he always said to me. Often, he was crying about missing the Emirates," Prashant said.

His father was particularly embarrassed about needing to send his four young sons to the local akhara, a community pehlwani training grounds, to make ends meet. Behsti was the word his father always used: shame. Behsti that he couldn't command the same wages in India. Behsti that he shipped his children off while he worked long hours at odd industrial jobs. Behsti that he sent them to the akhara less for the wrestling training and more because they offered free food to eat. And so, to alleviate this shame, at the age of twenty, Prashant made the decision to leave for Dubai and work as a lorry driver himself.

"I continued what he could not finish," he said.

We watched a group of fishmongers tarry on the opposite side of the market, waiting for a bus to take them back to their accommodations on the other side of Dubai. It was the first Friday of the month, probably payday for most of them, and I remembered parking outside Western Union that morning next to a snaking queue of men clutching little slips of paper smudged with bank numbers. The workers were sending wages home after months, years, even decades away from their families. In the stretch of lingering quiet, I did the math and realized that Prashant had officially been residing in the UAE for longer than he had ever lived in his homeland. I wondered, after twenty years in Dubai, if he even knew any people in this city of transience who had reached such a milestone themselves. But I was curious also, after so many years, how much family he actually still had left back home.

As though he anticipated my questions, Prashant put his hand on my shoulder and locked eyes with me for the first time since we sat down. "I have not seen my wife for five years," he said.

The waiter arrived with Mohammed close behind, and the two men spread a layer of newspaper on the cement, dotting it with plates of fish and doughy Egyptian khubz. I wanted Prashant to continue, but the potential hazards of pursuing this line of conversation were foregrounded when I noticed that our food sat atop the Courts section of the local government-owned

Arabic-language newspaper, *Al-Ittihad.* I pulled my plate toward me to cover up an article about a Filipino couple's sentencing for extramarital relations, punishable in the UAE by a minimum of one year in prison. By the time I mentally crafted a carefully phrased question about Prashant's wife, the topic had already switched back to pehlwani.

Even after the conversation shifted to safety, I was struck by how close Mohammed rested his hand near Prashant's body. As the meal progressed, he brushed his hand against Prashant's hip each time he leaned down to take a bite. When the waiter brought more food, Mohammed quickly moved his hand away, only to replace it again once he departed. For the rest of the dinner, whenever anyone walked past, I watched Mohammed repeat this same pattern: withdraw, return, withdraw, return. I recognized the studied ambiguity in their movements and the hypervigilance as they scanned for passersby. It was, after all, a dance I had been doing since my own arrival in the UAE four years earlier.

When the waiter returned again to clear our plates, I watched Prashant fold his hands and place them in his lap, out of Mohammed's reach. Several fishmongers began to linger near us, and I felt our chat grow halting and stilted as our privacy dissolved. In one last attempt to keep our conversation flowing, I lowered my voice and tried to ask how the two of them met. Though Mohammed flashed Prashant a quick smile, neither answered. And so, enveloped once more in silence, we sat facing the sea and watched boats navigate away from the sharp breakwaters. When I finally turned to look at them, Prashant had shifted his weight to his other hip, casting his body away from Mohammed, perhaps in a furtive attempt to steer a conversation that he felt had come too perilously close to the shore.

▽▽▽

When the last of the fishmongers scrambled to catch their bus,

Prashant walked across the street to buy a pack of cigarettes, leaving me to sit alone with Mohammed beneath a swarm of moths girdling the fluorescents. I expected another bout of silence, but he filled the vacuum with a sharp inhale and began to speak. His words tumbled out with an urgency I did not anticipate.

Mohammed explained that he had arrived in Dubai from his native Pakistan two years earlier. Before he left, he was hearing an uptick in stories from friends and acquaintances again finding jobs in the Gulf after the doldrums of the financial crisis. One neighbor was building a second level onto his house with the remittances sent back to his family. Another was able to pay for his brother to attend a business training program. But it wasn't a singular story that shook Mohammed into migrating. "I didn't say one day: 'I am leaving.' I was thinking about it, day by day. And then, slowly, I came here, just like this," he said, pointing beneath him and smiling. While he was speaking, he had inched from sitting along the edge of the newspaper to a new spot at the very center of our improvised table setting, close enough that I could feel his breath on my face as we spoke.

At home, he had been living with his family, who goaded him to marry, but at the age of twenty-five and without steady employment, his parents found it difficult to cast Mohammed as a suitable groom. Under the looming pressure, he retreated to a place he had spent much of his childhood: his local akhara, which had produced several of Pakistan's most legendary wrestlers. While training, he struck up a friendship with a fellow athlete whose brother worked construction in the UAE. He gave him the number for a job recruiter. "I thought I could be good in construction because I am strong," he said, pounding his chest. "And my friend said I could also make money as a wrestler here." He explained that many of those who gathered to watch wrestling each week would also place bets, illegal in the UAE.

Shortly after Mohammed arrived in Dubai, he began to attend

the weekly pehlwani matches in Deira. Initially he only spectated, but when he finally worked up the courage to talk to someone about competing, Prashant was the first person he happened to ask. The two men cast aside their national and religious differences—Mohammed was a Pakistani Muslim and Prashant an Indian Hindu—in favor of their commonality: both men hailed from the Punjab region of their respective countries and spoke the same ethnic language. "He said he would train me every week," Mohammed said, "but then we started meeting more often. And then," he added a little softer, smiling, "we met for more than training."

I was sure he would stop there, his story trailing off, but his next words were definitive. "We are lovers," he said, placing his arm around my shoulder.

His disclosure staggered me. I had met gay and bisexual people in the UAE, as well as those who casually engaged in same-sex relations, but this was the first time I was sitting in an interview with a man who wanted to talk about his physical and emotional relationship with another man. With a cagey Prashant still on a cigarette run, I recognized the uniqueness of this opportunity. I could ask all the questions I had started to formulate when Prashant guilefully referred to Mohammed earlier as his "good wrestler." And maybe, in front of this man who had shared such a deep secret with me, I could finally unfurl a longer list of questions—the dark-night-of-the-soul kind about migration, sexuality, and belonging—that had been circling in my own head for years.

Instead, before I knew it, I asked, "Isn't it harder for you here?"

I felt it flop out of my mouth like spat food landing on someone's shirt. I immediately wished I could recall it, this presumptuous question that my editor had posed to me, but Prashant returned, clutching a pack of Indian Gold Leaf cigarettes. He stood on the cement landing, glancing from my notebook to Mohammed and then back to my notebook again. Neither Mohammed nor I needed to say anything; I could see in Prashant's uneasy expression that he already knew our topic of conversation. He sat down, clutching a Gold Leaf to his pursed lips.

This time, the silence was too much for me. "I asked if all this—" I pointed feebly between the two of them. "—if it was harder living here than home." It sounded even cruder as a statement, a binary—here, there—I did not fully believe in and which I was now perpetuating. Rashly, whether as an act of apology or overcompensation, I said something that, outside of a small trusted circle, I had rarely divulged to anyone in the UAE: "I'm also in a relationship with a man here."

Discussing my sexuality with two men I had just met while sitting by the sea half a world away from where I was born was not a scenario I could have imagined even a few years earlier. I had grown up in a small, conservative farming town, grasping at vague dreams of living in a big city and meeting others who pined over the same unspeakable desires as me, but I had mostly encountered words for these people slung as hateful insults. Depictions of men who shared my speech patterns and mannerisms were limited to quickly flicked-off sitcoms and seemed so few and far between that I couldn't grasp the concept of being part of a group, that I might one day share their language of experience and exist in an ecosystem of others like me.

But, perhaps more worrying, what remained even more opaque than the idea of a queer community within the homogeneity of those formative years in Midwestern America—and even further into my life, far longer than it should have—was the notion of migrant communities: people and groups that disassembled and relocated their lives for a kaleidoscope of reasons, reemerging in a different place, potentially with entirely new and complex relationships to their homes, their families, their identities.

It was easy to read about the horrific court cases and punishments for "sodomy" in the Gulf—fines, deportation, a potential ten-year prison sentence for Mohammed or Prashant under the

Dubai penal code if they were caught having sex—and proclaim the region the worst place in the world to build a queer life. But it was much more difficult to figure out why the question "Isn't it harder for you here?" rang so false in my ear. Exploring the parameters of the question would push me not just to contend with the shortfalls of my education and media, but also to the limits of my own empathy and toward the outer edges of how I understood myself as a queer person, an American, and, later, as a title I gave to so many others but never considered applying to my own circumstances: as a migrant myself.

▽▽▽

For nearly a decade, I met queer migrants like Prashant and Mohammed who built a life in the Gulf, a corner of the world where same-sex relationships, being transgender, sex outside of heterosexual marriage, and cross-dressing are all deemed illegal. Some I interviewed, others I befriended; numerous struggled, plenty thrived. I witnessed their gains, sacrifices, and compromises—in acts of both concealment and coming together; in life and in love—while living in a foreign country with active laws that threatened their freedom, livelihood, and existence. I heard language weaponized, hedged, and reclaimed; I witnessed power wielded, laws skirted, expectations subverted—mine included. This book is, first and foremost, an amalgam of these stories. But it is also a personal account: an appraisal of what I myself reaped, lost, and—as a white American choosing to live in a place where human rights abuses occur each day—how I was complicit as well.

For some of the queer migrants I met, the experience was just a blip: a few months' project, a failed job search. For most, it lasted several formative years, long enough to build a house or lose a family. And for a few others, their Gulf migration story encompassed the better part of a lifetime. I met most of them in the UAE because this is where I spent the majority of my time in the region, but I also encountered them in Oman and Qatar, in Bahrain and Kuwait, and Saudi Arabia, too, because this urgent movement between countries and jobs is the very nature of migration for so many in the Gulf: a couple years chasing income in Riyadh, a year's posting in Doha, a few more in Dubai. This period comprised nearly all of my twenties and then some, an entire beginning to an adult life, built in a place that was not my own. This is an attempt to reckon with what that passage of time has meant to me and to others, as well as what we as queer migrants wrought by living a reality that I have heard people label paradoxical, counter-intuitive, reckless, and stupid.

Why do you wanna go live in a place like that?

I was asked this question in the form of a one-line, subjectless email from one of my high school teachers a few days after I announced on social media that, upon graduating from university, I would be taking a job in the Gulf. I remember staring at my laptop, unsettled by the uncanny resemblance her message had with all the questions I had heard spouted about queerness growing up in the Midwest. *Isn't it wrong? Isn't it unnatural? Isn't it dangerous?* They were framed as questions, but they did not feel like questions at all. They felt like a kind of masquerade, judgments hiding behind false openings for earnest dialogue.

That evening at the fish market, I realized that I was bothered by what I had asked Mohammed—"Isn't it harder here than it is at home?"—because, though I had framed it as a question about sexuality and living away from where he was born, it was just as disingenuous as all those same questions that had been assailing me for years. I "asked" it to verify entrenched assumptions, ones I didn't even know I had, that had hollowed my inquiry of any genuine sincerity. Assertions hid at the center of my question: that sexuality factored into the intricate calculus of Mohammed's migration. That it was obviously easier for him to live a queer life elsewhere. That "elsewhere" was even a viable option. And, perhaps most insidious, that he couldn't have considered the Gulf—this place where he met his lover, this place he had been living for years—as a home in which he belonged.

So many of the stories I heard of queer migrants' journeys to the region were complicated, almost convoluted. Mine was no exception: I was a boy from small-town Wisconsin who pursued a degree in Middle Eastern history despite no previous exposure to the culture or language, studied Arabic in the capital of Yemen—a country dogged in American media by the qualifier "the ancestral homeland of Osama bin Laden" like some obligatory tagline—and then moved to the UAE after being offered a job at an institution that did not yet exist. A year after returning from my studies in Sana'a, and mere months after graduating, NYU would open the doors to its brand-new campus in Abu Dhabi, a controversial degree-granting campus allegedly funded with an initial $50 million from the UAE government and built by migrant subcontractors subject to exploitation and human rights violations. With most of my friends struggling to find jobs in the wake of the financial crisis, I was grateful for the opportunity to take an opaque, half-administrative, half-academic, catchall role halfway across the world that would have me splitting my time between the mundanity of a photocopier and more enriching work like conducting research on Yemeni performance traditions. And yet despite the security of my position, or perhaps because of it, I found myself drawn into precarious work of my own making: seeking out and archiving other queer stories of departure, arrival, or a place somewhere in between.

This unpublishable archive of conversations was conducted under the weight of several layers of potential illegality. I was undertaking work that wasn't authorized by my visa, pursuing journalistic interviews outside the confines of the region's tightly regulated and often censored media, and associating with groups who engaged in acts counter to public decency laws. And yet I was urged forward by the undeniable parallels I felt and witnessed between queerness and migration in a place where most residents are legal outsiders. The slippery nature of prescribed identities. The duality of hospitality and exclusion. The search for "chosen" family when bringing or building a biological one is impossible. The potential for even greater nuance and clarity in speaking across second or third languages to challenge entrenched categories, nomenclatures, and narratives. And—perhaps above all—the knot that binds opportunity, risk, subversion, and both the rhetoric and reality of assimilation.

This book is neither exposé nor direct rebuke. Instead, it will tell a queerer story. Then, perhaps, those that find these stories unimaginable—of people choosing to live in a place that persecutes them—might finally scrutinize the larger, pernicious forces that inform their expectations in the first place. About the Gulf, yes, but also about how we define home.

That night in Deira, after I asked Prashant if it was harder for him to live in the UAE than India, I expected him not to respond. He had invited me to dinner to talk about wrestling, and the evening had ended up with his male lover admitting the nature of their relationship to a complete stranger—a stranger who was now asking him presumptuous questions about how it must be for him here, a place he had called home for much longer than I had.

But Prashant eventually lowered his cigarette and turned toward me. I already had my notebook out from speaking with Mohammed, and I grabbed my pen off the newspaper flecked with crumbs from the meal we had just finished, ready to capture a quick soundbite that would verify my barely concealed belief that it was more difficult to be queer in the Gulf than anywhere else on the planet.

Instead of answering my question, he placed his large hand firmly on my shoulder once again and asked if I wanted more food. The request seemed so absurd at this late hour; the moon had risen, and I was already so full. I patted my stomach, confident this would convey that I was finished.

"But you must," he said, signaling for the waiter despite my protest. "We need so much more time to talk about such things."

PART I:

HERE

1: A RINK

(Abu Dhabi, UAE: Imran)

I ATE MY FIRST BREAKFAST in the United Arab Emirates sitting inside an ice rink toilet cubicle. It wasn't even a meal, really—just a confusion of snacks from a welcome basket that had greeted me on my kitchen counter the night before. And I wasn't actually sitting in the bathroom as much as hiding. It was the second day of Ramadan, the Islamic holy month, when eating in public spaces was illegal during daylight hours, so I huddled inside the fiberglass stall taking wary little bites from what felt like the loudest granola bar in the world.

When I'd flipped on the lights in my new apartment for the first time the previous evening, I'd glimpsed the little cellophane-wrapped basket of food before I saw anything else. I had arrived well after dark, and though I was famished and tempted to curl up in bed with the snacks, slipping ever lower onto a pillow as junk food wrappers accumulated around me, I wanted to investigate the condition of my figure skates first.

The skates had worried me for most of my journey. I knew too many horror stories of boots mangled or blades nicked on long-haul flights, so I dropped my luggage just over the threshold and rummaged through the sweatshirts and balled-up underwear I had used to cushion them during the thirteen hours from New York to Abu Dhabi. Sitting on the tile floor, I inspected the integrity of all forty leather eyelets and realized that these skates were now the most valuable thing I owned. *You will be provided with a furnished studio flat*, my contract had assured me, and so I had sold off everything inside my New York rental that couldn't fit into an oversized duffle, saving for last my little monochrome Inkjet that printed me a one-way ticket to another life on the other side of the world.

My initial glance around the apartment made it clear that living thirty floors above the Gulf would be radically different from my residential experience in Manhattan. Instead of rickety metal bed stilts jammed against a closet that couldn't open, I now had a king-sized wooden bed frame sitting at the far end of a spacious open-floor plan. In place of an illegal egress bedroom "window" with a view of my own living room, I now looked out sweeping floor-to-ceiling windows. And in lieu of a dank refrigerator that could never quite muster a temperature cold enough to preserve milk through its expiration date, I was surrounded by a horde of brand-new, stainless-steel appliances.

I felt a surge of relief spotting a welcome packet and highlighter sitting on the coffee table, grateful for directions that might guide me through the art of living in a place that wasn't a veritable shoebox squatting above an East Village dive bar. I collapsed onto the couch and read through the neatly bound documents, circling contact information that could prove important: the resident technician, the taxi company, the nearest hospital. The last thing I remember noticing, with some alarm, was the prominence of the phone number for the United States Embassy; it was emboldened and listed first, above the police, the fire department, and emergency services.

I jerked awake to a sharp pain in my side. I had dozed off, digging the capless highlighter into my ribs as I slumped over and, in the process, defacing the couch's pristine white fabric with a long streak of ink. I stared at the stain in horror. It was the same shade of pink as my beloved childhood Troll doll's hair, the one I knew even as a young boy to keep at the back of my toy shelf for fear that a more favorable position might arouse suspicion about why I liked it so much.

I frantically Googled "how to get highlighter out of faux leather" and set to work blotting the sofa with hairspray-soaked toilet paper, my closest approximation to the Internet's solution of rubbing alcohol and a towel. But the ink was more stubborn than eHow.com had let on, so I pored over the entire welcome packet, hoping I might find a section dedicated to furniture care. Instead, I came across the line: *We will contact you ahead of your departure date to arrange a final inspection of the apartment.*

"But I'm not going anywhere!" I wanted to shout at the page. This was my apartment; I had a twenty-four-month contract. It had seemed like such a long time when I signed it in New York—half of my university career, twice the amount of time I studied Arabic in Yemen during my third year at university. But then I remembered how the idea of two years had begun to feel so short even as I waited for my duffle at baggage claim that evening. Jostling at a luggage carousel with passengers arriving from an Indian city I'd never heard of, I watched flights disappear from the departure board and realized that we were taking the places of many of those outbound passengers, and that in two years, someone would do the same for me, too.

I started scrubbing harder, imagining an unannounced rap at my door from an inspector who would turn over my apartment like a Marriott hotel room for some other newcomer. How could I explain to him this stain set deep in my fabric? I became acutely aware of my utter lack of time—to figure out the rhythm of this country where I was both resident and also guest, to understand who I was sharing it with and who it all belonged to; and, most importantly, to hide the transgressions I had already committed and would surely commit again, before I would be held accountable in a place where my actions—and who I was—would surely catch up with me.

Allahu akbar, ashadu an la ilaha illa-llah. I heard the fajr call to prayer through my windows. I had lost track of how long I'd been cleaning. Fajr was the sunrise prayer, and as I looked up from the sofa, a creamy hue was beginning to filter into my apartment. Giving up on the stain, I cycled through channels on the wide flatscreen—Lebanese music videos, Saudi men in white robes circumambulating the Kaaba, a twenty-four-hour program devoted entirely to old broadcasts of camel races—and responded to an email from my boyfriend James, asking if I had made it safely. We had been dating since my return from Yemen a year earlier, and I was dumbfounded by our luck when he also secured a job at NYUAD as a writing tutor. He would be arriving in a few months and asked in his message what it was like. But whether he meant my new domesticity, the act of moving across the world, or what the shape of our relationship together would look like, I still didn't have an answer.

Settling on a histrionic soap opera—I counted three slaps in the first few minutes—I laid down across the stain and closed my eyes, trying to use the program's dialogue as white noise to soothe myself and coax a few hours' sleep. But the vocabulary and accents of Khaleeji, the Gulf dialect, tunneled deep into my ears, discordant with the Yemeni Arabic that had become so familiar to me. Surrendering to the firm grasp of insomnia, I considered venturing into the streets but found myself Googling the hours for the local ice rink instead. It was already open; I could go. A little exercise could shake loose the jet lag and anxiety, I reasoned.

Looking out the window to catch my first real glimpse of the city by the light of day, I grasped how high thirty stories actually was. My building was called Sama, the word for sky in Arabic, and it lived up to its name. I tried to follow the path of each pedestrian I could see, but clusters of satellite dishes and cell tower boosters on the rooftops of the buildings below me obscured my sightline. It felt like peering out of my airplane window.

More than anything, I wanted to be able to discern the faces of all those people traversing the gray pavers knitted together below, to know who they were and where they were going. But they were all too far removed from my lofty perch in the sky. As I spotted a tan minaret poking out between the towers across the street, I figured most people at this hour would be heading to prayer, so I decided it was not my time to wander. Instead, I grabbed my skates and went to the rink.

I recognized long ago that the ritual I had constructed in high school around figure skating was a kind of retreat into self-preservation: the physical act of driving away from my small town. The mental act of blaring pop music in my car to drown out the homophobic taunts I had left behind. The therapeutic act of arriving in a bustling city and stepping onto a new sheet of ice to carve my own path across it. But as I sat trying to silently eat in the toilet cubicle, I was aware that I had retreated *away* from a city—and then retreated even farther within a place that was meant to be a sanctuary. Instead of proudly taking to the ice, I was paralyzed in the bathroom, granola bar in hand, straining to listen for any approaching footsteps. Who the footsteps might belong to, I did not know. A muscled Emirati hockey player? An off-duty Zamboni driver? A disgruntled janitor who patrolled bathrooms for gluttonous non-Muslim heretics who couldn't last a few hours without carbohydrates?

It would take much longer for me to realize that everyone I tried to picture in those initial days—the man I feared might inspect my apartment, each pedestrian I tried to spy beneath my windows, the figurative Zamboni driver—was faceless. I could still not quite conjure up who lived in this place, and, if they encountered me, whether my differences—which seemed, like my queerness, so painfully obvious to me—would lead to their ridicule, their scorn, or worse. I rubbed my hands together to rid them of crumbs, lest I give myself away, and noted the highlighter stains still set deep in my fingertips. I finally put on my gloves and walked out the door.

The ice was busier than I expected. Most of the three dozen or so skaters circled the edge of the rink in a stuttering clockwise parade, grasping at the wall like the railing of a rickety staircase. A handful of fathers skated nervously behind their young sons, arms outstretched, ready to snatch them up should they fall. One girl, barely older than a toddler, took a few tentative steps away from the safety of the plastic boards, grinning as she ignored the consternation of her mother. But my eyes were almost immediately drawn elsewhere, to the sole figure swaggering across the very center of the rink.

The man standing on center ice looked a few years older than me and was wearing the electric-blue hockey skates I had seen at the rental counter near the entrance. And though his skates seemed chunky and ill-fitted for figure skating, the man was clearly working on spins, pulling his arms close to his chest as he tried to rotate on one foot in as tight an axis as possible. I darted through the other skaters to get a better look and watched for a few minutes as he concentrated on something in his hands before trying a few other moves. He didn't notice me as I started to warm up, but as I began to work on jumps, he surprised me by catching my eye and smiling, breaking the etiquette of what I always knew to be a silent, private appraisal between skaters. As he glided toward me, his paint-on black jeans strained over the boots of his skates and his tan jacket puffed out behind him like an awkward pleather cape, but he came to a seamless stop in front of me, sure-footed as any figure skater I had trained with in the Midwest.

"As-salamu alaykum," I said, extending the standard Islamic greeting I had learned to use countless times each day in Yemen, for everyone from my Arabic teacher to the street food vendors on my block. *Peace be upon you*, it offered.

"Wa alaykum as-salaam," he replied. Like the television programs I heard in the middle of my jet-lag haze the previous night, it was a different accent than I was used to, but I understood the universal response: *And upon you, peace.*

"Great moves. Are you a skater?" I asked in Arabic.

He cocked his head to the side and offered a shy smile without responding. *Damn it,* I thought. I knew the Khaleeji dialect would be different from the Yemeni I was familiar with, so I tried again, this time slower and in Modern Standard Arabic, the stiff, formal language I had studied at university, which was rarely spoken outside of television broadcasts. I had learned to use MSA, or foosha, as a sort of ancient language bridge when I first got to Yemen—poor but crossable.

He responded with a string of quick phrases that mystified me. The cadence sounded vaguely familiar but the syntax and words didn't coalesce. It was like we were standing on the opposite ends of a vast ice sheet breaking apart. I stood still in the middle of the rink, scrambling to compose a sentence.

"Don't you speak English?" he asked in a tone that struck me as more than a little amused. The smile that hadn't slid from his face throughout our whole bumbled exchange grew even wider.

"Yes, yes—of course," I blurted. I didn't mean to, but I took a step backward as though he had startled me.

His name was Imran and he was from Tehran, he explained in rapid-fire English. I realized then that he had initially tried to respond to me in Farsi, and the fact that he hailed from a Muslim-majority country that spoke a tongue other than Arabic explained why he was familiar with the Islamic-tinged Arabic pleasantries but otherwise unable to carry on a full conversation in the language. I was surprised to learn that he was a self-taught skater and had only been on the ice since his arrival in Abu Dhabi a few years earlier. As I listened to him apologize for his English even as he spoke with seeming fluency, I couldn't help feeling a pang of inferiority to a man who had picked up with such ease two things—skating and the Arabic language—that I had struggled to master.

But there was an even deeper sting of another failure that I tried to push aside. I had studied the Gulf and was aware of its large migrant population, but Imran made apparent the chasm between my expectations and the reality of who these people could be. I stood stock-still on the ice, trying to form a mental grasp around this man who had so unexpectedly approached me, but Imran remained in perpetual motion. Even as we spoke, he seemed to be practicing footwork that reminded me of Russian Olympic gold medalist Alexei Yagudin: his heels high in relevé, a feat made all the more impressive as he was balancing not on exacting toe picks but on a dull rental hockey blade. He kept his arms extended wide as he moved, cutting through the air with an elegance but also a surprising strength for a man so lithe.

"Do you dance, too?" He raised his eyebrows to make it clear that, though he posed it as a question, it was also a dare. As I hesitated, he crouched down and skated backward between my legs, grinning as he drifted away in a rap pose. I looked around and wondered who had seen his little display, remembering the rest of the skaters still winding around the edge of the rink. We stood center stage, and I was conscious that our conversation was becoming increasingly loud and showy.

"Come on, I think you can dance!" he egged me on further. I suddenly realized that, unlike most of my other skating experiences, this rink was entirely devoid of music on account of Ramadan. I missed the tinny treble of the Top 40 blaring from the speakers, remembering how my welcome packet listed both listening to music and dancing alongside eating and drinking as forbidden activities during Ramadan. So I played it safe, eschewing any flashy footwork that could be construed as dancing, winding instead into an intricate spin.

"Wow, you are so like him!" Imran said once I stopped whirling. I didn't understand who he was referencing until he retrieved an iPhone from his pocket and started playing a skating program by Johnny Weir, the American figure skater who had competed a few months earlier at the Vancouver Olympics. It dawned on me that this video is what he had been consulting earlier; he was trying to teach himself each move of the program.

"Have you seen this video? I love him!" Imran said, placing one hand on my arm to steady himself as he mimicked Johnny's outrageous hand choreography with his other.

Of course I had seen it; it was a video I knew well not simply because I was an avid fan, but also because it had caused a sensation in the figure skating world. The video captured Weir's exhibition performance at the 2010 National Championships, the day after he had been selected for his second Olympic team. Exhibition skates generally tended to skew more theatrical and lighthearted than competitive programs—less Rachmaninoff and more Red Hot Chili Peppers—but Weir's program to Lady Gaga's "Poker Face" reached another level. Even before he began—entering the rink in a skin-tight black outfit with cat-eye mascara over one eye and blue glitter ringing the other—the on-air commentators let out embarrassed chuckles. One introduced the program with the caveat: "but he was plenty serious enough to make the Olympic team," as though his mannerisms were an impediment, or a deficiency.

Their remarks stung because I recognized Weir's flamboyance in myself. He wasn't even "out," and yet just watching his performance had led one prominent Canadian commentator to remark on air during the Olympics, "We should make him pass a gender test at this point." The controversy had boiled over just as I was signing my contract and planning my move to the UAE. If one of the world's top athletes could face this, I had wondered—and in supposedly liberal Canada, no less—what would happen to me? What about my decision, which had seemed increasingly absurd amidst this fervor, to spend the next two years in a country where being myself could result in much graver consequences than on-air mockery?

"You are…like Johnny?" Imran asked. Before I could respond, he winked and whispered, "I am."

I was paralyzed. It was a question I knew I would probably face sooner or later, but it was something I thought I might be able to stave off, at least long enough that I wouldn't have to answer it during my first few hours in the country. Even as his confession heartened me, I couldn't help feeling disappointed that I had already given myself away. I had grown up as so many queer people do, learning tactics to deflect attention and scorn—pivoting the conversation to sports, inventing an out-of-state girlfriend—tricks that I had taken a step further in Yemen, including wearing a wedding ring. But I also knew, in this place where I would be spending the next two years, I needed to build a life. I needed to be able to explain myself.

"Do you want to go to lunch?" I asked it to avoid answering his question, another diversion tactic, but also because I wondered if perhaps this wasn't the right venue to discuss this, with other people around. I felt on display. Imran had been open with me so, I thought, I might be able to be open with him, just in a better place and at a better time.

"No, brother, it is Ramadan! I am fasting!" Imran exclaimed. Before I could even backtrack and apologize, he skated off. I had tripped over myself again.

I had finally started moving but no longer wanted to be navigating the ice. I felt like I was getting in the way of everyone. As a left-handed skater, I was supposed to be used to traveling in the opposite direction, but I couldn't find the flow of this rink's traffic; I couldn't tap into its rhythm.

As I gave up, turning to head clockwise along with the rest of the skaters, I suddenly collided with a small boy. I checked him in the chest with the full weight of my hip and he dropped to the ice, startled. I felt my cheeks flush crimson. I was supposed to be the expert skater. As his father swooped in to scoop him up, I clambered out of my gloves to help. Leaning down to help the boy to his feet, I saw the pink stains that still marked my hands, exposed for anyone to see.

▽▽▽

I spent much of my first few days in Abu Dhabi at the ice rink. My job wouldn't begin in earnest for a few weeks, closer to the time my boyfriend would finally arrive, and since the UAE government shortened the Ramadan workday to account for Muslims' fourteen hours of fasting, I had the freedom and spare time to skate. I learned to make my way through the inexperienced skaters on the ice, but outside the rink, I was soon confronted with more pressing issues of navigation.

Waving down a taxi after skating proved difficult in those early days. Though I initially tried to blame this on a scarcity of taxis during Ramadan, the problem rested more with my own inept wayfinding. The rink sat within a larger seven-square-kilometer athletic complex called Zayed Sports City, which was filled with tennis courts, martial arts studios, and cricket pitches. Its labyrinthine design often had me walking into the middle of a soccer field instead of toward the road.

The facility was named after Sheikh Zayed bin Sultan Al Nahyan, the man who united a loose confederation of tribal sheikhdoms into the United Arab Emirates in 1971 and served as the country's first president until his death in 2004. Negotiating my way to the taxi rank, I tried to use a billboard of Zayed's face like a kind of compass, as though the portrait of his wizened countenance—upturned chin, eyes gazing nobly to the left—might guide me in the right direction. But I discovered too late that multiple identical billboards were posted throughout the complex, and I would often start navigating away from the rink using one of Zayed's imposing royal portraits only to inadvertently look at another, scrambling my sense of direction and sending me back to where I had started like some kind of open-air hall of mirrors.

I began to wonder if my issues with navigation were rooted in the fact that seemingly everything was named after Sheikh Zayed: I skated at Zayed Sports City, my neighborhood was called Madinat Zayed; in my first few days, I also encountered a slew of buildings and institutions including Sheikh Zayed Mosque, Sheikh Zayed Bridge, Zayed Military Academy, and Zayed Cultural House. I was unsettled not just by this uniformity but by what it seemed to convey about the city's reverence for formality, rigidness, tradition, and—perhaps above all—authority. The first time I found myself hopelessly lost, I made my way to the largest building in the Zayed Sports City complex, Zayed Stadium. When I still couldn't find any taxis, I wandered to its breezy entranceway, drawn in by the stadium's striking design of cement arches that looked like a series of enormous galvanized staples strung together into a neat oval. Inside, I found no athletes, spectators, or even any security; I had the mammoth, forty-five-thousand-seat arena to myself. I took the opportunity to stretch my hamstrings atop its empty bucket seats and jog up and down the formidable staircases of this modern behemoth, its cavernous emptiness seeming to be a testament to the country's overwhelming newness.

I was fixated on what felt like the exceptional pace of Abu Dhabi's construction. I had arrived in New York a few months before the installation of One World Trade's first foundational beam and departed four years later when the tower was still less than half its final height. But here, construction seemed relentless, and I absorbed the city as one sprouting mass. Walking down the street from Sama Tower, individual buildings blended into rows of cement. A few blocks farther, emerging into a sweeping tract of neon signs, I failed to differentiate one marquee from another, registering only a tangle of color and brightness.

It was initially difficult to regard the city through any lens but its newness. Profiles, travel articles, and cultural journalism of the UAE trafficked in the same phrasing, recycling qualifiers like "gleaming," "shining," and "sparkling" to illustrate the pace at which the city was being built, encouraging the dismissal of any historical variance between its structures. It was all so *now*, the tumult of articles suggested. But I slowly became aware that much of what I read about the Gulf was penned by "parachute journalists" —writers who flew into an unfamiliar place to cover the story du jour. Some clearly had never stepped foot in the places they wrote about. Describing Abu Dhabi as a "desert gem stepping out of Dubai's shadows," one CNN article praised the Cultural Foundation as "a 'must see' for any tourist" despite the institution having closed three years earlier.

As I took my first tepid steps into my own neighborhood, I began to note the inadequacy of much of this coverage. Diagonally opposite my apartment building stood the oldest structure in the city, a mid-eighteenth-century defensive fortress and palace called Al Hosn Fort. From my window, I could peer into its sandy courtyard, and I liked to study how its puzzle of inner buildings knitted together. I was self-congratulatory for noting a fault in the narrative.

I was smug also in my early understanding that each major street carried at least two official designations: an Arabic name and an English number, odd for east-west streets and even for north-south ones. When I heard English speakers refer to my road as Seventh Street, I could barely hold back a smirk, assured in my special ability to drop its Arabic name, Shariyah Zayed al-Thani, even if it meant keeping straight another place named Zayed. I thought this gave me a distinct advantage—a superiority, even—in being able to tap into the city. But I soon found that using it aloud rarely got me anywhere. Lost between two unfamiliar mosques a few days after my arrival, I tried asking for directions back to Shariyah Zayed al-Thani from an Indian woman. When several different pronunciations of the Arabic name failed to unknit her brow, I tried saying Seventh Street in English. "Ah, you want Electra?" was all she asked, eyebrow raised, pointing in the opposite direction.

I found the name in my welcome packet when I finally made it back to my apartment: Electra Street. It was derived from a nearby old electronic shop, shuttered long ago. In my rush to spurn Seventh Street and embrace Shariyah Zayed al-Thani, I had forgotten this third designation, the name most used by the city's residents—one that wasn't quite in any language. It should have been my first inkling that there might be a queerness hiding in the heart of the city; that officialdom could be rejected two times over, in two separate languages, and an alternate reality could be created, embraced, and propagated instead.

▽▽▽

I arrived in Abu Dhabi during what felt like a period of unprecedented change in the way people moved about the city. The streets had transformed from having no public transportation system in 2008 to carrying several hundred buses two years later. The service was so new that the fare—one dirham, or about twenty-seven cents—had only been introduced a few months before I arrived. Free public transportation, for nearly two years, seemed so outrageous that I struggled to comprehend how narrowly I had missed out on the opportunity. Whenever I began to flounder—unsure if I was walking east or west, whether I was strolling toward or away from the sea—I daydreamed about what it would have been like to arrive just a few months earlier: hopping onto a bright teal bus at no charge, slowly familiarizing myself with the texture of the skyscape as I looped for hours around the city.

But the complete overhaul of Abu Dhabi's taxi service felt perhaps the most seismic. In 2007, the General Manager of TransAD, the semi-governmental transportation regulatory body, introduced a major overhaul to the taxi system, heralding a new era of "high standards in passenger comfort, safety, and style." By the time I arrived, eight thousand sleek new silver taxis were already in the process of replacing the citywide fleet of old Corollas with once-distinctive green-and-gold paint jobs now battered and rusted by years of sand and salty sea air. The notoriety and rough-and-tumble reputation of the old taxis was only heightened by an official communique released by the British Foreign and Commonwealth Office just before my arrival warning residents not to use them because "they can be badly maintained and erratically driven."

My welcome packet also encouraged me to take advantage of the new taxis, but I was traveling to the ice rink fifteen kilometers away so often that I couldn't afford to keep paying the roughly thirty-dollar round-trip fare. The nascent bus system didn't yet have a convenient route to Zayed Sports City, so hailing one of the decaying jalopies, with their lower flagfall and much slower meter, seemed like the only way to make sure I didn't run out of money before my first paycheck arrived.

Despite the meters, many drivers of the old taxis often tried to cajole passengers into negotiating an agreed price before the journey began (or, if the driver was particularly shrewd, after he'd already put his foot to the pedal.) I had come to enjoy this kind of banter in Yemen as I improved at asserting myself in Arabic, but I found it harder to engage in these kinds of exchanges in Abu Dhabi. I told myself the problem was that I just hadn't yet learned the art of negotiation in my new home, but this papered over the reality that I struggled with more than just the quick volley of a good-natured haggle.

Like Imran, most of the drivers could employ basic Arabic or Islamic greetings, but they all had such diverse first languages—Urdu, Malayalam, Nepali, Tagalog, and more—that each conversation I began was filled with new linguistic pitfalls I hadn't before encountered. Modulating between a pidgin of broken English, broken Arabic, and the native tongue of whoever I was speaking with, I was frustrated that I couldn't seem to find the cadence of any dialogue I entered. And so, in an attempt to preempt all small talk, I increasingly made a show of pulling out a book as soon as I jumped in the car and burying myself in its pages.

In those early days, I was reading a work by Indian author Amitav Ghosh called *In an Antique Land.* The book was billed as "a subversive history in the form of a traveler's tale" and unraveled the eight-hundred-year-old story of an Indian slave in Egypt in parallel with Ghosh's own narrative as a young researcher living in the country during the early 1980s. I read it partially because Cairo sat at the top of my travel wish-list, but mostly because my encounters with Egypt's historic and cultural touchstones far outstripped my experience with the Gulf—not just in the standard pharaonic imagery I had loved for its exoticism as a Midwestern child, but also in the way Egypt had been embedded in my studies from the moment my first Arabic lecturer showed us black-and-white films from the country's golden cinematic era. I was enamored with Egypt and thought I knew it—or perhaps I was enamored precisely *because* I thought I knew it.

So I was struck reading Ghosh unpack a history of Cairo, a city that had so fully captured my imagination in university, that I was completely unaware of:

> *In its original conception, al-Qahira (Cairo) was a planned capital, an early forebearer of New Delhi, Canberra, Brasilia, and other such haunts of officialdom...In time the character of al-Qahira was to change entirely and it was to become a frantic, crowded district, the bustling nucleus of the conurbation of Cairo. But all that came later: in the early years of the twelfth century, when Ben Yiji first came to Masr it was probably still a relatively solemn, bureaucratic kind of place....(the) capital was still largely a ceremonial and ad-*

ministrative township.

I had been taught—or thought I had been taught—that the capital of Egypt, if not the entire Arab world, had always been a teeming, frenetic city. I remembered reading an article in the *New York Times* shortly after I started studying the region that the city of 18 million residents was one of the loudest places in the world, with an average daytime volume hovering at 85 decibels, or "a bit louder than a freight train 15 feet away." Somewhere early in my studies, I realized, I had made the leap that even if Cairo wasn't always that noisy, it had at least always been that buzzing—a quality I had been admiring in cities since my days driving away from my languid hometown for a bustling city ice rink, dreaming of New York. What I didn't realize was that implicit in this leap was my belief that the relative calm and order of a place like Abu Dhabi made it a city somehow less capable of possessing layers of history worth studying, or of revealing intrigue worth pursuing.

Abu Dhabi stretched out across a long, thin island, and my frequent taxi rides took me from my apartment at one tip, jutting far out into the sea, to the ice rink at the other, just across from the mainland. Though I had begun a cautious exploration of the surrounding areas, I realized, shuttling back and forth, they might as well have been portals to one another for all I was noticing in the spaces in between. Reading Ghosh dissect Cairo as we coasted past strings of low-rise villas, I felt my first glimmer that perhaps the city could someday morph from the staid bureaucratic capital I perceived it to be into a thronging, unpredictable place like the vibrant cities I loved.

All of the changes I was witnessing around me—from the buses to the taxi I sat in—seemed to be ordering the city further into another "haunt of officialdom," but I wondered if it all might someday shift in a way I couldn't yet conceive. As I began to take longer glances out my window along my route, I was drawn to the silhouette of one building in particular, an odd blockish tower with porthole-like sunshades sheltering rows of neat balconies. But each time I pulled out my phone to investigate the structure, foraging for answers in both English and Arabic—when it was built, who built it—I failed to uncover any information at all.

An architect, a history, a name: they seemed like facts that I should be able to easily find about a twelve-story tower standing in the heart of the city. But like the queer third names of each street, I did not yet realize that this information might not be as simple as a binary—old, new—but uncovered instead by troubling these simple delineations. And that the answers lay not in any official record but with people like Imran and the taxi drivers I silently sat next to, my head lowered as they navigated with ease and precision that which still confounded me.

▽▽▽

I found his number sitting atop my skating bag.

Imran must have written it hastily on the bathroom counter. The ink was smudged with water stains and scrawled on the same grainy paper towel I'd used to cover my food wrappers before shoving them deep in the trash can.

Imran's abrupt departure from our conversation had convinced me that I'd offended him with my caddish question, so I was relieved to see his message and rushed to send him a friendly text as I unlaced my skates. His replies flooded in so quickly that I scrambled to silence my phone, embarrassed by its constant pinging.

hi HELLO
nice to meet you
let's have dinner
i would like to get to know you !
use bbm much?

Suddenly, the whole situation became horrifyingly clear. The admissions and questions about sexuality, an awkward exit, Imran's hastily jotted phone number, his urgent messages: this was a textbook crush. I was mortified that he had misconstrued my invitation to lunch, interpreting my desire for a more private setting to respond to his question about my sexuality as some kind of romantic overture. Later that evening, lying on my bed surrounded by a chaos of Lebanese takeout containers, I stared at his flurry of messages, mulling over the most tactful way to tell him that I wasn't looking for a boyfriend.

I had read about a similar phenomenon, I realized; I had even encountered an article about its prominence in Saudi Arabia while I was living in Yemen. It was called "numbering": young men from the Gulf would lurk in one of the few public spaces they could interact with the opposite sex—say, a mall—and then drop their numbers onto the floor in front of a girl or, if they were feeling especially cavalier, directly into her shopping bag.

I felt sure that Imran had done the same, tucking his number neatly under my folded jeans. The article I read had only examined "numbering" among young heterosexual men, but I figured that certainly didn't preclude the phenomenon from existing among queer people. Recalling how wide his eyes had gotten when he said that I reminded him of Johnny Weir, I thought it obvious why Imran might want to "number" me: the pressure he would have faced must have been tremendous. I remembered reading quotes from Mahmoud Ahmadinejad, the president of Iran, shortly after I started studying the region declaring that "in Iran, we do not have homosexuals." It seemed likely that, between Iran and the UAE, Imran had potentially never met an out gay man in his entire life. Perhaps he was as scared as I had been, hunched in the toilet cubicle eating my granola bar.

I kept my messages to Imran warm but succinct, deciding it

would be better to tell him in person that I wasn't interested in dating. The opportunity to put this misunderstanding to rest came mercifully soon: within a few messages, Imran was insisting that I meet him at an Iranian restaurant that weekend. I googled its location and found it along the road between my apartment and the ice rink, sitting in that in-between space midway between Sama Tower and Zayed Sports City that I had yet to explore. Perusing the map, I noticed with a start that the restaurant also sat a few buildings down from the city's police headquarters.

In my first week, how had I agreed not only to an unwitting gay date in a country where that was illegal, but also to one that would unfold down the street from the largest concentration of cops in the city? As if that weren't enough, I would also be attending my first iftar, the dinner meal in which Muslims break their Ramadan fasts. The entire reason I had surrounded myself with greasy takeaway boxes that evening was because, nearly a week into my time in Abu Dhabi, I was still unfamiliar with the meal's etiquette. Without someone to show me its procedure, I had been too terrified to make a mistake in public, so I ate all my dinners in my apartment. To assuage my anxiety, I tried to read everything online I could about the dos and don'ts of the meal: listen for the boom of the mighty cannon just outside the Grand Mosque, start the meal with the humble bowl of dates placed at the center of the table, and, above all, don't even think about eating before the call to prayer. But even as I searched the internet for answers about iftars, I was slowly coming to realize that online research about practicalities in the UAE often felt as effective as trawling the Gulf with the fishing net of a child.

I left my apartment unreasonably early that Saturday and arrived before the neon in the restaurant's sign had even been illuminated. Too antsy to sit down, I skirted the edge of the block, walking between an insurance company and a mammoth health clinic, careful to avoid heading toward the police headquarters. It was my first experience of street level at dusk, and I was surprised by the unrelenting heat so late in the day; it was as though the energy radiating from the sun all summer had been stowing away entirely between the concrete buildings of this block. By the time I rounded the street corner, I needed to turn back: I had already pitted through my collared shirt, and sweat was beginning to drip down my calves from the creases behind my knees. I darkly rationalized that if there were a silver lining to showing up to the restaurant having sweated through all of my clothes, it was that it might be so off-putting to Imran that I wouldn't have to directly confront him about dating.

The restaurant was already brimming when I pushed through its heavy glass doors. I scanned the far walls, hoping Imran would have been astute enough to secure a table tucked away in some corner, but I was suddenly greeted by his frantic waving almost directly in front of me. He was sitting at a large table nearest to the door, in full view of all the patrons and directly along the traffic flow of the restaurant.

As he leaned in to greet me, I steeled myself to be assertively platonic, but his kiss on the cheek was quick, his embrace surprisingly neutral. I prepared to fold my hands and cast my glance downward, following his cues to match the level of solemnity he conveyed out of respect for the holiday. But as we sat, Imran threw his arms out wide. He was animated and louder than I had anticipated.

"I can't believe they are late," he said, tapping his foot.

"Sorry, who is late?" I asked. Before he could respond, the call to prayer rang out, and Imran unceremoniously devoured his dates and apricot juice as two men burst through the door, rushing toward our table.

"Sorry, traffic was so bad," the taller of the two said, pulling out a chair and sitting next to Imran. The other man popped a date into his mouth before collapsing into his chair next to me. Only then did I register that our large table held four place settings.

Imran introduced his friends. Ali, the taller of the two, with a handsome five o'clock shadow that rose higher than his sculpted cheekbones, sat next to Imran. Bahar, a brawny man with an impish smile and black hair styled into a rockabilly coif, wedged himself into the table beside me. Both stuck their hands out in greeting at the same time. I shook Ali's first and Bahar playfully rolled his eyes. "I do all the good work, and he gets the first greeting from the new guy," he groaned, kicking Ali under the table.

Bahar explained that the two of them were late because they had been volunteering, handing out free iftar meals to taxi drivers idling at busy intersections. "Ali only did it to smile at the hot men," he said.

Ali rolled his eyes back at Bahar. "So," he said, turning to Imran but glancing at me, "you found another gay to collect?"

Imran must have seen the confusion etched into my face. "You are so bad at your phone, my friend," he said, making me pull out my Blackberry. Imran grabbed it from my hand, showing me that he had sent me an invitation to a group chat with several of his friends. Fretting over his melee of messages that I had read as flirty, I'd completely missed that he had only been trying to connect me with other queer people.

We tucked into our dinner and the conversation shifted to the merits of their favorite childhood iftar foods. The three men slipped into easy chatter about Ramadans past, and I was grateful for a new topic; they had all been so cavalier about speaking the "G" word aloud in public. As I tried to process what it meant that Imran and I were suddenly *not* on a date, Ali pivoted toward me, asking me about my impressions of Abu Dhabi. I straightened up in my chair, conscious that this was my moment to impress these potential new friends with my astute assessment of the city.

"I think it could really become as exciting as Cairo someday," I said, telling them what I had learned from Ghosh's book about the history of the Egyptian capital beginning as an austere kind of place. Even though I was struggling to navigate the city in its present form, I thought expressing my hope for Abu Dhabi's future might demonstrate the kind of worldliness I wanted to project sitting at a table with three bilingual migrants who had uprooted their lives to be here. "We're so lucky to witness all this change," I offered proudly, backing up my analysis by mentioning the rapid changes I saw in the city's transportation—new parking schemes, new buses, new taxis.

Imran laughed. "You have crossed Al-Maqta, yes?" he asked. When I sheepishly replied that I had not, he explained that it was a bridge just beyond the ice rink connecting Abu Dhabi's major island to the mainland, including the outer rims of the capital and the rest of the country. I felt foolish when he stressed the bridge's location—so close to where I was taxiing most afternoons for skating, yet I hadn't even seen it—especially since it inadvertently revealed the fact that I hadn't even left the island.

"Did you know Abu Dhabi used to be more like a peninsula?" Imran said. "Before the bridge, people needed to wait hours for low tide so they could cross onto the island." I watched Imran set down his fork and spread both his hands out wide in front of him, an action I recognized as something my father used to do at the dinner table when he particularly wanted to get through to me. "Don't you think that bridge was a big change?" he asked. "And what about when we Persians first came here?"

I met his question with a blank stare. Imran and Ali tried to fill me in on two hundred years of exchange between the Persian Empire and what is now the UAE as they scoffed down biryani. It was a cultural dialogue I had been completely unaware of. To redeem myself, eager to prove that I wasn't one of those people who thought the UAE was completely devoid of culture and history, I mentioned how wise I thought it was that the country was preserving Qasr Al Hosn. "It's some of the only history you can see," I said.

I saw Imran exchange a smirk with Ali as he dug into his pocket and pulled out a two hundred dirham note. He held it up for me to study. I immediately recognized the building on the back of the bill by its distinctive shape—those imposing concrete arches that looked like giant staples. But I didn't understand why Zayed Stadium featured so prominently on one of the country's major units of currency. He explained that even though it was fewer than forty years old, it was the oldest stadium in the Gulf, a national icon with an impressive pedigree that had hosted major events including the FIFA Club World Cup.

"This place is history, too," he said, stuffing the bill back into his pocket. All I could think about was how I had used a landmark building as my own personal warm-down gymnasium a few days earlier.

Bahar started quizzing me in rapid fire about what I had seen of my neighborhood so far. He mentioned Hamed Centre, the oldest place in the city to go shopping, "an architectural marvel" adorned with concrete brise-soleil, just down the block from my building. I had dismissed it as an unremarkable cement tower wedged in a row of other concrete. A couple blocks further, I learned I had also missed El Dorado, the city's oldest cinema; he described a green marquee that had been welcoming audiences for over forty years. I hadn't even differentiated its sign from all the other neon surrounding it. He rattled off several other buildings that had been standing for decades, a few even predating the founding of the country, places that I had assumed had all sprung out of the ground recently.

"You know, your Statue of Liberty—it's nothing compared to two thousand years of Persian history," he said, brushing his hands together. "But we still call it history."

He was right. I had thought Abu Dhabi was still at its inception, that we were watching a city truly bloom for the first time. I recognized two-hundred-year-old Qasr Al Hosn as history because it looked like what I thought history should look like, but it stood in my mind as an outlier. I didn't see history as a continuum that we were in the midst of, that change had been happening for years, that it was all around us, complex and nonlinear. Hamed Centre, El Dorado, and all the buildings I had dismissed—they too stood as testament, even for those like me who didn't know their history.

I wanted to take the heat off of myself for a while, so I asked Bahar how he knew so much about my neighborhood. "I lived near you," he said, describing buildings along Electra Street using the kind of landmark navigation I was slowly coming to understand. I thought I wasn't going to be able to pinpoint his old building—another failure on my part—until he started speaking about a structure with porthole-like sunshades hiding rows of neat balconies. It was the building that captured my attention on my taxi rides to the ice rink, the one I couldn't find anything about online. I wanted him to tell me everything.

"People call it the Al-Mazru'i Building," he said, after the owner. Bahar explained that much of the information about the buildings built in the 1970s and '80s—the names of the contracted construction companies, their design houses, and sometimes even their architects—was often lost to the ages. I remembered the weathered face of the Indian shopkeeper who insisted on calling the area around the university the Old Fish Market despite him never seeing it in his life. It was these migrants who preserved these buildings, I realized; they were the ones who told the city's story.

Glancing over at Imran and Ali, I realized that they were already deep in a parallel conversation. Conscious that Ali had not contributed much to our talk—though I realized then that it was less a conversation and more an education for my benefit—I suddenly felt like the person who appears in a group and asks what everyone is talking about, only to force the discussion back to its starting point.

As we scarfed down another plate, I noticed a few patrons leaving their meals to go pray outside. Wanting to seem accommodating after having misjudged Imran's religious devotion at the ice rink, and eager not to let Ali and Imran float too far from our conversation, I offered that they could go pray if they needed, assuring them with a wave of my hand that I would be fine by myself for a few minutes. Perhaps I also offered so I could have the chance to take a few minutes alone and recalibrate after the shame of needing their world explained to me like a child.

Imran only laughed again. "Oh no, brother, we don't pray."

I must have left my fork sitting motionless atop my plate for some time, my food growing cold in front of me. Bahar pointed to my plate with his own fork. "Do not judge Iranian food because of this one restaurant alone. It is only a buffet," he grinned, and Ali and Imran laughed. And with that, the conversation moved back to childhood iftars.

All three of them seemed so convivial, so loose, and though I no longer needed to carry the anxiety of being on a date, my unease shifted like an awkward weight upon my back. Even as I worried about the ramifications of the topic re-emerging, I wanted the conversation to circle back to queerness. In the hopes of bringing it back up organically, I asked them about their childhood, hoping to seamlessly transition from their talk about holidays past to queer memories growing up together. Ali put down his fork and punched Imran playfully with his fist.

"We met here on a volleyball team two years ago," Ali said. None of them knew each other before they arrived, meeting instead through mutual friends who joined the same team. Ali went on to describe a team composed of Filipinos and Brazilians and even a Nepali who always told the same funny joke about all of the great spots in Kathmandu for beach volleyball. "No husband though, these two Persians were the only other gays," he said, laughing before pulling out a phone and taking a selfie to send to the group.

A volleyball team. It was not the clandestine meeting I had expected for three gay men in the UAE. But then again, I realized that I wasn't quite sure what I had expected. Or, perhaps, I had a vague idea of what I expected: a story about shame, heaviness, and burden. But burden is what I suddenly felt, from my own ungainliness, from all my assumptions being revealed. About this not-date, about this city I clearly didn't understand, about these three men sitting in front of me who I thought would be something else entirely—in their religion, their manner, their every facet. We were off the ice, but it was slippery here, too, and I was slowly becoming aware that the very act of living in the Gulf would require a constant interrogation, not just of the place itself, but also of why I thought about it the way I did.

"My problem was that not only had I not known much about the Middle East, but what I *did* know, and how I *did* think, had been an obstacle to original and accurate and moral thinking," I would later read in American journalist Suzy Hansen's account of her time in Turkey, and of the surreal game of catch-up she played abroad grappling with her previous unawareness of the reaches and effects of American exceptionalism and cultural illiteracy. It was a sentiment I was beginning to feel about what I thought I knew of the region, as well as both queerness and migration.

Later, filled with chelo kebab and sareshk polow, we pushed our chairs back from the table and walked out into the night heavy with humidity. Shoulder to shoulder, we strode down the block, taking up the width of the sidewalk and filling the air with our silence. It was the kind of pervasive quiet that usually foretold the end of a night's festivities, but Imran cocked his head to the right and motioned for us to head inside the block.

Ducking off the main street, another world emerged. Where moments earlier we had been walking along a six-lane highway studded with sleepy lamp posts, we were suddenly in a snarl of low-rise commercial buildings: cafés slinging chai, men sitting curbside in little clusters, and even a Pakistani confectionary selling sweets despite the late hour. Children were still running barefoot through the parking lot, their parents lounging on unfurled blankets, enjoying the Ramadan festivities. I had seen only a languid city, but the bustle here was inside the block, stirring up the heavy nighttime air.

Imran led us to an Indian embroidery and sewing accessories shop. I was just beginning to look at rows of flashy threads and spools of intricate trim when I saw Imran, holding a little paper bag folded once at the top, already beckoning us at the exit. "We have to get to the tent," he said. Some of the friends on the gay BBM group were already waiting at suhoor, the post-iftar meal and hangout session that often extended to the wee hours of the morning before the day's fasting began anew.

As we headed back outside, I motioned to his bag, and Imran delicately pulled out four golden tassels. "Don't worry, there is another great shop like this just behind your building," he said like it was my most pressing concern. I wanted to ask what Imran was going to do with four golden tassels. I wanted to ask him about his queerness, about why he was here. I wanted to ask him so many things.

Instead, Imran asked if I was joining them for suhoor. I looked at my watch. I wanted to stay with them and meet his other friends. It felt silly—wasteful, even—to miss this opportunity, but I explained that I had scheduled a Skype date with my boyfriend and that I was already late. As I bid the three men farewell, I had a sudden urge to be honest with him about my expectations for the evening, as if speaking this awkward truth might offer some kind of recognition for everything that they had explained to me tonight. And so I leveled with them: I thought Imran had invited me on a date.

"A date!" Imran asked. "Who do you think I am?" he joked,

pulling me in for a friendly parting embrace.

I thought about that question as I walked away. I remembered my sureness that Imran had "numbered" me based on an article I had read in the *New York Times*, as though that alone could make me know him, his motivations, this place. What I did know was that I wanted to understand who he was and why he was here. But instead, I walked home alone through the darkness, retreating to the comfort of familiarity with James—a comfort I would need to let go of sooner than I ever could have anticipated.

2: A CRUISE

(Abu Dhabi: Tahsan)

HAVING TWO SEPARATE APARTMENTS in the same building was a funny thing.

When my boyfriend James arrived in Abu Dhabi a month after me, he moved into a studio five floors beneath me. Most afternoons after finishing work, I dropped my bag just across my threshold and made my way downstairs to meet him. The lifts always took ages to arrive. While I waited in the cavernous elevator bank, I often thought about a secondhand rumor I heard during my first week through the friend of a colleague, an American employed by the city's urban planning council. The story went that after the architecture firm for Sama Tower had completed its final design, the main contracting company had strong-armed massive changes to the structure, doubling the height of the building without accounting for any additional elevator shafts.

I grew restive listening to the whirr of machines roll past me in both directions, never seeming to land on my floor. How could a twenty-five-story residential building swell into a fifty-story tower to house double its planned number of tenants? I wondered whether the lift doors would ever open, but when I heard the elevator chime closer to my lobby, I fretted also whether someone might suddenly appear from behind them. Even when James's plan for the evening amounted to little more than tearing into a bag of Doritos during a repeat viewing of *The Devil Wears Prada*, heading to his apartment always felt illicit. I made a point of wearing my work clothes as I traveled from my front door to his, hoping they might act as a sort of international signifier, that a man in stiff loafers and a starched button-down could deflect any curiosity about why he was wandering between residential floors.

I discovered the tower's staircase tucked off a corridor one afternoon while trying to find the trash chute. I started ducking into it to make my journey downstairs, savoring the emptiness, grateful that the low hum of the interior ventilation shaft masked my descent from landing to landing. I relished the feeling of the roughcast concrete steps on my feet and the gritty unpainted walls as I traced them with my fingers. It was an aesthetic that divulged a secret: this stairwell designed not to be seen. Discovering this emergency exit, and realizing that a hasty getaway existed just down the hall, slackened the unease that gripped me walking to James's apartment. But what, exactly, unsettled me—the health and safety implications of the tower's alleged rash changes, its sheer number of residents, the peril of so many watchful eyes—was obscured. I felt a kind of calm in that empty stairwell the same way I experienced the rumor of the building itself: as something I internalized without interrogating it fully.

James's studio was smaller than my apartment, with a bed that abutted his coffee table, but we spent most nights at his place. I didn't think much about why we whiled away those evenings curled up on his loveseat when we had an ample corner sofa waiting five floors above us, but it reminded me distantly of the way we had cocooned ourselves within his New York dorm the previous year. After he had asked me out, I spent entire weekends with him tangled in an unwieldy Ikea duvet, smoking joints and studying Christina Aguilera music videos on repeat, subsisting off delivery McDonalds and only leaving the apartment to buy more rolling papers from a corner shop in the East Village. Even then, I teased him about the ironic nomenclature of our relationship—"dating," "going out"—when in fact we rarely greeted the city together, two boys blinded to the bright world of Manhattan by a windowless bedroom.

We lived a similar existence those first few weeks together in Abu Dhabi (except for the joints, which, like homosexuality, featured prominently on the laundry list of activities illegal in the UAE)—devising ways to wring comfort out of makeshift familiarity. He ordered us delivery Pizza Hut. I torrented all his favorite Meryl Streep films. And when we failed at ordering our favorite board game, Settlers of Catan, to Abu Dhabi, we handcrafted it in its entirety, piece by painstaking piece.

One evening, while cutting little hexagonal cardboard pieces with dull kitchen scissors, I suggested a quick excursion to the nearby Indian embroidery shop to source some more materials for the board game—lurid glass gemstones and cheap plastic chains like I had seen with Imran. When James insisted on staying to whittle the most important game piece from a wine cork, I joked that he had the resourcefulness of a prison inmate. Settling back into the loveseat, the call to prayer rang out but he continued hacking away at the cork with a cheap butter knife. Nothing could fracture his singular focus. I instinctively looked out his window to watch people head toward the mosque, but there was no reason for him to look up, I realized; from his vantage point, he had no view of the city other than the darkening sky.

Holed up in his apartment those first few months, I was dimly aware of wasted opportunities to figure out Abu Dhabi's landscape, but I tried to let any agitation roll off me as I did when our intercontinental phone date made me miss my first suhoor with Imran. I had felt claustrophobic by the end of those weekends crammed together in his New York dorm, and restless also earlier that summer sitting down to dinner every night at his parents' house upstate, but we had always emerged. And whether it was for a walk through the West Village or a drive down the smooth tarmac of the I-87 outside Albany, I would grab his hand and feel grateful for that cloistered time, aware of how unreachable building a life with another man had felt even just a few years earlier, before leaving the Midwest.

At my most impatient, as Ramadan wound down and I left texts and invitations from Imran's BBM group unanswered, I wanted to ask James if he would have taken his job if I hadn't been offered mine first; if he really would have left his tight-knit family behind and stepped into this new life with me. But I held these questions back, throwing my energy instead into helping him nest, into creating a domesticity for us so that we might emerge here together, too. I reminded myself that it had taken time for me to find my way into the streets alone, and that we would also now have to fashion an entirely new kind of rhythm in public as a foreigner couple, something I told myself Imran could not advise on as a single man: a sort of reactive syncopation to the unfamiliar cadence and meter around us.

My early forays into work in Abu Dhabi were littered with similar unease and handwringing from Americans. Like the teaching assistants, most of the administrators at the university had been poached from leading liberal arts schools across the States. The only glaring exception was the new chief operating officer, an austere and surprisingly willowy former Navy Seal who chaired a weekly meeting for something he called the Master Work Plan. Though he didn't have any experience working in higher education, he imported an elaborate traffic light Excel document from his deployments to Iraq and Afghanistan to project manage the logistics of getting the university ready for students' arrival.

Sitting at a wooden boardroom table with professionals for the first time, I listened to several administrators inquiring about an item that seemed to have perpetually stayed in the untouched "red" category on the COO's document: mental health services for the university community. An uncomfortable silence pervaded the room; no one seemed to be able to speak to what, if any, private or municipal services might be available for faculty and the administration outside of the university's own health professionals. The task of finding out was finally delegated to someone, as the COO put it, who "had been on the ground" the longest and had had "their eyes on the frontline." Even as we filed out of the conference room behind him, his militaristic language seemed to hang in the air like we were preparing for an unexpected siege, or protracted trench warfare.

After the meeting, I stood in a snaking lunch line behind two administrators lamenting the state of their hair. Both middle-aged women had arrived a few months before me and were looking for a stylist, worried about finding someone who could match the skill of their hairdressers "back home." Grabbing a plate of mashed potatoes, one woman suggested checking out an online message board she had heard about called ExpatWoman "for military wives and trailing spouses."

Later that night, while James used his newly acquired copy machine access to print hundreds of black-and-white images for our board game, I pulled up the forum on my laptop. ExpatWoman: the name made me cringe, it sounded so suburban. But I also figured that I might use some of the advice myself, at least for a haircut. My last trim had been a few days before graduation—a shoddy hack job in a Lower East Side basement barber shop open a few hours once a week for heavily discounted but questionably executed student cuts. But in order to access the forum, I needed to first register an online profile.

I quickly dismissed keying in some variation of my name or initials. The hours I had spent lurking in online queer message boards and chat rooms as a pubescent kid had taught me both the safety and thrill of creating a fake online persona. I thought about the language and signifiers I had heard that day spent interacting almost exclusively with Americans, trying to inspire my message board handle: "Military wives." "Boots on the ground." "Frontline." *Why had we marched out of a university conference room behind an Iraq war veteran whose "regional experience" was in two countries thousands of miles away?* "Trailing spouses." *Was that James?* "Expat." *Was that me?*

On the table next to James sat the neat stacks of images he had printed. In Catan, players fight over five resources to determine control over burgeoning cities. Merciless expansion and shifting empires propelled the game, and we decided to change the resources to five that felt more regionally apt: camels, sand, palm, gold, and oil. These were the denominators we saw, the prism with which we understood our new home. We called our version Settlers of Abu Dhabi.

Stumped for a fake online profile name, I thought about AbuDhabiSettler, but it seemed too on the nose. I settled on CatanExpat instead. "Expat": it wasn't a word I had known to use on myself; even in Yemen, I had seen myself as a student. Expatriate was a word for British people; expats had mosquito nets and drank quinine by the gallon. It was a word for conquerors and exploiters recreating home amidst what they viewed as a hostile, inhospitable place.

As James stuck tiny paper images of camels and gold to the game board, I spent a few minutes trawling the message board and jotting down any phone numbers I could find for hair stylists recommended at the Sheraton, the Hilton, and a handful of other hotel chains. But after placing a few calls, it was clear they were all outlandishly out of my price range; I hadn't even yet received my first paycheck. Reaching for my phone again, I decided to message Imran for advice. Though I'd been ignoring his messages for weeks, his response came through in moments.

You want a barber? They are on every street. Walk outside brother!

I read his terse suggestion again: walk outside. It seemed so obvious. The thing I wanted to be doing; the one thing I wasn't. Softly running my hands through James's unkempt mane, I asked if he might want to find a barber with me, but he was adamant about finishing his glue job.

I looked down at the scruffy game board, our piddling cuts to each sheet of cardstock, suddenly aware we had made the board much too small. But I wasn't sure I had the fortitude to tell him we might have to throw the whole thing out—or that I didn't think I had the resolve to recreate once more the fragile little world we'd built.

▽▽▽

It was the creativity inherent in the barber shop names that initially caught my eye, and then the patterns that emerged from the torrent of neon signs. I first noticed the idyllic-sounding ones wedged inside tight residential blocks: Green Hills Salon, Happiness Gents. Then there were the three named after sparkling gemstones—Diamond Bright, Ruby, Red Emerald—strung like a bracelet along a perfect five-kilometer axis I walked parallel to Electra Street. And, seemingly everywhere, the curious propensity of shops inspired by weather patterns and the cosmos, scattered across the city with a vastness their very names evoked: Clouds Gents, Uranus Saloon, Half Moon, First Star.

Most of them were entirely glass-fronted, and it was the energy inside that kept me in rapt attention whenever I walked past: men in crisp white smocks unscrewing jars filled with a rainbow of lotions, rushing to slather men with velvety shaving cream or layer them with steaming cotton towels. Globular vanity lights rimmed wide mirrors, lighting up barbers as they fussed over clients like makeup artists brushing up actors backstage. Whenever I mustered enough nerve to take a step toward a window for a closer look, the bright, illuminated mirrors always created the uncanny illusion that, even as I stood frozen on the sidewalk, I was somehow already inside.

I felt particularly drawn to one barbershop crammed between a mosque and a currency exchange around the corner from my apartment. Full-length windows lined the shopfront, frosted along the center so that I could always see the tops of barbers' heads but never any patrons, their chairs reclined in an opaque haze. Only the narrow doorway was fully transparent, offering me one furtive glance inside per day on my stroll around the block. In my wariness not to be noticed, I could only make out the sound of laughter and the mint green of the shop's walls, never precise movements or to whom they corresponded. I was reminded of the voyeuristic contrivances I felt on an ice rink, attempting to size up other skaters while simultaneously trying to mask my curiosity.

One evening, as I tried to take my casual peek into the shop just after dusk, I was met by the unblinking stare of a barber in the doorway. He stood, smocked arms folded, with his nose nearly touching the glass, his eyes cast on me like security floodlights. The intensity of his stare made me feel as though he had already been keeping tabs on me, like he had not just clocked my daily glances weeks ago, but that my curiosity about the inside of his shop was embarrassing in its conspicuousness. I checked across both my shoulders in hopes that he was actually looking at another passerby, but there was no one else; his hard stare was meant for me alone.

When I turned back to him, his face softened and he pointed to my hair, ushering me inside with an urgent wave. I thought I had been walking past this shop for over a month because I wanted to know what was happening to all the men beyond the clouded glass. But as the barber pushed the door open for me, I realized that what I really wanted was to be concealed along with them.

Only one of the five chairs was unoccupied, and yet the stout barber still physically directed me to the empty station, clutching me by the forearm all the way to the far-left corner of the shop. I completed the set: a patron for each chair, a chair for each barber, and a barber for each washstand with matching green ceramic sinks and ovular mirrors. Confronted by the reflection of my own wild hair and a barber staring expectantly at me, I realized that I didn't actually know what kind of style I wanted. I had always been notoriously fickle with my haircuts, binding myself to roughly two-year cycles in which I attempted to grow my hair to my shoulders. Since the release of "MMMBop" in 1997, I had aspired for Taylor Hanson–like locks. Though my initial quests were hampered by a series of unfortunate mullets—my flawed understanding of hair growth as a child meant I thought I only needed to grow the hair on the back of my head—the real truth was that I never mustered the diligence to make my long locks work. For years, I had impulsively colored, chemically straightened, or dramatically chopped my hair into some new style, always finding a way to sabotage myself along the way to my ultimate goal.

The barber smiled at me for the first time, his thick mustache rising high on his face to reveal two rows of gleaming teeth. When it was clear I would only be meeting his smile with a vacant stare, he made a scissors motion with his fingers and cocked his head to the side. Remembering my awkward first encounter with Imran, I finally replied in English that I wanted my hair short on the sides and longer on top. It didn't seem like the right time to start another cycle of aspirational Hanson hair, I decided. My barber responded by wordlessly rifling through his drawer and pulling out two different clipper lengths, a number two that he held above my ear and a number five he pushed into the forest of curls atop my head. Before I had time to nod my approval, he turned on the shaver and mowed past my temples. As he sheared me, he began humming a harmonic third above the electric buzzing of the shaver.

The laughter I had heard so often walking past crashed over the shop in waves as I leaned back in my chair. Two chairs over, a man spoke with his barber about plans for the Eid al-Adha holiday. The two men on the far side of the shop shouted in Arabic about the soccer match blaring from the screen mounted on the wall. And the patron to my right watched his barber deftly swirl two wooden sticks through a bubbling vat of black goo like a concessions worker gathering cotton candy at a fairground. Without hesitation or ceremony, the barber pried open the man's nostrils and shoved both sticks up his nose. As the barber pulled them out—along with clumps of nose hair—I tried to offer the man a smile of solidarity, but I saw it materialize in the mirror as an involuntary grimace. His only reply was a quick, stoic wink.

My barber shaved the sides of my head with the same confident resolution and speed as the nostril-cleaning beside me. But when it came time to cut the hair atop my head, he carefully pulled scissors from his drawer and hovered mere centimeters above me. Seeming to take five snipping motions for every hair he actually trimmed, my barber fretted endlessly from side to side, checking every conceivable angle for symmetry. Before he had even finished half my head, the four men in the seats around me had been replaced by four more; by the time he held up a little handheld mirror, four more had replaced them as well. As I inspected the back of my new cut, I realized that we hadn't spoken once during our forty minutes together. Leaning forward to rustle my wallet from my pocket, he grabbed me by the forearm again and yanked me back into the chair.

"Massage," he said simply, gently closing my eyelids with slow, circular motions of his fingertips. I was taken aback by the sureness and care of it all—the quick work with the electric shaver, the meticulous crafting with his scissors, the thoroughness of the massage. I couldn't remember ever being touched by another human on my eyelids, and yet he was applying the perfect amount of pressure on one of the most sensitive areas of my body. With my eyes forcibly shut, I remembered meeting his knowing stare outside, how it felt like he had clocked my curiosity before I had even said a word.

The tempo and etiquette of the mint-colored shop started feeling more familiar as I began returning—initially twice a month for haircuts but then, soon after, twice a week for hot-towel shaves. There were no appointments; to enter through the opaque glass was to submit to a merry-go-round of five distinct barbers with five distinct grooming techniques, like how the barber closest to the door was the only one to use a shaving brush (the rest softened my hair follicles with vigorous rubs of their open palms) or how the man in the right corner enthusiastically incorporated neck cracking into his massage repertoire.

I started recognizing the cultural touchstones for requesting hairstyles, which were far more nuanced than my decade-long vacillation between "Hanson" and "not Hanson." The barbers kept rows of pictures of both Khaleeji and Indian singers posted above the cash register for creative consultation, though new stars with even more geometric, precision-crafted beards seemed to be swapped in every few visits. The television was also a frequent reference point, with men often explicitly seeking out a hairstyle that mirrored the particular football player dashing across the screen (usually Ronaldo with his shellacked faux-hawk). In the afternoon, the TV was reserved for Bollywood movies. Malayalam, Arabic, and Tagalog-speaking customers would drop in to ask for cuts inspired by a Hindi film playing on a Tamil-dubbed movie channel switched on by a bunch of Bengali barbers.

The protocol I had the hardest time adhering to was the one that involved order. When the barber chairs were full, as they frequently were, men waited their turn on a metal bench along the far wall, grabbing from a multilingual pile of newspapers. When a chair became free, I was often unsure where I sat in the queue, having gotten lost in my head working to translate one of the Arabic papers. The image I had of the Gulf—of bustle, of movement, of so many migrants coming and going into and out of residences, shops, the region itself—made me quick to jump, as though I needed to assert myself and declare my place. So when I stood, I usually cut in line. I saw my error in the way the other men waved me to the chair even after I had raised my hands in *mea culpa*: I had made my assumptions apparent, and it was already too late to sit back down.

Whether out of conscientiousness or just plain embarrassment, I started paying closer attention while I was waiting. I began to notice one man in particular who seemed to be on the same schedule as me, always showing up during the height of the shop's most hectic hours, just after dinnertime. Most weeks, he would open a paper but almost immediately fold it across his lap, leaning back against the bench and closing his eyes. I could never tell if he drifted off or just sat in silence, but he somehow always seemed to end up with my first barber, the one in the far-left corner. While I was shuttled from barber to barber with each consecutive visit, it was like he was shooting dice and kept throwing a pair of sixes, ending with the same fortuitous roll every time.

I sat next to him one evening, watching him settle into his familiar chair as his barber laid a gown across his chest. The bright smile on his face curled into a near smirk as they pattered chirpily in Bengali. When the barber turned to set the spray bottle on the washstand, I saw the man reach out from beneath his gown and pinch him in the ass. The barber yelped and grabbed the bottle, spraying the man in the back of the neck, water dripping past his shirt collar. As the men giggled, I cautioned myself not to make assumptions by recalling Imran's banter with me—how it had seemed so forward and insistent but was entirely platonic. I thought the teasing would continue, but when the man leaned in for another pinch, the barber shot him a wide-eyed look, yanking his head to the side.

In the mirror's endless series of reflections and obstructions, I couldn't tell if he was signaling that I was watching or that someone else in the shop was. The only other face I could see was the same photo of the UAE's founder that was plastered across Zayed Sports City. But here, Sheikh Zayed sat both behind and in front of me in the same moment. As my barber angled my chair backward, the portrait seemed to actively loom over me, inspect me, remind me that whenever I was doing the watching, I was also being watched.

I had begun to chat a bit more with my barbers; the man with the trimmer to my temples was telling me about his plans to briefly return to his village that summer for three weeks to get married. Our conversation often lacked nuance, but we had learned to cobble English and Arabic, second or third languages for us, breaking our dialogue down to common denominators and then building it back up, testing each other with new vocabulary and linguistics gradation as we went. But even when we spoke in clipped, periodic phases, our chat was also layered with another language whenever he would furrow his brow or jerk his head at me and I instinctively obeyed, tilting my head for him to clean up my neckline or sideburns.

Cast your chin downward, his nod said as I stared at the playful men, the same way *Cut it out* was conveyed by the barber to the pinching man beside me. We could see it in the eyes, watch it in the mirror, sense it in the air; commands hadn't been uttered aloud but they also had somehow already been spoken. It's what finally put me at ease in this place behind the frosted windows, I realized: that even with all the noise around us and all the different tongues spoken, we didn't need to open our mouths to be understood. It was a skill I had learned easier than any spoken language, a wordless fluency I cultivated all those years ago.

▽▽▽

I don't remember the first time I stood at a urinal and met the eyes of the man next to me.

But I do remember, very young, being drawn to spaces where I could surround myself with the bodies of men. Even as a kid, I would loiter in the YMCA dressing room, fiddling with my hair in the mirror, my combination lock, my swimsuit drawstrings—anything that gave my eyes time to wander. Or, as an adolescent, when my father set me free at the local hardware store, I would dawdle near the checkout as men who smelled like diesel and sawdust walked into the restroom, watching them with something I didn't yet know to identify as longing.

When I could finally drive, I started going out of my way to discover more of these spaces and figure out the best time to visit them. In tenth grade, I feigned a sudden interest in after-school weightlifting so I could spend most of my gym sessions in the steam room, where men who just finished work dangled towels lazily around their thighs. Afterward, I roamed the back roads in the surrounding counties, pulling off at parks and rest stops, hoping to catch another driver on his way home idling at a trailhead or lingering outside a grimy stall.

Just off the freeway sat the mall, the place I visited the most, not out of idle teenage boredom but because of Hobby Lobby, a crafting store favored by octogenarians. By puttering up and down its Home Storage & Organization aisle, I could always keep the mall's bathrooms in my line of sight. For hours, I would pretend to inspect the storage products: woven nylon baskets, two-toned willow baskets, little trunks of faux wood designed to look like miniature treasure chests. When I saw a man stride toward the bathroom, I would rush into the lobby and follow him to the urinals, hoping to feel the familiar weight of curious eyes as I unzipped my jeans.

I frequented the mall—dying in the way most American malls in the early aughts were slowly dying—most days except Sunday, when Hobby Lobby was closed and my intention felt obvious, with little more than a nail salon and a claw machine to provide cover for my pacing. It would be years before I would learn that the store's Sunday closure was in accordance with the beliefs of its evangelical founder, the same man who would lobby the US government for exemption from laws prohibiting LGBTQ discrimination and would also later need to return nearly 12,000 stolen artifacts from the Middle East from his "Museum of the Bible." Back then, the basket aisle of a store founded by a bigot and a pillager—where I could tuck myself away, hidden but in plain sight—didn't seem more unwelcoming than anywhere else, because everywhere felt inhospitable.

Before I knew the name for cruising, I felt these places vibrate with a kind of ineffable possibility that I couldn't find anywhere else. In rural Wisconsin, I didn't have any gay role models who could teach me about the history of the practice, let alone know any gay peers who could engage with me in the unspeakable activity I so craved inside these spaces. Trawling chat rooms and online messaging services, I explored virtual spaces, too, but to find them, I needed to acknowledge that my queerness had a name. At a time when articulating my desire felt inexorably tangled up with the words others used to denigrate queerness—inferiority, shame, danger—I could return instead to the mall, to rest stops, to the locker room and explore with my body without ever having to say a word.

I didn't consciously choose to return to cruising in Abu Dhabi. As days of drinking Tuborg and playing board games on the tile floor of James's apartment turned into weeks, I was grateful for my own place. On the nights we spent together, after everyone had left, James would often fall asleep on top of me, fully clothed, his breath hot with stale beer. After his fourth or fifth tallboy of the night, I had learned to check that the air conditioning was set to maximum; his heft, which had felt so comforting in New York, felt stifling as I lay sweating under him in the darkness.

One night, when I felt the muscles in his chest relax, and his shallow breaths gave way to gritty snoring, I threw his weight off me and climbed out of bed. Dodging takeout containers, I looked at our makeshift board game pieces that littered the ground. I tried to lean up against his window to see through the dark the embroidery store where I had bought the plastic gemstones, but it was hidden out of view. The barbershop sat just beyond it. I thought about how I'd still been unable to convince James to come to either shop. I checked the bedside clock—barely eleven—and looked at the compressed, fetal shape under the covers. If nothing had moved him then, I knew I wouldn't rouse him now. Slamming the door louder than I should have, I ducked into the emergency staircase, tracing my fingers along the unpainted walls as I descended thirty floors.

Reflexively, I began to wander toward the barbershop. I passed two men drinking tea from Styrofoam cups, sprawled on the curb of the new parking scheme where cars had been parked haphazardly only a few weeks earlier. One of the men leaned against the new parking machine, obstructing the coin slot, the other against the sign announcing the amended parking laws. His back obscured the hours, but I had read it when it was first installed. Midnight: that was when the parking enforcement stopped, when the dead of night eclipsed the forces of regulation.

The barbershop was shuttered. I didn't really expect, or even want, I realized, for it to be open. Instead, I kept walking—across the street, then on and on—finding myself in a block I had never been. Neon signs for travel agencies and tailors and internet cafés all sat dark, the sidewalks empty. Still, I wandered vaguely north, unmindful of a precise direction and yet goaded by some internal compass that nowhere was ever really empty of people or promise.

After emerging from a long, tiled underpass two kilometers from Sama Tower, I found it: a section of seaside promenade sitting at the very tip of the island. The Gulf bobbed in front of me; behind, waterfront towers twinkled, separated from the walkway by the six-lane highway. The promenade felt both part of and removed from the city, a bit of land jutting out along the sea, dangling precariously as though it might detach from land at any moment. There was activity here—a family on bicycles whizzed past; a few couples sauntered along the blue tiles, hand in hand. Dotted with people, the walkway stretched out as far as I could see, a gallant, unbending path that hugged the Gulf.

But I noticed immediately that I could also descend a level farther. I followed a set of stairs down to an even lower walkway that kissed the water's edge, so intimately close to the sea that I felt the salt settling into the back of my lungs like a lover nestling into the crook of my chest. The lower promenade wasn't a strict straightaway like the upper one was; every few hundred meters, the walkway wound around raised landscaped terraces that extended into the water like little miniature peninsulas. Everywhere else I had seen the Gulf, it had been motionless, but sitting on one of the benches that studded the edge of the water, I heard a constant churn, as if the waves couldn't hold their breath any longer, as if the sea itself yearned to divulge a secret.

The lower promenade buzzed too with activity, but the energy shifted perceptibly, and I knew immediately what this place was. It was a space where men appeared to busy themselves. At first glance, the half-dozen figures all seemed occupied, even rapt in their individual activities. One sat on a bench, his face illuminated by the green glow of a cell phone. Another rummaged through a bag of pistachios. Several others decked in gauzy sweatpants stretched, touching their toes or propping one leg up against a bench. But the authenticity of their actions fell apart upon closer inspection—the man with the phone kept setting it down; the bag of pistachios only had shells left inside; the exercising was all too convulsive, the hasty arch of limbs belying that these men yearned to move them in other ways. I had seen this before, this commotion that sat somewhere between rehearsal and performance, as though the men weren't sure whether they were still waiting in the wings or had already been thrust on stage.

But what really gave the lower promenade away as a cruising ground were the furrowed brows, the deep, penetrating looks. A steady stream of men paraded in both directions, faces etched with searching and also an awareness that they too were being searched. Some leaned against the galvanized wire railing along the water's edge, peering not out at the grandeur of the sea but back toward the possibilities that lay within the shadows along the walkway. I joined them long enough to begin to recognize faces; men were ambling the length of the promenade and looping back around to complete a circuit—walking, watching, waiting, vacating, returning. It was not so much a stream, I realized, but the lapping of waves. I had not yet swum through the Gulf, and yet I had already been submerging myself in this same water thousands of miles away for years.

The hundred meters between the little peninsulas felt like a fashion catwalk, a walkway where dozens of men strutted, dripping in both confidence and coyness. But it felt also like a catwalk in the theatrical sense, dangling a hundred feet above a proscenium, where every movement was tempered by the presence of danger. The walkway was called the Corniche, French for "road on a ledge," and though the precipice implied in the name was the sea, for those of us cruising, the danger was in the parallel upper promenade with its bikes and its families, separated from those who were searching for public sex by only a four-foot retaining wall and some sparse shrubbery.

I could see immediately why the men were gravitating toward the little peninsulas that stretched farther out into the water, buffered from the upper walkway by long, landscaped terraces. It reminded me of the thrill of finding the perfect, cloistered restroom in the Midwest, one at the end of a long, echoing hallway, where the sound of heavy footsteps traveled faster than the men they carried. Even at a distance I could tell that the peninsulas would be the kind of place that offered those critical few extra moments—enough time to hastily buckle a belt or throw a meter of distance between two sets of hips. They would provide the difference between slapdash camouflage and complete exposure, where even the thinnest veneer of plausible deniability was better than the alternative.

The globular lamp posts that reminded me of the lighting in the barbershops fell away as I rounded the bend of the lower promenade onto the first peninsula. Leering into the blackness, I had to skirt right against the recessed benches to see whether anyone was using them. When I did meet the eyes of a sole dark figure, our bodies were already so close that there could be no doubt about our intentions. It was like a match to a stovetop already leaking kerosene, too late to pull away without a singe. But even as he fumbled with his drawstrings, I kept moving; it was too early to be engulfed. And anyway, I could see in his eyes, and knew from my own experience cruising in the Midwest, that I could return later if I wanted. For now, I was relishing the movement, the pace, the prospects, and then the back and forth—six or seven circuits—careful at first rounding onto each of the five little peninsulas, but then dropping my hand from my waistband lower and lower with each consecutive lap, the tug of possibility pushing away the fear of getting caught.

I started returning to the Corniche at night more frequently, often tacking on a jaunt after heading to the barbershop just before it closed. A few weeks after my first midnight, I sat again with a razor to my cheekbones next to the patron with the wry smile and his regular barber whom he'd grabbed by the ass. The money exchange next door had long shuttered and the shop was also quiet; the other three workers had already left for the night, and even the television had gone dim. The patron and his barber spoke Bengali with each other in a hushed largo, even their relative whispers filling up the empty shop. There was no pinching or spraying, but I still watched them, struck by the barber's prolonged eye contact with his friend in the mirror even as he held a blade to his neck, as though he knew intimately the precise shape of this man.

I had a sudden urge to tell them about the place in the dark near the sea, a place where they could navigate the contours of each other's bodies. I didn't really have a plan for how I would inform them, except that I found myself abruptly requesting a haircut on top of my shave—a service I didn't really need—just to make sure I didn't leave the shop before they finished. I asked for an elaborate fade, a style I knew would chew up time. I thought that if I left the shop alongside them, we might be able to start talking, and perhaps walking, suddenly arriving amidst those searching eyes along the shore, a place they would be grateful for and would immediately understand.

"Na'iman," my barber said to me after another half hour passed, spinning me around in my chair to inspect my new hairstyle. It was an Arabic word I loved, one often used by barbers. *You're fresh, you're clean*, it imparted, a blessing that felt like a perverse invocation for my two-kilometer journey to the Corniche.

With a little stalling on my part, all four of us walked out of the shop together. As my barber locked up, I watched the two men continue talking and grinning. For a moment, I thought we would walk off together without a hitch, that all I would have to do was join in their conversation and steer them toward the sea. But in an instant, the men parted, heading in opposite directions, and I was left waving goodbye lamely at my barber even though my feet weren't moving. I had so wanted to gift these men a space; it felt like a kind of duty to inform them, but they were already gone.

Late one night a few weeks later, stepping over the cans of Tuborg that had begun regularly spilling from James's counter onto the floor, I opened the door and walked again to the sea. I had left his familiar form sprawled across the mattress nearly a dozen times, compelled by the anticipation of what I might find instead on the Corniche. As I descended to the lower walkway once more, I could just make out a hunched figure sitting atop the terrace of the first peninsula.

He was actually sitting in the landscaping. Surrounded by wooden stakes and rows of rubber drip lines, I thought he might be a municipal gardener, one of the team of South Asian men in bright green jumpsuits who trimmed plants and tinkered with sprinkler systems, often late into the night. I noticed their odd hours because of the way their meticulous labor affected the rhythm of cruising: as they moved from the landscaping of one terrace to another, it would take one peninsula out of commission, pushing more men into less space.

I prepared to walk past him, but he already held one hand outstretched when I rounded the bend. From his perch on the edge of the terrace's retaining wall, I couldn't make out whether he had the fire in his eyes that I was so used to seeing among the men who prowled the Corniche.

"Hello, how are you?" he asked in English. He spoke quickly, confidently, and I responded in kind, letting him know that I was fine. I kept my phrasing succinct, not out of fear of a language barrier but to make clear that I wasn't really interested in conversation. To convey what I really wanted, I lowered my eyes and rubbed my hand on my lower abdomen, but when I looked up, I realized that he still held his hand out in greeting. This would be the moment, I thought. Once our skin touched, he would know that I was here for the same reason as him.

His handshake was firm but didn't linger. I had to awkwardly half-climb up one of the benches to reach his hand but then wasn't sure whether to keep standing there at his height, with my head also poking out conspicuously for anyone on the upper promenade to see. I decided to climb back down to try and entice him to move lower to where I wanted him.

It was hard to get a lock on his eyes, but for the brief second when our hands met, I saw that he was handsome, older, perhaps in his early forties, with a jaw surprisingly wide for a man so thin. I noticed also that he wasn't wearing the green jumpsuit of the gardeners, his lithe frame swallowed up instead by a thin, checkered button-down. I watched his pant legs billow in the light wind.

I tried to guess where he was from. It was something I would do walking back and forth on the Corniche, less an erotic curiosity, I would later realize, than something deeper—a feeling that if I could somehow know where he was from, I would have a greater sense of who he was, as though that were deducible. I thought he looked South Asian. I craned my head around to the next peninsula; there was no one else walking. It was one of those quiet nights of midweek. I decided I could indulge him in a little small talk if it might get me what I wanted.

His name was Tahsan and he was an accountant from Dhaka. He explained that he lived for six years with five compatriots in a shared flat not far from Sama Tower, pointing in the direction from which I had arrived. I wondered whether he was from Dhaka proper or whether, like one of my barbers, he was from somewhere just outside of it, a suburb or town that seemed to orbit around a metropolis. I had just learned from my barber that Dhaka had eight million inhabitants, a fact that struck me because it was roughly the population of New York and yet seemed so much more unwieldy in my head. As a kind of shorthand, I told him that I was a New Yorker even though it wasn't really true. It was easier to declare myself part of something I thought people might already have an idea of in their heads. But I didn't really have any meaningful sense of Bangladesh, my perception of it colored by how I exclusively encountered its citizenry abroad, milling in the barbershops and money exchanges of my neighborhood. It seemed like it must be a place of toil, a place from which one needed to escape.

As Tahsan spoke, I noticed that he rested his hand across his inner thigh but wasn't making any overt movements. He hadn't said anything erotic or sexual, and yet I could feel the magnetism of this place; I knew what it was for. Maybe he was nervous, I thought; perhaps he needed to know more about who I was before he would indulge.

"All of my barbers are Bangladeshi migrants," I offered lamely.

I couldn't see the expression on his face as he towered over me, but I did hear the waves in the darkness. His distance from me, perched up on the terrace, suddenly seemed so vast as I waited for a response that didn't come.

Men started appearing around the bend. I wasn't sure if I should continue investing time in a conversation that I didn't really want to be having, whether I could still salvage the outcome I wanted. I weighed sunk and prospective costs, watching his legs dangle just over the bench. He really wasn't actually that far, I wagered; if I could get him to climb down, I could have him right there on the wooden bench. I was trying to satisfy his desire for words even as they threatened to complicate that all I was really craving was a body in the darkness.

"I'm an American expat," I said suddenly. It felt even more inexplicable than my comment about my Bangladeshi barbers, calling myself an expatriate; even the shape of it felt unfamiliar in my mouth. I thought about the ExpatWoman forum. Most of my encounters with the word "expat" had been in written form, and even those had always seemed to intimate Britishness. In my America, people didn't travel across the world, let alone live there, and now I was attaching the word as some kind of signifier to define myself to someone else. I had a sudden image of my high school Spanish textbook open on my desk to a chapter on travel vocabulary. "Libre de impuestos." "Duty-free." I had needed to raise my hand to ask what it was. I had never been abroad before; I didn't understand the concept of international zones, of exemptions and duties, of systems and infrastructure that were exerting forces upon me and which I was also operating within and upholding. How was duty quantified? Did I have a duty to understand what felt like the farthest reaches of the world?

Tahsan hadn't even asked where I was from, but it had felt like an obligation to define myself in relation to being away from a place—a place I wasn't sure whether I was apologizing for or using to entice him. As a queer boy, I had once been pulled to a city of eight million, and I thought about how he had been pulled nearly four thousand kilometers away from his own urban ecosystem. I wondered what I could do to pull him two feet closer to me, down into the darkness.

"We are too much expatriates here," he scoffed, kicking his dangling legs. I thought he sounded apologetic, too, perhaps not just for the parade of men that had started to thread between us on their way across the Corniche but for all his compatriots across the country. There were an estimated seven hundred thousand migrant Bangladeshis in the UAE alone—a community nearly the same size as the entire Emirati population—though the exact number was obscured by the transience within much of the workforce of construction workers, drivers, and other unskilled laborers arriving for finite contracts.

Two years later, there would also be a reported stoppage of work visas offered to Bangladeshis for obscure reasons, though the UAE government would offer various explanations: a profusion of fake travel documents among applicants, "security concerns," the notion that there was no visa freeze at all. Why exactly did a country stop welcoming an entire population? Many questions like this would come to me later—ambiguity hiding behind supposed revelation—forcing a recasting of previous encounters, a reconsideration of past conversations, a rethinking of knowledge I thought I had. Another example: a year later, I learned that the word "too," an adverb of degree usually connoting negativity and excess, is often used by many South Asian speakers of English in place of the adverb "so." It was only after revisiting my journal entry about my first encounter with Tahsan that I would reevaluate what he meant by that statement, "We are too many expatriates." Was it possible that I had misunderstood the very first interaction with a queer person I wrote down? In uttering "too much," Tahsan had almost certainly meant "so many." It seemed likely that what had first rung in my ear as a kind of apology might in fact have been a statement with a different sort of intensification—one tinged not with unease but perhaps something closer to pride, as in, *There are so many of us here.*

But I wrote down our exchange in my journal that night after I snuck back into James's room because what really struck me was the other word he used: expatriate. The first time he said it, I thought he was parroting, a tactic I had learned from a friend in Yemen when we met to practice each other's languages. After I used a word or phrase he didn't understand, he would make me define it and then spend the rest of our meeting trying to work it into our conversation, often comically shoehorning it where it didn't belong. (He once tried to say that a man and woman having sex were "burning the midnight oil together.") I thought Tahsan was doing the same thing, taking a word that felt to me in that moment like it didn't belong to him—expatriate—and misappropriating it. Bastardizing it.

I realized later why the word stayed with me. I would have used a different word for him: *migrant.* "Migrant" or "guest worker" is what I had been calling my Bangladeshi barbers, all the patrons within the barbershop, the figures I watched walking thirty floors beneath my apartment window, the parade increasingly staring at us along the Corniche. The former suggested figures in motion; the latter, a kind of conditional presence hinging on hospitality. "Expat," on the other hand, seemed to carry a kind of potent agency, not to mention a cultural cachet. Though I had uttered it aloud, I didn't feel ready to call myself an expat, and I certainly wasn't ready for him to call himself that, either.

On the Corniche, two men had stopped to lean against the railing and were watching us talk. I watched one grab explicitly at his crotch. I thought about the word *queer*—how it had been a word in Wisconsin for others to use, to weaponize, to fire at me, and only in New York did I decide that it could finally be mine to use, too.

Tahsan's hand sat unmoving on his thigh, though I thought I saw him make the kind of eye contact with both men which betrayed the real reason for his presence on the Corniche. I knew why he was here, and yet he gave no indication that he would offer me what I wanted. There was as much ambiguity in his motions as in his idiosyncratic phrasing. I looked over at the one rubbing himself. I let the silence overwhelm my conversation with Tahsan and then followed the man around the bend to the next peninsula. I don't think I even bade Tahsan farewell.

▽▽▽

In the sea of men flowing across the Corniche, I found him every few weeks sitting among the same landscaping, unmoving.

One Sunday, I completed three or four circuits of the lower promenade without passing another man with the hunt in his eyes. I had only arrived at midnight, and suddenly it was after one thirty, then nearly two. I had left James passed out in his bed for almost two hours, and I needed to get up early for work in the morning—nearly one hundred copies of a fifty-page document had been mistakenly printed uncollated, and it had been decided that instead of reprinting, I would spread the pages out across a conference table and arrange them. It wouldn't be a difficult task, but I wanted to at least project the appearance of a semi-functional adult, so I decided to take another chance with Tahsan instead of waiting for something else that perhaps wouldn't come.

I climbed up the bench and sat atop the terrace with him,

pushing away fears of being so exposed. I tried to sit as close as possible to him, but when he didn't move, I began talking about work, abandoning my plan to graze my pinky along the length of his trousers. I didn't know why I brought it up; I didn't know how to explain that I had been relocated on a business-class ticket halfway across the world and given a furnished apartment, all so I could shuffle some papers from one place to another. If the conversation was again to turn to expatriates, I wasn't sure how I could justify that my visa had labeled me a skilled worker, unlike most of the men who paraded nightly across the Corniche.

Since I couldn't articulate what pulled me here, I asked what brought Tahsan. Remittances from the UAE alone totaled more than half a billion dollars per year; it seemed like this could be the only thing that drew all these men here. Even if my barber from Dhaka hadn't told me that his payday was the first Friday of the month, I could have guessed it; it was when I saw men queued up at ATMs and exchanges across the city. They were as suffused as the barbershops.

"This is my tree for sitting," he laughed. He pointed to it as though I couldn't see the branches looming above both of us. I wondered how deep the soil went beneath the tree before its roots hit brackish water, or whether a concrete slab protected it from drowning in the salt, nestling all its soil in a concrete basin to prevent it from withering and dying. He was still smiling at me. He hadn't really answered my question, but I wasn't sure whether he had understood it in relation to coming to the Corniche or the UAE. Perhaps I really had meant both.

"What do you want here?" I asked, more exasperation leaking out of my question than I had intended. I grabbed lewdly at my dick. I had had enough of his equivocation.

"I want people to stop releasing under my tree," he said, making an obscene little arc from his groin to the ground next to him. "And I want men to stop doing this," and with that he jumped down off the terrace and mimed wiping his dick on the retaining wall. It was true; I had seen men do both. Cruisers made a mess of the Corniche, especially on Fridays when it was at its busiest, after some men had spent on alcohol much of whatever they didn't send back home. It was the only time I didn't come to the Corniche, a reverse of how I hadn't come to cruise Hobby Lobby on Sundays.

Why didn't he want me? I didn't think I looked like I would do either of those things to his tidy little spot, trying to push away the fact that I thought there were people who looked like they would behave a certain way. I was suddenly struck by how he called it his tree, and that I had already somehow internalized that this was his territory, too, like he was its host, like only he could invite people here. In some ways, I supposed, he did—I'd never seen him move, let alone get kicked off his terrace by cruisers or gardeners. But he was down off the ledge for the first time. I thought perhaps we were finally getting somewhere.

"Do you want to go somewhere else?" I asked. A few men had started to gather, and I noticed then that Tahsan was looking at one man lingering in the corner. The moon lit up the night, and I saw that he was young, clean-shaven, with striking cheekbones that accentuated his dramatic fade. I rubbed my hands across my own new style. For the first time, I saw a rise in Tahsan's trousers, and he adjusted himself overtly while looking at the young man.

I felt the rolling boil of frustration. I had had no trouble attracting the attention of any men on the Corniche; in fact, the only one who forced me into conversation seemed to also be the only one with no interest in me at all. He shot a look to the other two loitering men, and they made a courteous exit, sauntering along toward the next peninsula. I watched Tahsan take a step toward the other young man and pull him into the crevice next to the bench. In the dark, I could just make out him waving his eyes from side to side at me, and then I understood. He wanted me to be his lookout.

I had seen this before: a neutral man keeping an eye out for passersby on behalf of the men who were otherwise engaged mere feet away. I had always viewed this peculiar relationship as a kind of queer courtesy, helping to raise the alarm so a couple wouldn't be caught *in flagrante delicto*. The arrangement could also be one of facilitation—catching the attention of the couple so they could decide whether they wanted to expand from a pair to a group. I had been on both sides of this: the host and the guest, the inviter and the invitee to make a couple something more. But being the one on the outside, the security, was an entirely different kind of triangulation. I wasn't sure if I was witness or participant.

It was erotic, the watching. And though there was a pang of jealousy too—watching Tahsan grab a fistful of the man's hair as he kneeled down in front of him—I also took a kind of pride in my vigilance, that I was potentially their only line of defense between safety and peril, between ecstasy and catastrophe.

They had to pause four times for men walking past, and each time it was clear that Tahsan had a different metric for danger than me, ignoring my increasingly frantic whispers to stop as another man drew nearer. He waited until the sound of footsteps were already on him to push the man away, button his fly, and start innocently humming a tune I didn't recognize. He didn't even bother zipping up.

Tahsan waited so long for the last passerby that I thought he wanted him to join them. But as soon as the man walking by slowed down, Tahsan turned a cold shoulder and instead engaged with his conquest in a conversation in Bengali.

These were such short installments to get to know a person, like clipped little episodes: the time it took for a man to walk between peninsulas, for two men to achieve orgasm together. The time it took for a stranger passing by to lift his hand to your dick for you to decide if you even wanted him to. Both the opportunity for gratification and the risk of danger came in fits, with decisions undertaken in less than a moment.

In trying to understand myself—why I came to places like this, what I was searching for in this darkness—I had read an account by Australian gay rights activist and academic Dennis Altman years earlier about the potentiality inherent in cruising that had struck me: "The willingness to have sex immediately, promiscuously, with people about whom one knows nothing and from whom one demands only physical contact, can be seen as a sort of...desire to know and trust other men in a type of brotherhood far removed from the male bonding of rank, hierarchy, and competition that characterizes much of the outside world."

Cruising as an act of desire seemed obvious, but less apparent had been the notion of knowledge and trust. Was this the issue when Tahsan first met me? I thought about my quick decision to mention my barbers, as though that anecdote might draw him closer, as though through them, I could already know him. Perhaps my framing of who he was and who I thought I was became too immediately apparent, repellant enough to dash any chance of an encounter.

As soon as the passerby moved on, I watched Tahsan coax the young man back to his knees. He refused to heed my urgent hissing as a biker turned the corner round the nearest peninsula. Instead of disengaging, Tahsan just grinned and pulled the man's head further into his crotch as the biker rode past, leering. I turned away and pretended to look out to sea.

"It's no problem. I know my place here," he said, sighing, finally pulling the man off of him. "All of these bachelors are too thirsty," he said.

I sat in silence with Tahsan for a few minutes after the young man wandered off, looking dazed but grateful. I was thinking about how "knowing one's place" usually meant behaving and adhering to respectability politics. For Tahsan, he clearly had no issue staking his claim here even in the most dangerous of circumstances. I asked what they had been speaking of in Bengali.

"He is a bachelor from Dhaka, too. A wife and two babies," he said simply.

For all his ambiguity, Tahsan's use of the word "bachelor"—even to define the married father who was sucking his dick—did not confuse me. It was a word I had seen everywhere in the UAE, from the newspapers piled high in the barbershop to official press releases. Men like Tahsan, like his compatriot, were all defined as such here. It didn't matter if they were in fact married or whether they had one child or ten; if they were living in the UAE without their families, they were known as bachelors.

I sat by myself on the Corniche staring out into the sea, thinking about how the collective obligation of sending home half a billion dollars per year weighed against the personal obligation to one's deepest desires. I thought about the consequences of betraying either: a family with no income, a life with no passion. I recognized the impulse to take what you could, when you could, where you could. I thought also about everyone I went to high school with, how so many of them already had a spouse and a kid, how few of them had traveled, let alone abroad. I wondered precisely how many miles the young man was from his wife; I wondered whether, as he walked along the Corniche, he was getting closer or farther from her. I thought about James lying two kilometers away in our bed, about all the invitations I had accepted into the beds of men wearing wedding rings in Wisconsin. *Libre de impuestos.* Duty-free. What precisely were my obligations, and what was I exempt from? I thought about the potentiality for these words again: *bachelor/partner, queer/straight, expat/migrant, witness/participant*—their capaciousness, their beguiling imprecision.

We didn't speak of identity, but these labels and signifiers ghosted through our conversations. I thought again about "queer," about how I had heard others, like academic John Howard, define it: "Queer is a useful rubric…to aggregate varied persons based on their myriad experiences of difference and outsider status—a coalition of the marginalized. To look for queer...might well result in richer and more accurate histories of deviancy and normalcy and might help denaturalize their present-day iterations." I wondered how strong that coalition could be.

I didn't get home until nearly three. I wrote down the encounters I had, tucked my journal into my bag, and climbed into bed, though my heart was still racing. I could just make out my belongings purposefully arranged around the room: my meticulous bookshelves, stacked notebooks, the mirror I had hung on the far wall. Other than inexplicably holding onto a big pile of winter clothes that I had shipped over despite how ill-suited they were to this climate, I had otherwise finally finished moving in; the apartment really felt like mine. This place was meant to be my sanctuary, as was the man I laid with most nights, five floors beneath me.

I had been told for so long this kind of stability was the ideal, and yet it felt so foreign to how I had learned queerness. I wanted to be out of this room; wanted even less to be downstairs with the man who held me too tightly in his bed. I kept looking at the clothes on the ground, how stifling they all were, and thinking about James's parties, where we sat together on the tile floor surrounded by Tuborg and Americans. I thought about our version of Catan, our made-up resources, the things we thought we valued—all of it—over and over. I couldn't have slept if I wanted to.

At work the next morning, the American woman who assigned me the collating task commented on my fade haircut even though it was already growing out.

"I don't know, you have so many styles, I can't keep you straight," she said. She asked where I got my haircut, and I told her about my barbershop.

"Oh, god, you go to a place like that, with the migrants?" It was hard not to process it the way I had heard it, the way I had received it, as though just by going there, I was somehow doing something wrong. She didn't have any coded language to shelter her; she was loud and clear in her meaning, in her judgment, in her categorization and prejudices. I thought about the impression I might have given Tahsan when I first spoke to him.

My hair became something of a running joke—how impulsive I was, how inexplicable my choices were. I tried to explain that it was cheaper, what I got to watch on television, how relaxing the massages were. But as hard I explained, none of it precisely captured the entire truth, which contained elements of all of those and more, including darker things I didn't say about my lifelong impulse to be surrounded by the company of men. If I couldn't articulate my hair choices, how could I ever articulate something as bewildering, as seemingly risky, as cruising? I thought about the stories Americans told each other about Abu Dhabi: the rumors, the height of Sama Tower, the fear about the car-bashers. I wondered about the journey these stories took across the world. The administrator who expressed horror at the idea of me walking into a Bangladeshi-operated barbershop and asking for a haircut would only stay in the UAE for a year. I would wonder later what kind of stories she brought back with her.

One night, when the heat refused to abate and it was clear that spring was turning toward my second summer, I crossed the tiled underpass and made my way to the Corniche. I expected to see Tahsan sitting atop the terrace but, when I rounded the corner, I was greeted instead by a different face I recognized: the barber from the far-left corner of the shop. The one who first pulled me into his shop, the one who intimately knew the shape of his most loyal patron's head. The one I so desperately wanted to tell about this place.

He was followed closely by his four colleagues, but it still took me a moment to place them. I had started branching out, trying the other barber shops around the city that caught my eye: Diamond Bright and Red Emerald, Green Hills and Happiness Gents.

I wanted to think I was doing it because I was getting more curious about the city, but several of the shops were just closer to the Corniche and stayed open later, though none of them had the same opaque glass. The impulse to be cloistered inside and obscured was fading.

Whatever conversation the men were having in Bengali abruptly halted, and we all exchanged looks—the kind that conveyed everything they needed to, the kind we all knew so well. Before anyone had time to say anything, the stout barber took me by the arm and led me to a recessed bench. He had the same conviction as when he pulled me into his chair that very first afternoon. Three of the other barbers peeled off. He started fumbling for his zipper.

I had the sudden urge to ask him a thousand questions: whether he was romantically involved with his patron, how he first heard about the Corniche, whether he called himself an expatriate, why the barber who was getting married in a few months was both acting as our lookout and rubbing his crotch. But I didn't need to ask anything. I saw the futility in my questions, the flimsiness in my categorizations.

As we waited for our lookout to give us the all-clear, I realized we were sitting under Tahsan's tree. I never found out how deep its roots went, or the precise arrangement that kept it alive. But I did learn, months later, that the entire Corniche was built on reclaimed land; hundreds of thousands of tons of earth had been moved to this very spot, rising out of the depths to make visible these five peninsulas where I spent so many of my nights. I wondered if my urge to ask so many questions was because I was sitting in Tahsan's spot. Because I had finally displaced him.

When we were finished, there was no barbershop mirror to inspect myself in, but I still half-expected him to toss me a little handheld mirror and declare *Na'iman. You are fresh, you are clean.* I started walking slowly back toward my bed, back toward James.

Perhaps I wanted him to say it—I had recently learned that the word's Arabic roots were in the word *paradise* or even *bliss,* though no one used the word that way anymore. I bade farewell to my barber as he wiped his dick on the retaining wall. I would have to tell Tahsan the next time I met him. Except I never did see him again, on the Corniche or anywhere.

3: A LANDING

(Abu Dhabi: Shivani)

I CUPPED MY EYES against the glass door and tried to estimate the distance between the floor and the ceiling. Even though I was squinting into the darkness of a windowless room, I could tell that the bell-shaped light fixtures hung low from their mounts—too low. The thin matting would be a problem too. Its slipshod installation left some edges overlapping and others yawning open to expose cheap plastic tiling. I tried to imagine tumbling across the narrow room on the other side of the door, but it felt entirely feasible that I could both crash into the ceiling on the way up and fracture an ankle on the way down. No, this room wouldn't do at all, I decided. I banged the glass in frustration, turning my heels on yet another space that seemed inadequate in every conceivable way.

A tiny karate studio tucked above a grocery store on the second floor of an old residential tower wasn't exactly what I had initially envisioned, but my search was getting desperate. The one-year anniversary of my arrival in Abu Dhabi was a few months away, and in all that time I had been unable to locate a gymnastics training facility anywhere in the city. In the last week alone, I had taken unsuccessful reconnaissance missions to a girls' public school, the former recreation facility for the UAE armed forces, and—in a moment of particular desperation—a toddlers' play area complete with a sad approximation of a McDonald's ball pit.

Gymnastics had been my first love. I trained seriously and competed nationally until the age of thirteen, when I catastrophically mistimed a tumbling pass, landing first on my neck and then in an operating theater. The surgeon who fused my top two vertebrae and somberly conveyed how close I had come to quadriplegia ruled out my competitive return to the sport, and after an arduous four-month recovery largely confined to a hospital bed, I took up figure skating, the only other sport I had any real interest in. But when I arrived in Manhattan a few years later and compared the price of admission for the nearest ice rink to the cost of a weekly adult gymnastics session, I headed back to the gym, risk be damned. I thought it would be easy enough to find a gym in Abu Dhabi too.

One more place on my list offered a glimmer of promise: a jiujitsu studio near the ice rink. Imran had mentioned it to me a few days earlier, as we walked off the rink and I vented my frustration about my fruitless gym searching. While we unlaced our skates, he explained that jiujitsu had practically become the national sport of the UAE with the establishment of an organization called the Abu Dhabi Combat Club less than a decade earlier. It was only a few buildings down from the ice rink. ("Also, there are cute men in tight pants," he assured me, which certainly didn't hurt.) A bit of Googling on the taxi ride home confirmed it: the emirate hosted the world's largest and most lucrative competition, the annual Abu Dhabi World Professional Jiujitsu Championships. The sport was even embedded in the curriculum of many of the emirate's schools, and the city was home to dozens of top-tier coaches from around the world.

I didn't bat an eyelash at this discovery. The proliferation in the UAE of foreign entities and practices seemed unremarkable. It was one of the things the country was most often lambasted for in the Western media; perhaps the most frequent criticism leveled at the UAE was its lack of homegrown heritage, its propensity, it was alleged, for importing other cultures wholesale as a means to make up for its own deficits. The American gaze upon this perceived phenomenon was one of vicarious embarrassment—*What wacky, incongruous thing would the UAE import next?*—and it reeked from headlines that labeled Abu Dhabi "vapid" or nicknamed Dubai "Disneyland." But I was starting to notice it even in subtle ways, like the ubiquitous photos in Western publications of Emiratis in traditional dress eating at American fast-food chains, as though there were some inherent contrast or novel incongruity between the traditional and the modern on display.

In the week between my learning of jiujitsu's existence in the UAE and my next trip down to Zayed Sports City to visit the facility, I started seeing the sport everywhere. Advertisements for jiujitsu lessons. A message board posting by a jiujitsu practitioner. A new gym popping up on the other side of the city. *Had those signs always been there? Was my blindness of the sport a failure of knowledge, curiosity, or imagination? And what else wasn't I seeing?* I wondered. Maybe gymnastics was staring right at me, and I just hadn't looked in the right place.

With this hope in mind, I pushed my way through the heavy doors of the jiujitsu federation training facility with my ice skates slung over my shoulder. The sport's popularity was apparent as soon as I stepped inside. Despite visiting during the middle of the work week, dozens of athletes were training, squatting low to the ground and throwing each other to the mat. But my heart sank. The mats looked far too hard—maybe even worse than the lackluster karate studio—and I couldn't find any non-jiujitsu equipment. I tried to make my way to the door but had already been spotted by a man who waved me over. I attempted to explain what I was looking for and was passed from person to confused person. Finally, someone beckoned over a sweating coach.

"I'm looking for a gymnastics gym. *Gymbaaz*," I said, using the Arabic name in case that rang a bell. He squinted in apology. "Sorry, I just thought since jiujitsu's from Japan and popular here, maybe gymnastics would be too," I said, making a lame attempt at a cultural connection before I left.

He squinted at me again and pointed to a sign on the wall. *Brazilian jiujitsu.*

"Brazilian jiujitsu is from Brazil," he said, laughing and explaining that this style of martial art had been born in Rio de Janeiro. I looked apologetically at his waiting students as he launched into an extended diatribe about how a group of Brazilian brothers had developed "BJJ" at the turn of the twentieth century after a Japanese expert settled in the country.

I didn't know how to respond. *Had the signs I'd finally noticed earlier that week for jiujitsu mentioned Brazil?* It was literally in the name of the sport. *How had I missed this too?* And how could migration take a sport from one country on an entirely different trajectory in another, and yet I couldn't find a damn pommel horse anywhere?

I thanked him and turned to leave.

"Go to the Corniche," he said, wiping his forehead with a towel. "On Fridays, you will find the gymnasts there."

▽▽▽

The Corniche. Though I hadn't strolled it much during the daylight hours since I started cruising, I was sure I knew every inch of the beachside walkway. I had a sudden flash of visiting Muscle Beach in Santa Monica as a twelve-year-old, knowing even then that my urge to stare at all the shirtless men climbing ropes and hanging from rings was an aberration to be suppressed. I tried to imagine a similar outdoor gymnastics facility along the Corniche—men sweating through low-cut fluorescent tank tops as they swung to handstands on metal parallel bars—but I was fairly certain I wouldn't have missed a scene like that.

The next Friday, I walked west along the promenade, skirting the din of Friday mosque traffic. This section of the Corniche had only been a paved walkway for less than a decade; I had learned that it was reclaimed from a tidal beach where boats carrying migrants had docked right in the sand. I walked past the quirky architectural features installed to provide cover from the relentless sun along the eight-kilometer path: tall hedges, sleepy kiosks, billowing sunshades designed to look like ship sails. Like the little peninsulas along the section of walkway that I most often frequented, I knew all these as hiding places, and the other kind of cover they provided in the darkness.

I made my way to one of my favorite features on the Corniche, a series of chaotic stairways and spiral accessibility ramps leading down to an underpass. Each one was partially enclosed by large, tiled walls that created a kind of concealed labyrinthine chasm from walkway to tunnel. One of the ramp's exits inexplicably spat people out mere meters away from its entrance. The whole place felt like an Escher painting come to life.

As I approached, a young man in black swim trunks and a cutoff T-shirt suddenly appeared, landing on the edge of a wall like a mischievous cat. He caught sight of me and smiled before jumping into the abyss. Only as I drew closer could I see he had jumped onto another wall, just a few feet lower, and was balancing in a handstand on its precipice. He looked like a high diver ready to jump off the edge of the platform and disappear beneath the waterline, lost to the depths.

I spotted more people in the abyss below, climbing, balancing, and propelling themselves up, down, and sideways onto the next manmade obstacle: raised fountains, sloped walls fastened with railing, landscaped terraces of varying heights built up around stairwells. One man was jumping from the spout of a decorative waterfall installation. Two more used the bright blue railings to practice handstand pirouettes. Still more took turns leaping over each other and landing on the edge of high, narrow walls like acrobats along a tightrope. I had seen a concealed ecosystem, the cruising ground, emerge from a public walkway under cover of darkness, and here was another in the same location, operating in plain sight.

I descended a half flight of stairs and approached a group of young men and women standing in a roughshod line. They were leaping from a short wall onto another several feet higher, separated by a running fountain. I watched a few rounds of their jumps, each one infused with a kind of defiance that manifested in their hearty fist pumps after each successful pass.

I found myself edging closer, wondering if I too could bridge the gap. There seemed to be no consideration for queues or turns; it was like jumping into a double Dutch skip rope, gauging the precise moment to enter the fray.

In a moment of inactivity, I found myself suddenly clearing the lower wall and leaping to the higher one. It was only as I landed on the upper wall, my center of gravity pitching backward, that I considered the formidable drop beneath me. I quickly knelt and steadied myself on the wall. I had made it—just. I didn't let myself think about how narrowly I had escaped a more dire fate. I had long ago learned to cast that kind of thinking aside.

We each took a few more turns. A few started trying more daring maneuvers, like grabbing a leg or adding a half twist mid-jump. They knew how far they could push themselves. It was one of the things that had drawn me to individual sports. Or rather, I had never felt entirely comfortable in team sports, had never felt—like in my queerness—the stability of a group's support on or off the field.

I walked over to another clutch of athletes scaling a rectangular, tower-like structure. They hoisted themselves onto the metal protrusion—all slats and screws—and jumped into the air, flipping and twisting before landing on the walkway. I weighed doing it myself but wasn't sure how I could conquer the thing without knowing what it was. But then suddenly, like the walls a few minutes earlier, I was climbing it anyway. I stood precariously atop its sloping metal frame, unsure whether my ankles could handle the torque from landing on the unforgiving concrete below.

"*Yalla! Aawi qalbak!*" I heard behind me. I turned around gingerly, careful not to slip. It was a young woman decked in Adidas activewear, an orange headband, and an impish smile.

I had never heard the second Arabic phrase before, but it was easy enough to grasp its meaning: *Stay strong*. But it was the way she exclaimed the familiar *yalla* that caught my attention. It was a phrase I had heard countless times, one of my favorites used across the Arabic-speaking world regardless of dialect. In the same way *Let's go* could be tinged with impatience or encouragement, could start a conversation or end one, *yalla* was beguilingly multifaceted in its possibilities. I still translated Arabic conversations back into English in my head, the crutch of someone without native fluency, but it was the comradery inherent in her delivery of the phrase "let's" that captured me. Unshackling the contraction heightened the solidarity in the phrase: *Let us*. I was the one standing atop this particular unfamiliar summit, but it felt in that moment that she was on the same dangerous terrain as me.

"Do you speak Arabic?" she asked in English.

Yes, I replied. I was suddenly aware that this was the same conversation I had with Imran, except the roles had been reversed.

"Then yalla, "she repeated, a smile betraying her faux impatience. "Let's do it," she said, code-switching between the two languages.

I smiled at her. I wasn't sure if she had seen or had felt my hesitation, but I recognized the warmth in her encouragement. I leapt, twisting and flipping once through the air. The landing stung, but I was on my feet. She walked over with a triumphant arm outstretched.

"How long have you been doing this?" I asked in too-formal Arabic.

"My whole life," she said with the same mock impatience.

"We all have."

These athletes must be Emirati, I reasoned. Starting with the wrong foot or making one wrong hand placement could spell disaster, and it was clear in the way they jumped from obstacle to obstacle that they knew the topography of this place, its every nuance. This was their landscape. After meeting so many migrants, I had finally met a group of people who had known this place their whole lives.

A few of them started to peel off toward the tunnel back into the city, and they beckoned for the young woman to join them. She explained that some of them were going to mosque, and the rest would be wrapping up for the day, too. Summer was coming, and the noon heat was already stifling.

"We will return again next week," she promised. I knew in that moment that I would too, that the lure of being part of a community would bring me once more to another stretch of walkway along the Gulf.

▽▽▽

I looked forward to my next Friday Corniche trip all week. I had already upped my midnight visits, grateful that the increasing number of nights I was spending away from James in my own apartment allowed for my escape. But this standing daytime visit meant an opportunity to hang out with people that seemed to truly be part of the local community. I had been subverting the Corniche under the cover of darkness with queer migrants, people who doubly didn't belong. Now I was looking forward to what felt like the chance to finally get to know the fabric of this place in a way I hadn't yet: getting to experience another facet of it with others by the light of day.

I walked toward the complex of stairwells I had visited the previous week. A dozen athletes were already leaping from ramps to stairs to railings. I moved slowly, relishing the chance to watch their individual maneuvers, how they jumped from heights that invited concern yet landed faultlessly each time. I scanned their faces and only recognized a few from the week before. In a city where only twenty percent of the 1.5 million residents were Emirati, I wondered how many of these local athletes there could actually be.

I caught sight of the familiar orange headband vaulting over two benches. By the time I approached the young woman, she had climbed a narrow wall above another staircase and was balancing on one foot, her back toward me. I wanted to greet her but recognized this particular moment of precarity where minute adjustments and split-second decisions were the only way to avoid catastrophe.

The young woman executed a one-foot, 540-degree turn and was suddenly facing me. We made eye contact, and she immediately brightened, reaching out a hand in acknowledgment despite standing on the edge of a five-foot drop. I was lost for words. We still didn't really know anything about each other. I didn't even know her name. The only line that came to me was by reflex: *Where are you from?* It was the one I heard employed each day across the city as a kind of greeting, an entry point into conversation used by everyone from taxi drivers to shopkeepers. People began dialogue and grew personal relationships by discussing their positionality away from this place, but her nativeness to this city felt as though it scrambled that equation, and I was left with my mouth agape.

She stood above me, motionless in the blazing daylight. I thought about all the nights I tried to size men up in the darkness along this same walkway. I positioned myself beneath her so she would block out the sun, but she jumped without warning—one flip, a half twist—and landed closer to me than I anticipated. I startled, and she laughed. I wondered how she learned that—the hard landing, the fearlessness—but I knew from all the stupid things I had been asked over the years about gymnastics that it would be an insipid question. There was no easy answer, no pithy response that didn't flatten the calculations and years of toil to get to this place of knowing one's own capabilities, and limits.

"I like your T," she said simply, standing up from her crouched landing. I realized that I had knelt down to be at her level without thinking about it. I was wearing an I LOVE BEIRUT shirt that poorly copied the I HEART NY logo in Arabic script. I had carefully selected it that morning hoping to get this exact acknowledgment, hoping it would help me belong.

She asked me how long I had spoken Arabic, and I explained my college studies and time in Yemen. "I need some Emiratis like you to teach me a bit more Khaleeji," I said.

"Oh, I'm not Emirati. I know my Arabic is good, but—" She cut herself off laughing. "I'm from Sri Lanka."

I cocked my head, confused.

"I studied it just like you, mostly out here," she said, shrugging and gesturing around her.

I didn't know what to say. I had done this once before with Imran—making assumptions about place and language—but I had been so sure this time. There was something about the way she traveled through this place that made me sure this was her country. Her carriage, her confidence.

"Third culture kid," she said, turning to scale the wall again. "I don't ever remember living in Sri Lanka. Moved here when I was three. I'm Shivani, by the way."

Third culture kid. I had never encountered the phrase before moving to Abu Dhabi but, like jiujitsu, I was suddenly hearing it everywhere. It was a term coined by American sociologist Ruth Useem in the 1970s to describe people who live through their formative years in a place other than their parents' homeland. Once upon a time, third culture kids were a phenomenon associated with the children of diplomats, military workers, or missionaries, but increasingly it was the children of parents who were migrating or had migrated, for economic or other reasons. Parents from one place, or two separate places, and a childhood spent in another. A mother and father from Brazil, say, a childhood raised in India, and as a result, an in betweenness. A belonging to nowhere in particular, I imagined.

"They are all TCKs, too," she said, pointing to the other athletes, using an acronym that made it sound like they were all members of an eighties new-wave band. Their numbers had grown since my arrival. I watched a group of athletes hurl themselves over a plot of landscaping and onto another ledge. I was taken by their nimbleness but also their easy smiles. They looked like children horsing around on a jungle gym.

What had struck me most about the term "third culture kid" when I first encountered it was the last word: kid. The title was still bestowed upon people well beyond childhood. It reminded me of how queerness and youth were often spoken of as intrinsically linked even into adulthood. I had spent my adolescence hearing how queerness was just a phase: anyone who identified "that way" would someday grow out of it, that they just didn't know themselves or the ways of the world well enough yet. I realized I harbored the same negative connotations with TCKs too; it rang in my ear as a kind of unfortunate affliction. But Shivani proudly wore the "kid" badge despite her age, in the same way I had watched all the older men who had survived a plague hold up their cocktail glasses and shriek in acknowledgment when a drag queen shouted "Hello, boys" in a New York gay bar. Perhaps TCKs—these children of migrants—and queer people alike were indeed in a kind of Neverland-esque suspended youth. But then, what were we searching for—or missing—and how long could it last?

"I'm carrying on the family tradition of displacement, a kind of belonging I'm finding harder to sustain as I grow older," writer Deepak Unnikrishaan would later publish about his experience growing up as a third culture kid born in the UAE. His words felt charged with a deep ambivalence, but also a beguiling ambiguity. Initially, they seemed to gesture to the difficulty of living away from one's ancestral homeland. But much later, I found them also suggesting difficulty even in establishing a personal definition of one's homeland. Maybe both could be true.

I watched Shivani's body in motion as she climbed back atop the wall and leapt off again. She was executing a move called, ironically enough, an Arabian. It featured two distinct moments of jeopardy. The first was the element's rotation, a horizontal half twist executed entirely before a flip on the vertical axis. Twisting before flipping pushed the head-over-feet movement—the greatest danger—to even later in the element, heightening the likelihood of catastrophic injury. But the other moment of peril came at the very end of the element: the landing. In gymnastics, it was called a "blind landing," when the gymnast is unable to spot the ground before their feet strike it. An athlete has to perfectly time everything and know the world and their relation to it based on feeling alone. There was no mastery here: there was simply understanding your position as you hurled your body through space, and then doing it again and again, lessening risk but never completely eliminating it. Perhaps arriving in a foreign country and not knowing how long it might stay the center of one's family alignment—be it months, years, decades—was its own kind of blind landing.

As Shivani kept training the move, I sat on a railing and watched some of the other athletes. A merciful breeze blew in off the Gulf, and I looked out onto the waves if only to relieve myself from having to wince at their hard landings on the concrete. They were all so close to the beach. They could have been training on much more forgiving terrain. I looked past the Friday traffic and into the tangle of buildings just a few blocks from the karate studio I had scoped out a few weeks earlier. These athletes found their gym here, on the Corniche, along the edge of the city. Training here, on the periphery, they were part of the urban fabric and yet also removed from it.

Shivani stayed silent as she continued training. I didn't want to bother her, though I had so many questions. She didn't say it, but I wondered if this location—this liminal space between the city and the sea—drew them here as much as the acrobatics did. How had the first of these athletes declared this as their place?

I thought about how I had been drawn here in the dead of the night to be both away from and part of this city; to surround myself with people who both were and weren't expats, were and weren't migrants, were and weren't queer. There was a tension between how labels such as these pushed against categorization and also became categories unto themselves. They could be given, rejected, reclaimed—sometimes all at once.

The sun rose higher and training began to wind down. I realized I was only a few hundred meters from where I had last seen Tahsan nearly six months earlier. I wondered how many of the disbanding athletes knew about what became of this place at night, how the same promenade they had fashioned into a gymnasium was later co-opted by what I thought of as an entirely different group.

"I have to go pick up my girlfriend," Shivani said to me suddenly, leaping off a wall. "But we should hang out sometime." She walked off as if she had told me something as mundane as the weather forecast.

▽▽▽

I had always regarded "we should hang out sometime" as a kind of Millennial nicety. It seemed like the sort of phrase reserved for acquaintances one might bump into just frequently enough to warrant maintaining vague appearances of aspiration toward a closer relationship. So when Shivani repeated the platitude again the following week after training, I expected noncommittal plans for a coffee date in the distant future, not for her to usher me into the passenger seat of her cluttered Corolla a few minutes later.

"Where are we going?" I asked as we sped south down the length of the island.

"Musaffah," was all she offered through her smirk.

I was grateful she didn't follow up with any questions about my experience in Musaffah, because the truth was that I didn't yet have any. I certainly knew things about it, or at least thought I did. That it sat on the outer edge of the city. That it was both an outpost of factories and also the center of industry and manufacturing for the emirate. And, most notably, that it was filled with low-waged, unskilled migrant workers from South Asia.

I had finally crossed over the bridge Imran had mentioned at iftar, Al-Maqta, but I had never taken the southernmost of the three bridges that connected the island of Abu Dhabi to the mainland that was home to the rest of the emirate. This was the bridge that led to Musaffah. Too far from downtown, the burgeoning bus system still didn't reach Musaffah conveniently, and a taxi ride would take nearly double the time of my already costly fifteen-kilometer journey to the ice rink. As a result, I knew the neighborhood mostly as the destination for the illegal share taxis that operated in the block adjacent to mine. Across from a hospital ambulance bay, groups of mainly Pakistani and Indian men in scuffed pastel-colored shalwar kameez would cram into vans as drivers and their touts shouted the names of the various landmarks that marked the end of their journey. None of their destinations were familiar to me; they sat like a hinterland at the outer edge of a city I was still coming to know.

We drove nearly thirty minutes before Shivani finally broke the silence, pointing out the window while dodging lorries, precariously navigating a shoulderless service road.

"That's the industrial grass yarn factory," she declared, smiling vaguely at a nondescript corrugated metal building.

I didn't have the faintest idea what "industrial grass yarn" was, but I nodded anyway, not wanting to seem disinterested or skeptical about the nature of our adventure. Though Shivani was an adept English speaker, I took the curious phrase as a linguistic slip-up. But as I looked for a sign or any kind of market on the outside of the building, she explained that that's what they call artificial turf.

"Grass yarn factory." She laughed. "It sounds like the kind of place where snitches make up stories, right?" I didn't track her cheesy, multilayered play on words at first, until I realized that she was employing English-language slang. Just as in her athletics, she demonstrated a nimbleness and sense of play that caught me off guard.

As we whizzed past more anonymous industrial buildings, she pointed out each one with the gregarious sureness of a city bus tour guide: here, a plastics factory; there, a shipbuilding site; off in the distance, a marine dredging company. We reached a larger road lined with a clutch of towers. I expected her to rattle off more obscure facts about office space and square footage, but she instead pointed to a squat one and explained she lived there with her girlfriend. Then she was already abruptly pulling off onto another service road, seemingly hopping out of the car while it was still in gear.

"Chickoo?" she asked.

I stared at her and wondered if this was something related to technical grass yarn.

"You know: sapodilla? Sapota? Wood apple? Naseberry?" She paused briefly between each word, waiting for one to register with me. "Juice!" she said, playfully rolling her eyes. "I'm getting us chickoo juice!"

We walked inside a too-bright shop with a metal counter and stacks of oranges and mangoes stuffed behind a plexiglass display. I stared dumbly at the peeling, discolored wallpaper of pineapples and kiwi that decorated one side of the shop. Like the barber shops, there was no menu. Shivani chatted with the man in a plastic smock who stood behind the counter. I wasn't sure when, or if, she ordered, and it was only when she came to stand next to me with two overflowing cups of brown juice that I realized I had taken two steps back from the counter. I had been standing behind her like a child, waiting for her to handle this interaction. I asked how she knew so many names for one fruit.

"I like languages," she shrugged, ushering me to follow her outside. As she took a seat on the curb, she explained she was studying at a local university to become a teacher. I wanted to ask more about her studies, more about why she was living in Musaffah, more about how she came to Abu Dhabi to begin with, but I wasn't sure what one to ask first. Every line of question felt like slightly the wrong place to start, as though each informed the other. Instead of any of those questions, I found myself asking which language she spoke with the man at the counter, cringing at the cluelessness of this particular line of inquiry.

"Hindi," she said. "He's Indian. But I speak Sinhalese." She explained that the two languages had enough crossover to enable an ease of conversation. "But also English," she added as an afterthought. "Khaleej, too," she said. "But there's always more to learn."

Shivani swirled her straw around the bottom of her cup, sucking up the last of her juice. She explained that her parents moved here when she was eight for her father's work and that she only remembered bits of pieces from living in Sri Lanka.

"I go back now to see some family, and I think I have a memory from when I was a kid, but I'm pretty sure my visits have imposed themselves on any memories I had from my time actually living there," she said. "It doesn't actually feel like home, maybe because I don't have any memories from the time it ever was."

"So this is home?" I asked. I tried to point to the towers around us, but from where we sat on the curb, parked cars obscured our view.

"Yeah, I think so. I mean, it's complicated. Hey, let's go," she said suddenly, picking up our glasses.

"What do you want to do?" I asked as she tugged me back toward the car.

"Right now or, like, in life?" she asked. She had that same impish smile; I couldn't be sure if the question was sincere. I wanted the answer to both but wasn't sure which one I wanted first. "Let's go jump over shit. We are in the right gear," she said, pointing to our gym clothes.

She had taken us this far, so I jumped back into the car wordlessly and let her drive. I watched her navigate the car by gripping the steering wheel with one hand.

"Here!" she exclaimed suddenly.

She jerked the wheel to the right, pulling off the road into an empty lot of industrially compacted sand. I instinctively gripped the door handle, but she brought the car to a remarkably controlled stop between two massive drainage pipes that framed a ditch and some broken fencing. Pushing through a feeble string fence festooned with orange warning flags, she explained it was supposed to be a new stormwater system, though work had been stalled for years.

"This place is my favorite," she said, before hoisting herself on the nearest pipe and kicking into a handstand. It was nearly four feet tall and just as wide. I tried to follow suit, but I didn't have the propulsion and landed hard back in the sand. I had to climb atop it, awkwardly gripping it with my legs like a hopeless toddler.

Shivani kept using the pipe as a kind of vault, leaping on and off an obstacle that seemed like such an improbable aid to get her so high into the air. She ushered me forth—as she had done so many times already that afternoon—but I realized that once I sat atop the pipe, I had the impulse to stay put. I watched and smiled but wasn't sure that I could follow.

For weeks, I watched the athletes on the Corniche drill one trick in particular. They ran along the narrow edge of a raised concrete planter box and leapt off the end, completing a midair sideways flip before landing on the ground three feet below. I couldn't figure it out for the life of me. I tried it again and again but always found myself executing a forward or a backward flip.

Keep your chest up, *Look outwards*, and *Shift your run* were some of the pointers I received in English and Arabic from earnest TCKs from Jordan, Lebanon, India, Nepal. I fumbled my way through attempt after attempt, trying to translate both their words and my visual perception of what they were accomplishing into a kinetic awareness, but I couldn't seem to commit to the basic mechanics of the move.

The problem was the very nature of the flip: a rotation on the sideways axis. As I tried to hurl myself into the trick, all the points of reference I used to develop a sense of where I was in the air were scrambled. I knew the skill as a "side-somi," and its sideways rotation meant it was a non-standard gymnastics move, one that never found its way into my regular repertoire. The athletes along the Corniche tried to teach me others, too: bent corkscrew turns, delayed backflips, forward flips that featured wild scissoring legs like an upside-down ski machine.

I had never been taught these sorts of moves. I began gymnastics after watching the US women's team capture a bronze medal in the 1992 Olympics and begging my parents to enroll me in classes. I wanted to capture the feeling I saw when those women soared through the air; I wanted that freedom. But over the years, as classes became training and attempting tricks turned into mastering skills, that feeling of freedom dissipated. Using women's apparatuses—the balance beam and uneven bars, two of the things that first attracted me to the sport—was curtailed by my coaches. Even my father began to bark at me when he caught me "doing those hands," flicking my wrists as I used the cracks between the wooden floorboards in our kitchen as an imaginary balance beam. There was no more room for variance, only the serious business of being a male gymnast. I was suddenly in the middle of something that required precision and certainty, regimentation and standardization in a way I hadn't anticipated. I felt it in gymnastics but began to feel it in the rest of my adolescence as well: the bifurcation of boys and girls, the marked difference I was beginning to feel in my curiosity about the bodies of men.

I returned with Shivani to Musaffah week after week. She drove us back to the storm drainage construction site, but also to others as well: a disused storage building with its shutters swung wide, an unfinished parking lot overflowing with parking blocks, another sandlot populated by overturned concrete road barriers. One of her favorites was an empty lot adjacent to a clutch of car repair shops. A pile of old tires sat in one corner, and she tried to teach me to flip from tire to sand, riding the small bounce from the tire to gain a little extra height. I was used to factory-crafted trampolines and springboards and marveled at the way she was able to develop such unconventional techniques.

While I fumbled, we talked more about her studies. She was both excited and nervous because she had only one year left of her degree. I asked her what she wanted to do, but winced when I remembered how insistent and overwhelming the question had been before I graduated.

"Well, I only have a few months to find a teaching job or I have to leave," she said. After her studies concluded, neither her student visa nor her parents could sponsor her anymore. Living in the UAE was contingent upon a work visa, and if she didn't secure one, she would need to face the uncertain future of being separated from her family and returning to Sri Lanka, a place that had never felt like home.

"When I was a kid, I remember a lot of my friends were here one day and then gone the next," she said, explaining that many parents lost their jobs during the Great Recession, which hit the UAE particularly hard. "I was just kind of waiting for it to be our turn. But then more than ten years passed, and it never came, and now I can't imagine being anywhere else."

I ventured to ask if she thought she'd feel different if she weren't in a relationship here.

"Everything would be different, I guess, but I'd still call this home. And now it's like, where else can I go that would feel right?"

"So, what's the deal with your girlfriend?" I asked. I tried to stay as nonchalant as I could, knowing that we hadn't really talked about her in any detail despite me admitting in one of our car rides that I, too, was gay.

She explained that her girlfriend, Yasmine, was Turkish and that she'd lived here for most of her life, too. She also identified as a third culture kid, caught somewhere between her upbringing amidst the wealth and opportunities of the UAE and her more modest roots from a town outside of Ankhara. They had bonded over their in-betweenness, first as friends and then as more.

"You just kind of know," she said, referring to her sexuality. She didn't have to explain anything more to me, because I knew exactly what she meant, having spent years looking in the eyes of men to see if they had that same curiosity as I had in mine.

We sat awhile on the tires. I asked what the hardest part of being in a lesbian relationship here was. I expected her to launch into something about familial traditions or pressures, or perhaps cultural expectations, but she laughed and simply said, "Finding a place to live."

Because Shivani was on a student visa despite living in the UAE for her whole life, she was only allowed to work a limited number of hours at the local retail outlet that employed her. Her measly salary wasn't enough to pay for housing on her own, but between her income and her girlfriend's equally paltry pay, they scraped together enough to illegally sublet an apartment. Though they resided on paper at their respective parents' homes, both sets had lived long enough in the country to understand illegal subletting and didn't ask any other questions about their living situations, assuming they lived with fellow students—which was technically true.

I asked Shivani how they had found the apartment. She explained that she quickly gave up on the online forums other students used and also didn't want to live in sparse university accommodation—"I didn't feel like I would be living in the city," she said—but then was daunted by the expense of trying to secure an apartment on her own. She first tried other unofficial channels, like cold calling phone numbers listed on any posters she found around the city advertising illegal room shares, but didn't have any luck there either.

"Straight people make it so hard," she laughed. She joked about the racial stratification she saw in all the posters looking for *Indian bachelor only*, or *Arab family wanted*, or *seeking single Filipina working woman* that papered the city's walls and lamppost. "Everyone is looking for themselves but then can't find it," she said.

As we walked around the lot, passing the car repair shops, she explained that after meeting her girlfriend, they made the brazen decision to try to find a flat together. In breaking the law together, residing in an illegal sublet, they had suddenly rendered a difficult situation easy.

"It's people like us," she said, meaning queer people, "and those who know about living in foreign places who know how to work the system." She proudly recounted how they had broken not just the illegal sublet law but also another major piece of UAE legislation: the prohibition of cohabitation among unmarried couples. "Double trouble." She smirked.

Until a landmark law change in 2020, only legally married couples could reside together. But it was their homosexuality,

Shivani reckoned, that made the ability to live "in sin," as she joked, paradoxically easier: no one suspected two women would be in a relationship. She gleefully described a recent encounter with her landlord and three repairmen who came to fix her stovetop.

"We played it up with them," she joked as she explained how they splayed across each other on the sofa and got as handsy as they dared in front of the men. "The repair guys kept looking back at us, like, 'Is that how ladies are when we aren't around?'"

She suspected her landlord knew the truth. "We only have one bed. One plus one equals two, you know?" She laughed, aware that even if he wasn't happy about renting to two lesbians, they were in a kind of legal and moral stalemate together because he was also doing something illegal by renting to them in the first place. She didn't say whether she was bold enough to attempt all this illegality because she was already breaking the law as a lesbian or because she knew the lay of the land as a longtime resident. Maybe the distinction didn't matter. Whether as a woman, a lesbian, or a TCK, she was able to hold as much power as her Emirati landlord—at least in this situation.

I thought of the two American couples I knew who rushed to get married before moving to the UAE. One relationship was already on the rocks because of that very decision.

"The bottom line is that I don't think I could live in Sri Lanka with my Turkish girlfriend, and at least I have that here," she said.

When we moved on from the tire lot, we drove to the very outer edge of Musaffah. The neighborhood was laid out in a near perfect grid, and after skirting roundabout after roundabout through one-square-kilometer blocks, the buildings gave way to packed sand and *sabkha*, evaporated salt planes that made it look like the earth was covered in the white-brown mix of receding February Midwest snow. After miles of flat land, I saw what looked like little mountains in the distance. We pulled over onto the hard shoulder. Shivani said that they were piles of construction waste: chunks of concrete and tarmac and rebar piled high into neat mounds. At the center, she explained, lay a tangle of metal troughs that fed it all into the country's only construction waste recycling plant.

I thought we would walk to an opening in the hills to try to peek inside, but she led me right past the ramshackle fiberglass guard's hut, waving at a figure in shadow inside, and into the center of the mounds. The troughs looked like little waterslides, and I watched men in hardhats and high-vis vests, standing atop a platform in the middle of the site overseeing the whirring machinery. She told me she knew one of the men who worked here.

I was still processing the fact that Abu Dhabi even had a recycling plant, let alone a plant specifically for construction materials; I could scarcely process that Shivani had brazenly led me into the heart of an active industrial site because she "knew a guy." The stories I had been fed about the excess of the UAE didn't allow for a place like this. The contempt and skepticism I had been told to foster meant I had assumed there was no value placed in reusing and reshaping, and also that a queer woman couldn't have the power or agency to be a part of a community here.

Shivani jumped atop a metal tank and waved me up to get a better view. I scrambled up and looked around, guessing which one of the men in the high-vis vests might be the one that she knew. I wondered where he was from and how long he had been here. I wondered also where Shivani might work someday—whether or not it would be a place she had, or would, or ever could call home.

She started egging me on to attempt a side-somi into a pile of dirt beneath us, playfully raising her eyebrows at me. Her encouragement was ceaseless. Each time I felt like giving up on the trick, I felt a beguiling pull I hadn't anticipated to try it again, week after week. And after searching for the right equipment for so long, I realized I had been seeking out the very regulation that I had once tried to escape. Perhaps here I could reclaim a bit of the looseness and freedom I once craved.

"Just feel it," were the words she used for the umpteenth time, as though I could shift my kinetic awareness, as though I could suddenly change how I moved through the world. *Could I?* I wondered. I stood motionless on the tank.

"We are not gymnasts, you know. Stop thinking like one," she said. It was an admission she had never made before and one whose significance I hadn't fully appreciated until that moment.

From my vantage point on the edge of the tank, I couldn't see beyond the tall mounds of crushed asphalt rimming the site, but I knew the towers of Mussafah, the place where Shivani lived, lay just beyond them. The plant in front of me, the industrial buzz just beyond it, the people who recycled and built and manufactured in this unknown section of the city: they all subverted the perception of the UAE strictly as an importer, not just of goods, but of culture as well. If Tahsan had shown me a slippage between migrant and expat, then Shivani and the type of acrobatics she did, and this place, intimated at something beyond that binary. If there really ever were migrants and expats, then Shivani and TCKs—and the gymnastics they were doing and the city they were building—were something beyond all that. I thought back to the Brazilian jiujitsu studio I had so quickly dismissed. Perhaps jiujitsu—or anything else labeled an "import," for that matter—could shift again here.

Years later, I would read about the emergence of a sociolect, multicultural London English in the UK's capital. Areas of London that had once been home to the familiar twang of the Cockney dialect were now the incubator for a new and still developing variant of the English language largely due to an influx of immigrants moving into previously white, working-class neighborhoods. "It is difficult to say if there is a direct influence from Nigerian English, or Jamaican Creole, because they are all in the mix somewhere," linguist David James explained. "It is language change not from the outside but from the inside—they are building it themselves." If this language had shifted, perhaps almost imperceptibly, through the mixing of young people coming to learn English from the varied linguistic touchpoints and rubrics of their own first languages, perhaps the same thing was happening in a place like the UAE. And perhaps it wasn't just limited to language, either. Perhaps they were building something more in other ways, too.

My phone rang. I let it ring and explained that it was James, probably wondering where I was again. I had told him I was skating. I hadn't told him anything about the cruising, but neither had I told him about my daytime visits to the Corniche, about the gymnastics, about Shivani. I had tried so many times to talk to him about getting out into the city with me; I had encouraged him to walk beside me as I wandered its streets. But our conversations and interactions were becoming increasingly rooted in transaction and routine. How had those two boys in New York gotten here—halfway around the world but more insular than ever? Wasn't our queerness supposed to surmount all that?

I silenced my phone and watched Shivani dive off the edge of the tank. It looked from the run-up to her jump like she was going to do a forward flip, but her rotation slowed as she jumped, and I audibly gasped, thinking she would land on her neck like I had once done. But in the moment before striking the ground, she tucked her chin and rolled through the mound of dust. It was a near carbon copy to the move that ended my career, except she had the awareness to execute it properly. I let myself think for a moment about the hundreds of gymnasts' careers that had ended like mine, not making it to the point of glory or recognition—just ending on a mat with no record. Perhaps queerness was like this too: all those, jailed and deported yet never making the news, who hadn't had the luck or fortune that Shivani and I'd had so far.

I watched her stand up and brush off her shirt like nothing happened, like she didn't come inches and seconds away from paralysis. I recognized the danger, recognized how people would think it was insane, recognized that people couldn't—or perhaps didn't try to—understand that sometimes danger was inherent.

So many people in my life misunderstood my participation in gymnastics—thought I had some pathological need for risk instead of an adeptness at negotiating its nearness. But what does a closeness to danger do? What does a lifetime spent in proximity to danger become? And for Shivani and others in precarity, what might it become over generations?

I stood over Shivani as she went to retrieve her phone from atop the overshirt she left lying in the sand.

"Yasmine said I'm sure we are having a good time and hopes to meet you soon," she said. "She also sent a few other things she said she'd like to do to me in the sand that I won't repeat."

I wished James had that same curiosity, that same sense of freedom. And although I recognized that my own queer acts along the Corniche demonstrated that same impulse and potentiality, they were still hidden and singular. Shivani, in her relationships and in her actions, felt eminently more public and seen. She wasn't just troubling definitions in the darkness, but building an entirely new form with those around her.

I tried the side-somi again and landed hard in the sand. The sun was already lowering in the sky, but maybe we had just enough time for me to try it again.

4: A STAGE

(Abu Dhabi: Sunil and Reggie)

I FINALLY DECIDED there was probably only the one band whose name was inspired by a lesbian sex position. But when I first read the headline "Scissor Sisters to perform in Abu Dhabi," my initial thought was that some unfortunate, two-bit girl group had unknowingly taken the same name as the queer New York glam pop rock band. The *real* Scissor Sisters sang about cruising and chemsex. The band's lead singer, Jake Shears, was an unabashedly gay former stripper seemingly always decked out in bedazzled hot pants. I'd even recently read an article about the band in which the journalist described Shears obscenely mashing his hands together to demonstrate the sex act that inspired the band's name. Surely, it couldn't be *this* Scissor Sisters playing in the UAE, a country where even kissing in public could lead to imprisonment and deportation? And yet, there it was, just below a campy photo of Shears rope-tied to another band member: a headline announcing the band's concert in the country's most popular English-language newspaper.

I had loved the Scissor Sisters since their cover of Pink Floyd's "Comfortably Numb" debuted seven years earlier, during my sophomore year of high school. The song was unlike anything I had ever heard on Midwestern radio waves, and I voraciously read everything I could online about the band's storied beginnings singing in grungy Lower East Side clubs dressed as rejects from Andy Warhol's Factory—scenes I could scarcely imagine, cloistered in my Wisconsin bedroom. I was also only tentatively beginning to acknowledge to myself that my interest in the band may at least have been partially rooted in the fact that four of its five members were gay. (Or, perhaps even more honestly, that my interest was rooted in the amount of time I spent studying photographs of Shears's body in skin-tight costumes.) Before I had heard much of anything about the LGBTQ+ histories and communities of New York, the Scissor Sisters allowed me to contemplate what queer culture—what "out" and what my own queer future—might someday look like.

I carefully considered who I could alert about their concert in Abu Dhabi—especially considering the tour was to promote an album with a cover featuring a closeup of a man's clenched ass in gauzy dance pants. I thought immediately of Shivani, but I still hadn't introduced her to James. She and Yasmine knew about my cruising on the Corniche, but the dynamism of their relationship made me embarrassed of the insularity of my life here with James. Inviting Imran wouldn't work either: perpetually and proudly single, he had been skeptical of my relationship with James since I'd first explained that a phone date with him prevented me from accepting the invitation to that first iftar. Imran's anti-James stance had only fortified after I'd confided in him about James's increasingly hermit-like tendencies.

"Tell him to get a dog if he wants to stay inside and be an American," was the advice he half-jokingly doled out to me on more than one occasion. "Go enjoy life here."

The Scissor Sisters concert seemed like a final chance to get James to enjoy life alongside me. I noticed him spending more and more time in front of the television or Skyping his parents, and he seemed to be intentionally steering more of our conversations toward how hard it was continuing to be away from the things he missed—his family, New York City, marijuana—in order to gauge my reaction. I thought the opportunity to see a band from New

York might be a way of getting him out in this city with me and yet still be part of something that felt familiar to him.

I kept scanning the local newspapers for different articles about the event that might excite him, but all the coverage seemed nearly identical. It was a phenomenon I had noticed soon after arriving, the media often relying on press releases to build their articles, resulting in a sometimes-glaring uniformity. It seemed, in many ways, understandable: in a landscape with one of the most restrictive media regulatory laws in the world—the UAE ranked 112 out of 179 that year on the World Press Freedom Index—censorship was rife, and criticism of the government was officially outlawed. Three years earlier, a brand-new newspaper, *The National*, was established with much fanfare to counteract international criticism that the country's media was tightly controlled, but it was still owned by an investment fund controlled by the government, and several of the journalists poached from leading American newspapers like the *New York Times* and the *Wall Street Journal* resigned within a year of the paper's establishment, citing censorship restrictions.

The coverage of the Scissor Sisters concert announcement felt equally constructed around a safe press release. I noticed two articles that offered vague mention of "controversial" performances, but neither actually elaborated on the source of that controversy; one dared to use the word "transgressive," which seemed to more explicitly hint at a conscious pushing of morality boundaries, but any mention of the band's overt queerness was unsurprisingly totally absent from any local coverage.

I sent James a one-line email of invitation to the concert as soon as I saw the announcement: *I'm going come rain, shine, or deportation!!* Dark humor seemed like the right angle to convince him to come along with me. It was impossible to ignore the fact that attending the concert of a queer group seemed immeasurably riskier than just sitting at home and watching another Meryl Streep film, so I figured it was best to couch any danger in a joke. He sent a one-liner response just a few minutes later: he would come along.

I couldn't quite believe that we would be attending—not just because I was skeptical about James finally coming out for the evening, but because it was difficult to imagine how the Scissor Sisters could ever take the stage in Abu Dhabi. The band had even bluntly stated they didn't think they could ever play in the UAE because of the inherent risk involved. Not six months before the concert announcement, I had read an interview in British music magazine *Q* where band member Ana Matronic declared, "I have it on good authority that I will get arrested in the UAE. Just by brushing up against some of my friends, I would have so much cocaine residue on my clothes I would have to spend the rest of my life in jail. I've heard you can go to jail for having trace amounts on your clothes, because the drug laws are so insane there."

The stories Ana Matronic had probably heard weren't exactly inaccurate; people were indeed prosecuted for seemingly minute infractions across the UAE. In 2007, British citizen Keith Brown spent four months in prison after Emirati customs officers allegedly found .003 ounces of cannabis in a joint stub stuck to the bottom of his shoe. And only a few months after that, notable British DJ Grooverider was arrested at the airport and sentenced to four years in a Dubai prison for possession of just over two grams of marijuana, which he blamed on a forgotten spliff in his pocket. He was royally pardoned ten months after his arrest during Ramadan—a month which traditionally sees select prisoners released—though intense media coverage in the UK likely expedited that process. Coverage of the UAE abroad was also fueled by salacious stories of Westerners caught up in sexual escapades: the infamous case of Vince Acors and Michelle Palmer, a British couple who were sentenced in 2008 to a three-month prison sentence for having sex on a beach in Dubai, was splashed across every British newspaper for months.

I was beginning to feel like the easy proliferation of these sensational news stories in the Western media was the very "good authority" that people like Ana Matronic relied on to understand the Gulf, and I was likewise just beginning to notice who was missing from these international accounts. I could find plenty of coverage of what were framed as undue punitive measures for minute infractions—like how a jail term for sex on the beach was an unjust sentence for a night of drunken passion between a pair of straight Brits—but never seemed to encounter stories about queer people, let alone articles about non-Westerners who were subjected to local law.

That is, until I started reading between the lines of local newspapers. There I found story after story of men engaging in illegal sex together and getting caught. A few days before the concert, I stumbled on an account in the Courts section of *The National* of four teenage boys being arrested for—well, what, exactly, was unclear. The entire episode was muddled. Initially, authorities took four teenage boys into custody, accused of the grave crimes of raping and kidnapping a man. But as the trial progressed, the most serious charges were dropped, two of the defendants were sentenced only for "homosexual acts." And then the trial became even more opaque: the remaining two boys were sentenced to two additional months in prison exclusively for masturbating atop the body of the victim. With few other details given, I wasn't sure how or what to think about the boys. Had they indeed committed a terrible crime? Or were they on trial primarily for engaging in sex with a man? Was everyone in the story a victim—and of what, exactly?

I couldn't discern the lines between these possibilities, if there even were lines in the eyes of the local authorities. And I saw myself in that undefinable space, too: all the times in high school I had coaxed gray-haired men off park paths and into public bathroom stalls, knowing exactly what I wanted them to do to me illegally in public spaces. I couldn't help feeling an empathy—or perhaps even an unwarranted sympathy—for the boys when I read the judge's statement, which referred to the act they were being sentenced for as "the secret habit," an English translation of an Islamic term for masturbation. The judge told them, "If a person practices the 'secret habit' in the privacy of their bathroom, they don't face penalties." Was this the issue: what was public versus what was private?

I wanted to shout at the newspaper that queer people had rarely been granted privacy as a space of safety; fucking in public had become a necessity for people like me. I returned to the story again and again, not for how it read to me like a parable for my situation in this new oppressive land, but for how eerily the story of these boys in the UAE mirrored the cautionary tale I had been taught growing up in the US: that queerness was something not to speak of or allow to be discovered—and if it was, it incurred penalties.

I pulled the story up on my phone and started reading it to James as he rummaged through his closet, deciding what to wear to the concert. He pulled out a crumpled yellow shirt from behind his overstuffed laundry basket.

"Can I get away with this?" he asked.

"It's a little tight. Maybe try something else," I offered as diplomatically as possible. I didn't know how to tell him that his gut hung conspicuously beneath the hem. It was his third prospective outfit for the evening. "Did you hear what I said about the court case?"

"Sorry, I'm kind of trying to sort myself out right now," he shot back, his tone rising with each consecutive word. I summarized the case again to the shadow peeking out from behind the door of his wardrobe.

"Well, obviously, they should hide that," was all he offered, turning a balled-up green T-shirt over in his hand like a worry stone. I tried to protest but he ducked his head out and cut me off. "Can you get me something from the kitchen?" he asked. "I'm kind of busy for this right now."

"Hiding it" didn't seem like the right answer to me, though I didn't have any idea how the boys should *not* hide their queerness. Certainly, we were hiding ours.

I walked into James's railroad kitchen, scanning the open snack boxes and chip bags for signs of sustenance. I wanted to keep talking about the case, but I knew he wouldn't really engage. I inwardly acknowledged that it probably wasn't fair to expect him to have the same connection to this place without studying the region or the Arabic language like I had, but I still felt his lack of curiosity taking an increasing toll on our relationship. I'd slowly initiated more and more time apart because of the claustrophobia I was beginning to feel, sequestered in his apartment covered in takeout litter. I suspected from his foul mood that he hadn't eaten much save for the empty chip packets on the counter since I'd made him dinner the night before. I rummaged through his threadbare cupboards but knew I wouldn't find anything. And anyway, I knew "get me something" meant "make me something."

"You have absolutely nothing in here that even remotely resembles food," I said, gathering up as many empty containers as I could and mashing them into his overflowing trash can.

I told him I didn't feel like I was helping much, and that I was going upstairs to my apartment. He didn't respond. Still buried in the wardrobe, I could only see the back of his head as I swung the door closed.

I returned to my own space thinking about those electric nights we spent sequestered in my tiny apartment in New York, dreaming of everything we could do together. That year felt like a gestation: two gay boys making plans of how to be together out in a world that hadn't taught them how. But as I opened the door to my apartment alone and considered them again, they suddenly felt like a harbinger for James's insularity.

While I was irritated—if not entirely surprised—by his behavior, I was at least partially relieved that I didn't have to actually help him choose his outfit for the concert. I didn't even know what the hell I was going to wear. Alongside the occasional stories of queer debauchery, I'd also come across stories in the Courts section about "indecent" clothes, as well as a proposed federal dress code. But an outdoor concert seemed like the perfect chance to step out and push boundaries. I pulled outfit after outfit from my closet in hopes of finding something even slightly transgressive, but I didn't have anything, and I couldn't exactly pop over to a Brooklyn thrift store in a pinch. I couldn't figure out how to pay homage to the queerness of the group without potentially imperiling myself, until I came to the very bottom of my lowest drawer and spotted a pair of trim pink shorts that ran just above my knee. It was all the defiance I could muster.

James and I barely spoke in the taxi and arrived at a sprawling venue that looked like an airplane hangar shortly before the band was due to take the stage. We were meeting a few of James's American colleagues. A group of my own colleagues was also attending, and though neither suspected anything amiss in my relationship with James, I was drawn away from James's crew—not just because they counted James as a friend, but because the other group had spent time in the Gulf and spoke Arabic. Plus, they were meeting a friend I had never met before, and I was craving contact outside of James's circle. I had tried to compromise with him beforehand by floating the idea of bringing the groups together, but his reticence at "investing in new people" meant I hovered between the two groups ten meters apart, like an impatient grocery shopper trying to hold space in two different checkout lines.

As much as I felt the tug of obligation to show James a good time, I also wasn't going to stand at the back of the concert with the same people I saw every day. So as the DJ amped up the volume and the two groups pulled apart, I let the jostle of concertgoers take me away toward the stage. I wasn't going to come this far and then not feel part of this. I offered an apologetic wave, but

James's eyes were fixed elsewhere.

I followed my friend Alana as the band strutted on stage, taking in their outfits. Ana Matronic wore a black polka dot dress with matching leggings. Jake Shears's jeans were shredded enough to look like they had gone repeatedly through a bread slicer, but I noted that his denim outfit was also markedly modest. We tried to push further toward the stage. I bobbed and weaved through concertgoers, slightly alarmed by how all the men I pushed past seemed to be decked out in polos and baggy cargo pants.

The crowd was less packed at the front than I had ever seen at a concert, perhaps unsurprisingly, given the band's overt queerness. As we slid into the second row, I noticed only one man dancing: a man in a tight gray T-shirt, directly ahead of me in the front row. As Jake swept across the stage, I kept my eyes on the man's black curls, loose enough to bounce nearly in time with the beat. His sturdy shoulders swayed back and forth, his hips moving only slightly, as though he wasn't sure how much he could move them in this setting. Alana mouthed *"That's him,"* and pointed to the dancing man, tapping him on the shoulder.

He turned around quickly and hugged Alana, though I caught him staring at me. He smiled wider, daring me to hold eye contact, and I grinned dumbly back. He tried to introduce himself, but I couldn't hear him over the noise of Jake Shears singing my favorite song from the new album. *Oh, let's see how far that we have run / I hear the warning sign / What would you do for more?*

I began to dance not so much next to him as with him. I tried to stand in parallel so it looked like we were just two fans of the band, but I also tried to subtly move my hips in time with his. It felt like we were the ones on a stage in front of thousands of gawking spectators, our shoulders cheating outward to the audience, our eyes meeting only to look outward again. As the song reached its climax, he leaned in to whisper something, and I found myself leaning back, trying to get as close to him as possible. After a moment, I pulled away to apologize for not hearing what he was trying to say, but when we locked eyes, he just gave me a knowing smile. I gave him a nod and leaned in once more, knowing he hadn't said anything at all, just grazed his lips along my ear. We held that position until the song ended. When the audience broke out into cheers, I looked back and remembered everyone standing around us. I pulled away to clap and cheer, but he motioned me to lean in once more.

"Alana said her friend Gaar was coming, but I had never heard your name and thought you were a girl," he said. I stuck my tongue out at him and asked if he was disappointed. He smirked and shook his head with an emphatic, "No."

I tried to concentrate on the concert. But I kept getting distracted by the energy I felt standing next to this stranger I suddenly wanted to know, who had introduced himself as Sunil. I found myself leaning over to him between songs and spontaneously hurling questions about everything from the genesis of his Scissor Sisters fandom to the name of his hometown. The vowels of his Australian accent bounced as much as his curls.

"Who did you think would come to this?" I asked. "I thought everyone would be a little more, you know…" I flicked my wrist and gave him a look, and he laughed.

He explained that the Scissor Sisters were big in the UK not because they were queer but on account of their electronica-infused glam-rock credibility. "I guess that's why I'm here," he said. "What's big in the UK is big in the Commonwealth." He laughed before adding: "Though I didn't think I would feel like the only brown person here."

I looked around the sea of apparently British men in cargo pants and women woohoo-ing like they were at a bachelorette party.

We stood hip to hip for the rest of the concert, willing Jake Shears to speak to us, but there were scant few moments when he engaged in crowd banter, electing mostly to jump directly from song to song. I realized I was disappointed; Shears was normally so gregarious. The band's famous rapport with the crowd felt lacking. Shears didn't mention queerness at all. The most political moment of the show came in the form of an awkward joke; in a quiet moment between songs, Ana Matronic faked exasperation and asked the audience, "What does it take for a girl to get stoned around here?" before adding in bad jest, "I don't mean *that* kind of stoned."

Sunil and I looked at each other and winced. Was that the closest the band would get to mentioning anything controversial? I didn't expect them to run out on stage waving a rainbow flag or engage in any Pussy Riot-esque stunts, but I realized that I did expect...something. Even the bumbling garage band The Black Lips had pushed more boundaries with their recent tour in India, reportedly getting chased to the state line by local police for kissing on stage. Is that what I wanted, some kind of performance—or at least acknowledgment—of queerness? I looked at their subdued outfits that felt like a poor imitation of straightness. The band launched into their next song, "Night Life." *When you're underground / You need a breakthrough,* Shears cooed. I found myself shuffling even closer to Sunil, wondering if that was the kind of defiance I craved.

After the concert, I stood in line for the modular bathroom pods behind Sunil, who invited everyone back to his apartment for a marathon of all three Scissor Sisters albums. James shot me his *Let's go home* face that I had seen so many times over the past year. I thought about my first night with Imran, of missing out on my first suhoor, and how much I had missed since then. A year and a half later, Imran had nearly stopped inviting me to anything at all. I didn't want the same thing to happen with Sunil. I watched men walk in and out of the bathrooms and wondered how many of them would be hooking up in the stalls at a Scissor Sisters concert anywhere else in the world.

"I'd love to go," I said to Sunil. I shrugged at James and told him I'd see him tomorrow. It was so easy. All I had to do was step out of the queue and file past everyone standing so dutifully in line.

▽▽▽

I felt like I was inside a Celine Dion music video. Electronic strings and heavy bass drums reverberated against marble walls as I picked at the upholstery on a velvet sofa. I tried to identify the song, but the heavy wooden door on the opposite side of the hotel lobby garbled the sound bleeding through from the bar. I looked at my phone, waiting for a message from Sunil.

After the concert a few weeks earlier, I'd taken a taxi with him back to his apartment, along with Alana and Sunil's British flatmate, Jonathan, the man Alana had her eye on. I sat in the front and watched in the rearview mirror as she flirted hard in full view of the taxi driver. I stared at the registration information dutifully displayed on the meter, unsure whether the Muslim name of the driver was preventing me from chancing it with Sunil. Alana was a nominal half-Muslim, half-Jewish straight Lebanese American; I wondered whether some alchemy of those identities afforded her the gumption to saddle up so close to Jonathan. I looked back in the rearview and thought about Michelle Palmer and Vince Acors, the couple on the beach, and whether they took up any real estate in either Alana or Jonathan's minds.

In Sunil's living room, the four of us had danced next to an artificial gold Christmas tree still standing halfway through January. He must have seen me staring at it glinting off his windows, which overlooked the four lanes of a major east-west thoroughfare. "I love that it blinds whoever drives past with its gayness," he said, pointing out the window with his middle finger. "'Make the Yuletide gay,' indeed." He'd smiled, and I grinned back, charmed that his act of putting up a campy Christmas tree felt like the same impulse I had to wear pink shorts.

Now my phone vibrated with a text message from Sunil, jolting me back into the hotel lobby: *Already inside!* I gathered myself off the velvet couch and tried to adjust my collar in the reflection of the sliding doors. I felt the dull flutter of nerves. We were meeting for the first time since the night of the concert, and I was relieved it was in a place where darkness and noise might cloak my impulse to be so near to him.

I flashed my identification to a bouncer and walked up the marble stairs to the bar entrance. The instrumentation shifted as soon as I opened the door. What sounded in the cavernous lobby like it might be a haunting grand piano sounded in the bar like a keyboard inside an empty tin can; the strings that seemed so rich and full were just a shaky, trebly synthesizer. It wasn't even a Celine Dion song, I realized—or any other song I recognized, for that matter. The cheap speakers were blasting a karaoke instrumentation of some sweeping Tagalog ballad. The only thing that sounded grand were the vocals. Whoever was singing was hitting each of the low, smoky notes with the panache of Toni Braxton. The singer's vowels were deep and clear with no hint of strain. I scanned the dark room for the singer but couldn't find her anywhere.

The bar was packed with revelers humming along and swigging Singaporean beer. I spotted Sunil waving at me, leaning on a tiny high-top at the front of the bar. The table sat directly in front of a small stage, but I noticed that the singer wasn't there either. I offered him a shy smile as I walked over, not sure how to greet him in a public setting. I stuck out my right hand, grimacing internally at the absurdity of a handshake. He pointed to a woman sitting at the far corner of the bar, alone in the near dark. I had walked right past her. I couldn't imagine such a powerful voice emanating from such a slight, unassuming frame. And with such a powerful instrument, I couldn't understand why she wasn't on stage.

I settled into the chair next to Sunil, careful to sit far enough away so as not to arouse suspicion or be tempted to touch him.

Like the concert, the music was deafening, and he leaned in to greet me. I felt his lips against my earlobe.

"What do you think of your first Filipino karaoke bar?" he asked.

I had felt embarrassed at my ignorance when he'd invited me via text a few days earlier. He explained that there were several in Sydney—that they were everywhere, really—and wondered how I hadn't been to one in New York. I hadn't even known where to look, let alone whether I should have found them on my own or whether I wasn't hanging out with the right people. I thought about all that time with James in my apartment.

"Well, may this be the first of many," he said, clinking his glass with mine.

When the woman finished singing, the bar erupted into raucous cheers. It looked like nearly fifty people had somehow jammed into the tiny room. Each seat at the two dozen tables was full, and two rows of patrons hugged the back wall, several of them clutching the rim of their glasses with their teeth so they could applaud.

Waitresses collected little scraps of paper with hastily written song titles from eager patrons. I scanned the crowd in anticipation of the next singer, but a stern bouncer clad in a black T-shirt took the microphone. Five Filipinos in matching blue outfits burst through the doors, snaking between tables to high-fives and wolf whistles. The bouncer set the microphone in a stand and carefully unhooked a velvet rope from its metal stanchion. The group sashayed on stage.

A man with a helmet of long shellacked hair and a baby-blue button-down opened to halfway down his chest grabbed the microphone. "Welcome back! We are the Diamonds!" he cried, nodding to the guitarist, who kicked off the unmistakable plucking at the top of "Rolling in the Deep."

"Oh, yeah—there's a cover band too," Sunil grinned.

I expected one of the two women to take the microphone

from the man, but he broke into the first verse, emulating the same smoky tone as Adele. His backup singers swayed in matching blue miniskirts as the guitarist and drummer offered periodic smirks to the audience. At the bridge, the singer walked to the very edge of the stage and winked into the crowd. I turned to see if he was looking at anyone in particular, but everyone was in shadow. Sunil grazed his leg along mine. I wondered, our table parked so close to the stage, how illuminated we were for the crowd behind us.

"Remember, you can request a song from us during any of our four sets," the singer coaxed once the applause for his pitch-perfect rendition of Adele subsided.

He walked to the corner of the stage and reached like a magician into an empty champagne bucket, where waitresses were throwing in request slips.

"Ah, I see someone has requested the same song as last week." He laughed, shielding his eyes and peering out into the crowd. A joyful shout of acknowledgment from a man in the far corner shot back at him. "Don't think we forgot about you from last week. I just need to pull up the lyrics, but I think we can do it."

The band huddled on stage while one of the backup singers pulled out a tablet. I looked at Sunil quizzically. "If you request a song the band doesn't know, they'll go learn it. You can literally pretty much request anything. Watch," he said, pointing to the singer in the button-down. "He is going to pretend he needs the lyrics, but I bet they've all learned it already."

The drummer broke into a familiar soft beat, followed by the guitarist strumming an irrepressible riff. The song didn't click until a few bars later: they were playing "Jai Ho," but singing the original Indian version. This Filipino man with the coiffure of Elvis and the timbre of Adele was singing a song with lyrics that cut frenetically between South Asian languages.

As Sunil suspected, he really didn't need the lyrics. When he belted the fourth "Jai Ho!" at the climax of the chorus, I expected the bar to erupt, but he held them entranced until he broke into the second verse, effortlessly modulating between intricate Hindi, Urdu, and Punjabi lyrics.

The band whisked through seven more songs—including a barnstorming rendition of "Hotel California," where the guitarist played his solo with his teeth—before they announced the end of their first act and exited the stage, promising to learn a new Nicki Minaj song. It was only when Sunil abruptly stood to grab a giant black blinder off the next table that I realized we had our arms around each other's shoulders.

"All right, what are we going to sing?" he asked with a gleam in his eye, eagerly pawing through sticky pages of songs listed in Tagalog, Korean, Arabic, and English. "What about some Scissor Sisters?" he smiled.

I told him if the band needed time to prepare a new song, I'd probably need a week or so to belt some "Comfortably Numb."

Sunil raised his eyebrow and winked playfully. "So, you want to do this again, then? What about that boyfriend of yours?"

Somewhere between dancing to Scissor Sisters songs at his apartment, I told him about how James wanted to return to New York and I, well, wasn't sure. Our two-year contracts were drawing to their conclusion, and James was increasingly badgering me about returning along with him. I thought about that first night in Abu Dhabi, defacing my sofa with highlighter hours after arriving, and how I would have to account for it to somebody. But I hadn't been found out, and neither had my queerness.

I looked around the bar. I felt here with Sunil what I did on the Corniche and also at the ice rink: a way through, a mode of operating that felt familiar. And viable. And thrilling.

I scribbled two Scissor Sisters songs from the book on a scrap of paper. Sunil grabbed them off the table to hand to a passing waitress, but I snatched them back and told him I'd only do it if he made a deal.

"If you keep coming back with me for a month, we can do it," I told him, trying to make clear how much I wanted to keep spending time with him.

"Deal. There have probably been enough songs already to last the whole night, to be honest," he laughed.

He was right; I couldn't believe how many people wanted to sing. The buckets for song requests were nearly overflowing with little slips of paper, like a soup made of confetti. A grinning bald man at a crowded high-top a few tables away took the microphone from the bouncer.

Sunil leaned in. "Watch this. He sings the same song, like, every week."

The man pushed aside a few glasses and a half-empty bottle of whiskey. As he carefully rearranged his chair to be more visible to the audience, I realized he was wearing a kandura.

"This song, I love it too much," he said in broken English, chuckling. "Sorry for my Tagalog." The crowd started cheering before the song, "Bakit Pa," even began.

"Apparently he learned the words just by coming here and watching other people sing it," Sunil said. "Everyone goes nuts every time he does it."

When Sunil invited me to a Filipino karaoke bar, I expected the audience to reflect that national qualifier. I knew Filipino migrants made up a large section of the population in the UAE, especially in the health care and hospitality sectors. But I was surprised how much of the audience was from elsewhere. Several of the tables were filled with men wearing non-Western clothing. A sign hung outside the bar—outside many of the bars in the city—officially outlawing "national dress" as a way of enforcing the law that prevented Muslims from consuming alcohol. Enforcement of this "national dress" law also served as a way of preventing men who wore shalwar kameez, the national dress of many working-class migrants from South Asia, from entering establishments serving alcohol. But here, both types of dress were present: tables of Muslim Arabs sat beside working-class South Asians, all cheering on a song with lyrics they most likely could not understand.

The lights dimmed. I could just make out the band weaving through tables in new matching pink outfits. The singer wore a pink button-down barely buttoned at all. White sneakers poked out from beneath pink crushed velvet bell bottoms as he climbed once more onto the stage and the lights rose. They had done a costume change. It was the kind of showmanship I had expected from Jake Shears.

"Thank you for coming! We are the Diamonds!" he repeated for the new arrivals. More people had somehow packed into the bar. "You might know this one," the singer cooed, giggling as he tucked his thick black hair behind his ears.

The guitarist sat at a keyboard and banged out the familiar intro to Lionel Ritchie and Diana Ross's duet, "Endless Love." The singer stood astride his mic stand with his face in dramatic profile, his left cheek gleaming in the spotlight as he nailed the first few lines of Lionel's mournful tenor. I waited for one of the backup singers to chime in a few bars later with the Diana Ross section of the verse, but the singer abruptly turned 180 degrees to reveal the right side of his face in full makeup. "My first love / You're every breath that I take," he sang, his lips accentuated with a slather of thick red lipstick. He flipped back and forth, a one-man comedy act, delivering both Lionel Ritchie and Diana Ross's parts. Each time he flipped to his Diana Ross side, he fluttered his one visible set of fake eyelashes and smoothed down his bell bottoms as though he were wearing a dress.

The crowd hollered. He hit his final "My endless loooove" and turned to face the audience head-on, finally revealing both sides of his face, one unadorned and one made up, as he blew a sensual kiss. He winked, and the audience rose to their feet. It felt more electric than standing at the front of the Scissor Sisters' crowd.

The singer held his face in profile for the rest of the set, hiding the made-up side of his face, but I knew it was there. I had seen it—the lipstick, the gestures. He had flaunted this queerness. I thought again of all the newspaper articles I had read about legal reprisals for transgressions like this and wondered how much this artist was risking. Why was he doing it? Maybe if I could ask him directly, I could find the answer for myself.

I turned to Sunil and told him I was going to approach the singer when the band broke for their next set.

"Don't you see the stanchions?" Sunil asked. "That's to keep us separate. We aren't allowed on stage, and they aren't allowed to talk to us."

"What do you mean they aren't allowed to talk to us?"

"We officially can't interact," he explained simply, like I was a child and this was the most normal rule in the world. "There's a law separating performers from audience members." He pulled an article up on his phone to show me: a Dubai government regulatory commission enforced a rule that "prohibits artists from mingling with the audience." Although the official cited in the article declined to state the motivation for the rule, it seemed to nod to the destabilizing potentiality inherent in performance: that those on stage wielded a particular power over their audience—of suggestion, provocation, or outright defiance of norms. Although a performer was not necessarily a political revolutionary, in a country where unauthorized demonstrations or public gatherings were prohibited, they perhaps came close.

The word "officially" that Sunil had used seemed slippery because the article stipulated that the law only applied to the emirate of Dubai, not the entire country. As the proprietor of an Abu Dhabi-based establishment, it was as though the manager of the bar enforcing the "rule" was self-censoring before any trouble could arise. Perhaps they recognized that this performance was already boundary-pushing—from the makeup to the fake dress, the singer had already broken laws, and been cheered for it. I thought about the delicate triangulation of performer, audience, and content, what wasn't just witnessed but also accepted—celebrated, even. If the singer had done all that for a crowd, I hoped he could at least speak to me for a few minutes after his set.

I looked at my watch. If it were any other night, I would still be on the Corniche. This bar had the same feel to it: an electric fizz, a joy in hidden potentiality. Like the Corniche, I would need to wait, to be patient. I would find a time and a means to connect with the singer. I watched the band hurriedly exit the stage and push silently toward the door, weaving past tables, the singer's lipstick still gleaming in the spotlights.

▽▽▽

Wedged between two backup singers clad in matching snakeskin jumpsuits, I leaned back against an industrial dishwasher and cracked open my notebook, trying to project a confidence I didn't feel. Stainless steel appliances cast reflections at new angles each time the overhead track lighting moved to a new setting. I couldn't figure out why a sketchy bar where I'd only seen people down beer and whiskey to fortify themselves for karaoke needed a kitchen in the first place, but the lead singer had told me to meet the band there.

The guitarist and drummer, both in Metallica T-shirts, flanked the women. The lead singer—this man who was both Lionel Ritchie and Diana Ross—sat across from me on the metal countertop, casually shifting his leg to rest atop a two-burner hot plate while I tried to conjure the right way to begin. I noticed his hands fidget as he waited. I wanted to cut him off before I even phrased my question, to tell him to be careful, not entirely unconvinced that he might accidentally turn a dial on the stovetop without noticing.

I was grateful that they even wanted to talk. A few nights after Sunil explained the real and perceived reach of the stage performance regulations, I decided to linger near the bathrooms between sets in the hope that one of the band members might walk past. I figured I had plenty of experience loitering outside men's rooms trying to look inconspicuous. When I saw the singer walking through the empty hallway a few minutes later, I reached out a wild hand and told him that I was a journalist and wanted to speak to him. He smiled but barely stopped walking.

"Come tomorrow two hours before the show. The bar will be empty except for the band," he said, winking as he breezed past just like he had after "Endless Love." He told me his name was Reggie.

I had forgotten to introduce myself and felt self-conscious that I led with the title of journalist, which still only felt aspirational. Though I was beginning to ask questions and think about publication, the designation wasn't yet quite right. I was curious about the band in the way any good journalist should be about a story, but I wasn't quite sure how to prepare for the task of actually speaking with them. I spent the night before the meeting fretting about how to outwardly perform the role of journalist. Bringing a recording device seemed too impractical for a place as loud as a bar, not to mention too off-putting for a first meeting. Instead, I packed a shoddy pen from a Midwestern motel, an old notebook half-filled with college Arabic homework, and a list of hastily jotted questions. I felt like I was preparing for cosplay.

I didn't know which of the questions to ask first: the one about the genesis of the band, the songs they pushed themselves to learn, the kinds of patrons who returned to the bar night after night. It reminded me of the laundry list of questions I'd had for people like Shivani: unsure of the right place to begin, my points of reference and framing scrambled by who sat in front of me. And though I wanted to hear about the band's background and their journeys to the UAE, I knew it was Reggie's overt flamboyance on stage that drew me to seek him out. It was this—how he navigated his queerness—that I most wanted to understand.

Like forgoing a recording device, I knew I also needed to start my inquiry somewhere benign. I stammered out a few basic questions, and the guitarist, Manuel, explained that all of them were from Manila and had been in Abu Dhabi for three years.

He spun a cutting board on its corner as he detailed their schedule: arriving two hours before they took the stage; performing a four-part, five-hour set six days a week; using breaks to learn new melodies, harmonies, and dance moves. As the drummer scrolled through a playlist on his phone, showing me the twenty songs they aimed to learn over the next couple of days—"I'm embarrassed we don't play 'Call Me Maybe' yet," he said—I heard a scraping sound and ducked my head around a cabinet. A man was placing stanchions next to the stage.

"He's the manager of the bar," one of the backup singers said in a hushed tone. "We can talk, but we should go a little more into the kitchen." The drummer explained that plainclothes officers had been known to come into bars and fine both the management and the performers for speaking to anyone during performances in Dubai, so the manager was especially cagey about the band talking to anyone offstage, even though they were working in another emirate.

As the rest of us pushed farther into the tiny kitchen, I noticed Reggie unmoved atop the hot plate. "What do you really want to know?" he asked, smiling, almost gossipy. It felt too early to ask the loaded questions, but his grin felt like a provocation.

I hedged, asking him when he realized he wanted to be an entertainer.

"I've always known," he said simply, flipping his hair. All different types of music—from the Righteous Brothers to 1970s Filipino-American band the Rocky Fellers—had been in his house growing up, he explained. But it was after puberty—he raised his eyes at me as he said this—that he realized he had an unusually high range. "I was different, and this helped me."

"But why here?" I asked, almost frustrated. I realized I was getting ahead of myself, but I couldn't understand it. I imagined there must be hundreds of better cities, if not a hundred better countries, to make a living as a performer.

"It's not so different here than any other place, really," he said. "I learn songs, people applaud, I make them happy. It is my job. No, it is my life."

"But it is different here," I insisted. I realized that I had pounded my fist on the counter, making the cutting board clatter. I knew that I didn't sound objective, that I had a bias, and that perhaps a real journalist could have been more able to nimbly phrase a less leading, more neutral question.

His eyes lit up, and I saw the other three look to him. "Ahh, you are asking about that," he said. "Tell me, this thing we both are—" I watched him look directly at me, into me, and recognize my queerness. "—you've always known this about yourself, right?"

I thought about my very first interaction with Imran on the ice, how he saw it within me, too. This time, though, I didn't freeze.

"Yes," I said. It was true; I could scarcely recall a single childhood memory that wasn't colored by my awareness that I was always, on the most atomic level, fundamentally different than everyone else.

"Well, same for me," he said, shrugging. "And I had the same feeling about leaving the Philippines to sing. I knew I needed to leave."

Filipino cover bands were an industry, Reggie explained. As soon as they were old enough to understand that they had musical aptitude, each of the band members began searching for an agency. But they were not looking to sign a recording contract or form relationships with producers. The agency they sought was more common; it was one that recruited solo musicians, formed bands, and relocated them abroad for what amounted to multi-year musical residencies. Growing up, they all knew about Filipino bands who played in Shanghai, Goa, Bahrain, Hong Kong. This was their image of success: a musician not popular in the Philippines but created specifically to entertain abroad.

Competition, usually at multinational hotel chain bars, was fierce. Filipinos made up one of the largest diasporic populations in the world, and performing artists made up one of the largest percentages of these migrants, second only to domestic workers. Reggie explained that he stood in a line for three hours before he was seen at an open call. He anticipated more hurdles but found himself a week later with these four other performers in an office not much larger than this kitchen. A manager was forming them into a group. They would practice for a few weeks and then put together a video to send to entertainment managers abroad. To their surprise, less than a month later, they had an offer to sign a two-year contract in Abu Dhabi.

They had not been seduced by one ad campaign. It was a wider system that they wanted to opt into as the most viable career option. During their first day of rehearsals, they realized they had all come to the initial audition a different way: social media, message boards, a poster, the recommendation from a friend who was in another band.

"I applied to another agency, but the phone line was disconnected, so I just kept trying until I found one that would hear me," Reggie laughed. "I could stay and try to be a singer for $5 a day, or I could be in a cover band and make $100."

I realized I had been waiting for some kind of sob story—a sick relative, a father unable to work—that precipitated their movement. But being a successful singer for Reggie was not about hearing one's own songs played on the radio; it was about having performance skills that enabled migration. And to make a living as a Filipino singer was to be away. This was not intermittent touring in support of music, it was a foreign residency to enable a feasible livelihood. They had no say where they were going to perform, Reggie explained. But it didn't matter: nearly half of the Philippines' 100 million citizens live on less than two dollars a day. Anywhere else was better.

I realized I'd had similar dreams of movement—I'd harbored a dim sense of New York as a kind of refuge, but I was driven by the more overwhelming awareness that I needed to leave where I was. The destination was shapeless. Only the departure was discernible: a specific need to be away.

"But what about the dangers facing people like us here?" As I asked the question, the manager shuffled nearer the kitchen, and the drummer signaled with a nod of his head that we would have to finish.

"It is dangerous everywhere. You can get killed for singing Frank Sinatra in the Philippines." Reggie laughed. "Come to the show tonight. Maybe you will see how I can make it okay here."

I bid them farewell and waited in the hotel lobby for their evening residency to begin, researching the killings that Reggie had mentioned almost as an aside. The "My Way" killings, as they were known, were a series of early-aughts murders in which a number of singers were killed, often on stage, while performing the famous Frank Sinatra song at karaoke bars across the Philippines. Several writers attempted to construct a pattern and narrative around the killings, blaming the incidents on the country's culture of machismo or even Sinatra's own brash lyrics, but I was most drawn to the accounts that pointed to the singers being murdered for not performing the song well enough. At one bar in 2007, a security guard complained to a "My Way" singer that he was off-key. When he refused to stop singing, the guard pulled out a .38-caliber pistol and shot him dead. I was transfixed by the idea that several people could harbor such protective, impassioned feelings, such ownership, over something—be it songs or sexuality—that another person's rendering of it was cause for murder. How even just being confronted with it was too obscene and needed to be stopped at any cost.

Reggie began his first set later to a full house beneath a single spotlight. "I'm," he breathed, as Manuel began a familiar riff. "Coming." I knew what was coming, and yet I was still jolted by Reggie's knowing smile. "Out." Manuel continued the riff and Reggie repeated his declaration six more times before further proclaiming that he wanted the world to know and would have to let it show. As in "Endless Love," he once again became Diana Ross not only in affectation—swishing his arms and shooting authoritative stares into the audience—but in the very timbre of his voice.

Perhaps this was the key: mimicry. Reggie had called it *wido,* a Tagalog cognate of the Spanish word for "to hear," as in, "to play music by ear." It was a title bestowed unto others in the Philippines, those with a particular aptitude. *Oh, they have the wido.* To excel as a Filipino cover musician was not just to sing the right notes but to fully inhabit a celebrated tune, from vocal inflections to mannerisms. It was a mimicry cultivated by history: already a music-loving culture proficient in Western church hymns after three centuries of Spanish colonialism, Filipino cover bands proliferated in the wake of WWII, filling a space to entertain troops around the world by perfecting American rock 'n' roll.

I watched Reggie finish his final note to thunderous applause. He had told me in the kitchen that he didn't have any interest in making his own music. This was the industry; this was the dream. To make a living adapting to the likeness of another.

"There is an international understanding of what the Filipino mimicry brand is: exactitude in copying, technically and aesthetically precise repetition, and giving people what they want and what they expect, every time," Abigail De Kosnik, Director of the Berkeley Center for New Media, would later write in her research on the proliferation and global popularity of Filipino cover bands.

Was this adaptation the same as assimilation? Was perfectly mimicking someone else a means—or a shortcut—to acceptance? I wondered how it related to more than just music when the Emirati man sitting at the next table leaned over to me after a few songs. I had seen him at the same table for weeks, and we had exchanged pleasantries, especially after he realized I had studied Arabic. As he motioned for me to lean in so he could say something, I noticed his arm around his Filipina girlfriend.

"He is..." He waited for a second as though unsure which word to use. "*Mithli*, no?" He used the Arabic slang for a gay man. I looked up, and he was smiling, clapping. He switched to Arabic. "His show is so good." He said more, mere inches from my ear, but I couldn't make out his words amid the cheers.

I realized that this man may not have recognized the performance for what it was—charged with the politics of a gay anthem explicitly declaring one's intention to live an openly queer life—but he did notice a flicker of something and was, at least, charmed. This was intentional. Reggie's queerness was obvious; he was knowingly and outwardly performing it. He wasn't just mimicking. He was infusing his performances with a just-there subtext, the very act that the law preventing singers and audiences from communicating was trying to avoid. Perhaps that was the power of a good performance in any realm of one's life: concessions that led to acceptance, all while holding fast to one's true identity. I thought again about Jake Shears on stage, still unsure if the Scissor Sisters had, in fact, done enough. At what decibel did subversion become audible to all?

Later, I waited for the band on the curb outside the hotel entrance like a groupie. I reasoned that even if we couldn't interact inside, we couldn't be barred from incidental conversation outside the bar. I was surprised to see Reggie push through the rotating doors alone.

"Sometimes, I need to be by myself after I perform," he said.

He looked tired but exhilarated, his eyes both a bit glassy and wild, the way I always felt after leaving a good concert. "Now you see? I am Whitney, I am Diana Ross, I can be anyone—a joke, a diva." He flipped his hair. "And maybe sometimes myself."

I told him I felt a little like a performer, too. I leveled with him: as much as I wanted to write his story, I wasn't actually a working journalist, though I hoped to be one soon.

"Well, I think you will make a good one. You ask good questions," he said, tapping at his temple. I walked side by side with him, hoping this was true. To fill the silence, I asked him what he thought made a good performer.

"The truth is, I think the best ones of us are gay," he giggled. "We are kind of like chameleons."

I walked with him a few blocks and noticed he was heading north. I asked him if he ever goes to the Corniche at night.

"In the past." He smiled. "But I am with Manuel now."

I said goodbye and started walking home, replaying the band's onstage antics. I had registered the queerness of Reggie's performances, and yet he hadn't displayed even a glint of flirtation with Manuel under the spotlights. He had shown what he wanted to and nothing more. Humming Whitney Houston, I walked back to my apartment under streetlamps that felt like stage lighting: first in shadow, then under the spotlight, over and over again until I reached home.

▽▽▽

"Well, this is it," I said, pulling the two crumpled slips of paper with Scissor Sisters songs on them from my pocket. "I can put these requests in if you want. Or," I grabbed a pen and a new sheet of paper at our familiar table, "you can trust me, and I'll try not to get us booed off stage."

Sunil looked at me and smirked. "I trust you," he said. "But will I know the song?"

I handed my request slip to a passing waitress. "Everyone knows it," I said. She snuck a peek at my song and giggled.

The bar was packed but not heaving. We had arrived early so we would be assured a chance to sing. After just a few songs, a waitress in a sparkling black dress approached our table with two microphones and told us we were next.

Though we had been coming for weeks, this would be our first introduction to this community as singers. I had started to recognize familiar faces and wanted to become one as well. I thought of the Arab man singing the Tagalog song, how he moved his chair, cheating out toward the audience. As we took the microphones, I told Sunil to grab his barstool and follow my lead. We walked a few feet to the very edge of the stanchions, taking up most of the narrow passageway between the stage and the first row of tables.

The bouncer wagged his finger and pointed to the stanchions, but I held my ground, placing our chairs three feet apart and turning them to face the audience. "Just watch, we won't go on stage," I told the bouncer. He reluctantly took one step aside. We were mere inches from the edge of the stage, and just eight inches lower than the platform. It was just enough room for us to maneuver.

"We're going to need to perform the shit out of this," I whispered to Sunil.

The guitar riff for the Backstreet Boys' "I Want It That Way" started. I dared to look at Sunil. He was grinning at me. I took the first verse, holding out my hand at Sunil in performative longing. He turned his chair to face me at the first chorus, allowing himself to be publicly cast as the object of my affection in this performance. His perfect harmonies caught me off guard. I didn't know he could actually sing.

We improvised hand choreography and reveled in the melodrama of the song by projecting furrowed brows and parted lips. I reached out to Sunil again with an overly dramatic hand gesture, and he replied with a soapy look of yearning as he gazed into my eyes, pretending to caress my cheek from a distance. Schmaltzy pop lyrics and campy choreography—they were the only way we could express our affection for each other publicly. It felt both insufficient and totally right.

The cheers were raucous. The crowd rose, offering us the same ovation as "Endless Love" had received. Even the bouncer was clapping. I pushed our chairs back, and Sunil raised his eyebrows in an expression that looked something like relief. I wanted to hug him but offered a wink instead. It was enough.

A string of people approached our table as we sat down, offering high fives and handshakes and a couple of rounds of beer. Sunil ran his foot up my leg throughout the receiving line. I saw the Arab man next to us look at our nearly intertwined legs, and he leaned over. "You guys were so funny," he said, smiling.

His Filipino girlfriend winked. "Very cute."

I could tell they both knew about us. We had both skirted the law that kept amateur singers off the stage and captured their attention with a visual performance. Even more, we had performed a kind of public queerness. Sure, we had couched it in ambiguity—were we making light of the idea that two men could sing this song to each other or was our presentation authentic?—but we had also devised a performance that allowed us to outwardly express raw, forbidden emotion while keeping ourselves safe. We had both worked within the limits and pushed against them.

This was the balance of assimilation and subversion I saw in Reggie. It was a calculation: a careful algorithm of pushing and relenting, honed and fine-tuned over years of performance that both acknowledged the reality of and flew in the face of respectability politics. Some might immediately recognize it, but everyone would at least be witness to it. Maybe performing this kind of queerness in front of this diverse audience was enough of a political act.

I got a ping on my phone. It was a message from Reggie; he was in the next room rehearsing a new Rihanna song. "I could not see you," he said. "But you sounded very good. And who was that other boy?" Maybe just being in proximity was enough, too.

I looked at my watch. I didn't want to leave, but I knew James was waiting; he had his repatriation flight scheduled for the next day. He had tried for weeks to get me to agree to a long-distance relationship. I couldn't imagine what it would look like. It felt like a poor imitation, a bad mimic of some straight ideal. I felt so much more potentiality for a different kind of queerness here.

Sunil grabbed the binder and asked if I wanted to put in another song. We flipped through the sticky pages, and I let my hand linger on his. It wasn't for long, but it felt like just long enough. I noticed a few conspicuous absences I wished were in the book, but there were surely enough songs to keep coming back week after week and do something new, I reckoned.

I sent James a message. I told him I'd see him in the morning before his taxi. I felt like I had just arrived for my own kind of residency, and I wasn't going to waste it.

PART II:

THERE

5: A SALON

(Dubai: Marie and friends)

"Did you notice the change?" Sunil asked, his hands drumming the steering wheel.

I looked up from the radio dials and squinted into the distance, scanning the horizon for a tower to emerge, poking out of the haze. Nothing. I felt Sunil take his eyes off the road just long enough to stare at me expectantly.

"No, you were too slow; look behind you, quick!" he said, laughing.

Dusk was settling. Since we'd left the island of Abu Dhabi and hit the mainland on the highway out of the city, I had mostly busied myself with the radio. There was little to see besides the occasional petrol station. The few towns that bled together, effectively forming the northernmost suburbs of Abu Dhabi, had fallen away nearly an hour earlier.

I turned around quickly to look out the rear windshield. Nothing again—just sand bifurcated by a six-lane tarmac that unfurled into the inky distance.

"The lights! Look at the streetlights!" Sunil cried.

I could see—something. The light that hit the asphalt seemed slightly different a hundred meters back. In the near distance, the road was cast in an incandescent white. What we were driving through now was murkier, a darker hue of yellow.

"That's the border between Abu Dhabi and Dubai," Sunil

said. I started to laugh, thinking he was telling some kind of joke, but he shot me an earnest look and pointed to the lamp posts that lined the highway. He explained that on both sides of the border, the poles were the same thirty-meter height, but that the lamps themselves were different. Abu Dhabi used six-thousand-watt globes in a circular formation, like a Ferris wheel turned on its side. Dubai's lamps were molded in a V shape with only four bulbs of a higher wattage. We were far away, but I could just make out the difference: the tops of Abu Dhabi's chevron-shaped posts emitted a languid yellow, which flattened out into the halos we were now driving under, bursting with incandescent white, as we passed into Dubai.

"You didn't feel the bump either?" He was genuinely incredulous. There was a tangible difference in the road at the border, he explained. Dubai used a different kind of pavement. You could feel a slight bump, like a crease or a seam, if you really paid attention. I watched him explaining it all to me, riling himself up just enough to gesticulate with both hands before quickly grabbing the wheel again. He had such an earnest buoyancy. I leaned in and kissed him.

Everything had changed so quickly. James had wanted to pursue a "long-distance relationship," but even the framing of this proposal felt inadequate. Though the distance itself might have been a hurdle, I knew migrants could sustain romantic relationships through blurry photos and prepaid phone cards. But "long" seemed to hint at an eventual end—one I could not yet conceive of, now that I had decided to stay in Abu Dhabi indefinitely. And "distance" felt like a flippant understatement in measuring the dissonance between his contempt for the city and the undefinable queer potential I was beginning to feel in it.

Sunil and I had spoken vaguely about where our relationship might go after James left, and we started dating the day after he left. With him, "dating" meant emerging from our apartments and into the public sphere in a way I never had with James; we were getting out, finding our way through. That morning of our first trip to Dubai, Sunil had called, telling me to pack some overnight gear. It was only when I opened the passenger door to his car that he told me he was taking me to Dubai to celebrate the publication of my first major article.

I had traveled to Yemen to write an article about the country's only activist rock band. Editors were eager to capitalize on the Arab Spring protests that had sent millions of people into the streets in over a dozen Middle Eastern and North African countries from Morocco to Oman. The demand for articles and photographs about places that had toppled decades-long rulers proved irresistible. Even outlets that had never before published about the region were getting in on the game, commissioning content about countries from Tunisia to Yemen. A story about Egyptian revolutionaries calling in pizza orders for protesters on the steps of the Wisconsin state capitol had gone viral. A region seemingly ignored in the Western media outside the lens of terrorism was now being breathlessly written about through the prisms of human rights and protest.

But I had to travel: little had happened in the Gulf in the way of popular protest. For one, both criticism of the government and public protest remained outlawed across much of the region. Regional protests resulted in some political reform, mainly economic concessions in Bahrain and Saudi Arabia and the resignation of the Kuwaiti prime minister, but very little else tangible had occurred.

In the UAE, construction on Qasr Al-Watan, the $500 million presidential palace spanning two million square feet, began mere months after the deposition of the leaders of two Arab countries; the construction site blighting much of the northwestern corner of the city felt almost like a provocation. The protests that did arise were almost entirely virtual: five bloggers were rounded up in 2012 and tried for defamation and insulting the state for posting material critical of the UAE government. Their arrests resulted in limited international news and almost no local media coverage. Much like how articles about the Scissor Sisters were neutered of any mention of queerness, given the illegality of homosexuality, mention of the Arab Spring was covered locally as a foreign problem, alien to the stability of the region.

With the media tightly legislated, no journalist working at a local media outlet could publish anything overtly critical of domestic policies, the economy, or religion under a 1980 law regulating printed matter and publications. Though a few international outlets maintained channels or limited bureaus in the UAE, like the *Wall Street Journal*, they were understood to operate with the tacit understanding that they would also play by the rules. Even the local bureau of CNN International was subject to frequent criticism for running PR for the nation and ignoring human rights concerns in favor of fluff stories. Moreover, journalists hoping to visit the country for work were sometimes denied entry; many of the pieces critical of the government were penned by those who had entered the country covertly on tourism visas.

But I was in a slightly unique, if precarious, position. I was subject to the same laws as other UAE residents, but I was also employed by a unique, high-profile institution, NYUAD, whose close links with the UAE government were established with the agreement that the university would have complete academic freedom both in the classroom and in faculty's areas of research. Though the university did not offer a journalism degree, it was a liberal arts university with a robust arts and humanities division, one I was affiliated with as a theater producer and instructor. And as a faculty member, I was given a research fund, initially leading research trips to Yemen to think about performance in the way I was thinking about performers like Reggie. I realized I had unique access and opportunity: I could begin to collect stories and publish my interviews—my research—as journalism that might offer more nuance than what I read from Western media and a slightly more critical eye than local outlets. It was a gray area, but one I thought was worth the gamble. I fashioned myself a de facto freelance journalist, writing long-form arts, culture, and environmental pieces from the Middle East and South Asia. I couldn't necessarily publish anything overtly critical, especially at first, but I could toe a line. Like my queerness here, I felt an opportunity for my work to exist between the cracks.

Buildings finally appeared through the windshield. I thought we would keep driving toward the city, but Sunil made a sudden turn onto a construction exit. He shot me a grin. We drove through industrial estates and past corrugated metal warehouses and arrived at a mess of gates and overlapping barriers. We couldn't go any farther. Sunil put on his hazard lights, cut the engine, and opened the door, motioning me out of the car.

The light was falling fast, but he pointed out toward the sea, another few hundred meters away, unreachable due to the metal barriers. He told me that this, the Palm Jebel Ali, was the project he came to the UAE to work on.

I had been to the Palm Jumeirah, a few kilometers up the shoreline, once the largest manmade island in the world, visible from outer space. Shaped like a palm leaf, it was a modern architectural marvel consisting of seventeen wide fronds—each its own little peninsula to maximize water frontage—an eleven-kilometer-long breakwater in the shape of a crescent, and ninety-four million cubic meters of sand. But the Palm Jebel Ali was over 50 percent larger.

An astonishing amount of the Palm Jebel Ali was constructed before a single building had been erected, he explained. Its final shape was complete, as were all of its land reclamation works. Some of the fronds still had piles of coarse sand, but most looked flattened. Sunil explained that this was called ground improvement works, and it allowed road infrastructure to begin. Some roads had actually already been built, and construction had also started on some of the planned 125 bridges that would link the fronds.

Infrastructure works began in 2007; workers began laying in the roads and lighting network and water, a mammoth undertaking of historical proportions because nothing had ever been quite built to this size before. This was the work that Sunil was brought over from Australia in early 2008 to do: manage the building of roads, digging of tunnels, laying of power cables. And yet, just a few months later, the entire project—one that had cost $12 billion before a single structure stood on the island—was stalled due to the financial crisis.

We looked out onto the island, the parallel bars of land like dozens of fingers that fanned out into the water. I felt a kind of vertigo as we stared in silence: visually registering the scale of this neatly organized behemoth and yet unsettled by how much more I could not see—intersecting pipes, miles of snaking wires—that men had built underfoot. It was exhilarating to work on a project so large when he would be doing small fry stuff in Australia. In Sydney, he would have been working on one city block—if he were lucky, he said. He felt like he had snuck in under the radar in 2007, an unqualified brown kid from Australia with no knowledge of the Middle East who had only just finished an internship at a toilet paper factory. I told him that I knew a bit what he felt like—even down to the toilet paper factory, one of the places I almost did temp work while making money for university. He sheepishly told me he knew the factory, Kimberly Clarke: it was the headquarters of the one he worked at near his home in South Australia.

"I didn't mention it before, but it seemed like an auspicious sign for us somehow." He laughed. "I was lucky here," he continued. "Everyone else got fired. I think they kept me because I was a graduate and didn't cost much." He explained that his job was safe now: there was a government plan called Emiratization to coax Emirati citizens from the bloated public sector into skilled private sector jobs, but he knew not every job could be taken by the local population, even with incremental implementation. His company couldn't get rid of him. He was necessary here, even as he felt under the radar and like he didn't belong.

"This is the kind of work I do," he said, nodding again out to the unfinished island. "I'm part of the things people don't see, and don't know they need."

In the silence, I considered how this might ring true for queerness as well. None of his colleagues knew about his sexuality; they couldn't, of course, as it was against the law. But he wondered, was that the thing that would most define him in their eyes if they did? He was so good at his job. He had told me he sometimes fantasized about going up to his boss and fessing up. Would his boss dare turn him in and lose him as an employee? And even if he were jailed and deported from the country, someone would need to fill his role. And what if she were queer? Even if the government desired a kind of purity not to have queer people as residents—and even if outsiders couldn't understand why they would come to this place—we would always be here.

We took one last look around the site, abandoned and yet alive. "People think there's nothing here, but there's so much," he said, kicking at the dirt. "Some of it's underground, but so much of it is visible, too, if you look. It all serves a function." We stood a few minutes longer, silent. As we got back in the car and drove away from the unfinished project, a little somber, I realized our little pit stop had felt to me a bit like a memorial service.

▽▽▽

He held fast to my hand atop a metal table while humming Nicki Minaj. I could not see his face. I had heard his humming echoing down the hallway minutes earlier, but he turned his back almost as soon as he rounded the corner and ushered me from the waiting room into his treatment room. He'd sat down to work right away, pulling out metal instruments and pouring astringent liquids into ceramic bowls, his thick swoop of jet bangs coming loose from behind his ears and falling in front of his eyes. He did not offer any chatter; he just grabbed me by the wrists and set upon my cuticles, picking and filing as a Tagalog soap opera played on the TV behind him. I could have watched the histrionics unfolding on the screen, but I was drawn to watching the deft movements of his hands on mine.

I had arrived at the nail salon by accident. I'd walked into a barbershop in Abu Dhabi the afternoon before we left for Dubai and noticed a slight Filipino man sitting in a massage chair in the corner. He shot me coquettish smiles whenever I glanced back at him in the mirror. When I stood to leave, he beckoned me over to his chair and asked if I wanted a pedicure. I apologized, explaining that I was in a rush, that I had just gotten a fresh haircut because I was about to drive to Dubai. *With my, uh, friend,* I quickly added, as though someone in the shop might somehow discern I was traveling with Sunil. Smiling again, he asked me to hand him my phone. I watched him type in an address to a salon in Oud Metha, explaining that his cousin worked there and that I should visit him.

I had only visited Oud Metha a couple of times for its sagging ice rink. It was an old neighborhood set just back from the creek on the edge of one of the city's most tightly clustered residential districts. The area had been a thriving, modern neighborhood during the city's ascent in the 1980s, but as I took in the clutch of squat, low-rise buildings that sat far from the glass towers of downtown, it was clear its degraded buildings once reserved for citizens were now being occupied by migrants of a lower socioeconomic status.

Building after building housed modest salons on the ground floor beneath stacks of apartments. I opened the heavy door at the address the manicurist had typed into my phone. On the floor crouched a man with the same gleaming black hair. He knelt over a basin, toweling off the feet of a man in a kandura, carefully holding back its starched white hem. Apologizing for being busy, the pedicurist pointed me to another salon just down the road.

It was full, too. As was the next, and the next. Like the barbershops I was now used to frequenting in Abu Dhabi, the salons in Oud Metha were all male spaces, filled with the bodies of men in various stages of waiting or luxuriating. At each one, I was kindly pointed to a chair where I could wait an hour, and then—when I politely refused—to the next salon a few buildings over. I was struck by how their hospitality felt communal: *Kindly make your way to our waiting room or down the road to an entirely different establishment where I'm not even employed.* Each manicurist and receptionist had long black hair that reminded me of my longstanding impulse to grow out my own hair, the impulse I was currently suppressing because it felt too feminine, too much of a queer dead giveaway.

In another salon with beige tiled floors, I finally got a walk-in appointment with the man with his hair over his eyes. I felt compelled to compliment him. It seemed so daring.

"I like your hair," I said, before quickly adding, "And your polish." It was just barely visible: a layer of clear shellac that made his long nails gleam. If I hadn't been staring directly at our hands, I may not have noticed. I leaned across the table to whisper it. It felt like the kind of compliment that would best be received if it were spoken conspiratorially.

The man finally looked up from my hands. He held eye contact with me and stopped moving the pick he had buried under my index finger. I waited for a jab of pain, a sign that we were both prying too deep, but it never came. He smiled and kept working, sure and confident as ever. I felt a knowledge pass between us.

He introduced himself as Marie. He flipped his long hair behind his shoulders and playfully batted his eyelashes, coyly proud to have received my compliment. His femininity—this thing that felt so glaring to me, this thing I tried to hide in myself—I watched him flaunt.

"Thank you. I sometimes want to use color, but I don't want to get into too much trouble for being a bakla," he said, giggling.

My ears perked up at the use of the word "bakla." They were a self-identifying group in the Philippines who were assigned male at birth and adopted a feminine gender expression, I remembered. Many of them also considered themselves a third gender, and were acknowledged as such by much of Filipino society, while still others identified as transgender.

In 2007, I had sat in a cramped dorm room to watch a film called *Paper Dolls* with other students from an LGBT student group I'd just joined at NYU. It was a documentary that followed a group of Filipinos who had migrated to Israel to work as caretakers for elderly Orthodox Jewish men. They called themselves bakla, wore their hair long, and shuttled between male- and female-presenting outfits, styles, and affectations depending on where they were—at work, at home, in public, at a Tel Aviv gay bar. The six characters shifted back and forth across a fine line: they understood that Israel had fairly liberal LGBTQ+ rights, but they were working within a conservative religious community. Furthermore, as migrants, they had to reckon with their own precarity; their residency visas would be revoked if they lost their jobs. And indeed, their ability to stay in Israel hinged on their sex: religious rules forbade Orthodox men from being touched by women, so their carers needed to be male, making both the baklas' evening drag performances and many of the documentary subjects' desires to have gender affirmation surgery even more fraught.

The film and the term bakla expanded my idea of what "queer" could be at a time when I was still figuring out how I could operate within LGBTQ+ community and history. The term could be conditional and contextual—pliable and playful, even. Some were this, others were that, still others lived within the slippage between signifiers. I asked if he had seen the film.

"I think every bakla has heard of this movie." He laughed. "Are you wanting to know about Sally?" I didn't know who he was referring to, but he carried on as though I had nodded. He explained that Sally was one of the stars of *Paper Dolls.* "I didn't know her, but some of my friends did. She was murdered on the street in the daytime a few years ago in Dubai."

Marie left the room to retrieve another tool, and I pulled out my phone, smearing it with nail-soaking liquid. I quickly came across an article dated November 2007 from the local UAE press: "Hairdresser found dead in Sharjah." It stated that a body was found on the street outside an internet café and that "there was no sign of assault." But I found another article from a Filipino newspaper a month later: "Noli asked to intervene in death of Pinoy Hairdresser in Dubai." The family of Sally slammed the inaction of the Philippine Embassy and the authorities in Dubai, accusing both of a cover-up and stating that an embassy worker had referred to Sally as "the one whose head was bashed." I noticed also that the Filipino papers referred to the deceased as Sally, but in the UAE, they used masculine pronouns and used her birth name. Marie returned and set back to work on my nails. I asked him how he felt about his safety.

"I wear this, and it's no problem," he said. He pointed to his tight pink scrubs, jamming his chest together and putting his hair up in a ponytail. "I only wear a bra and makeup at night," he said, grinning. "I can look like a girl and get compliments from men. But when I am working, I look like this," he said, letting his hand go and his hair flop to his shoulders while frowning, before letting out a hearty laugh.

"And my boyfriend is a policeman, so he will tell me about the campaigns." Marie explained that there were occasional campaigns to rid the city of crossdressers. Later, I would read about a one-week campaign from a few years earlier called "Preserve Our Social Values," in which the Dubai police chief at the time was quoted in a press release as saying: "We have noted an emerging trend of men dressed as women and vice versa in the UAE markets and streets. Several men in women's dresses and makeup have already been arrested from shopping malls and residential buildings." But another release by the Dubai police stated that their campaign was "targeting transsexuals," demonstrating a conflation in the eyes of the authorities of those who wore clothing perceived to outwardly signify another gender and those who identified as trans. Marie explained he had several bakla friends who had been deported simply for looking too feminine.

"They know bakla are parloristas," he said, using a Tagalog word for the stereotype of bakla as flamboyant, campy crossdressers who work in beauty salons. "This is our main job here, so sometimes they come looking."

He showed me his ID photo. He had a slender jaw and long flowing hair. Even in a photo taken to look neutral—the final step for a residency permit—the left side of his lip turned up into a near smirk. It was like he was goading the camera, daring whoever was looking at him to take in his feminine beauty, his wily smile, and not offer him a work visa. *You need me,* the photo said.

His phone vibrated. He said it was from a friend living in Manila who was badgering him about how he could come to Dubai, too. "I know so many bakla wanting to come here." He showed me his Facebook page. There were dozens of messages with friends asking about Dubai. "I tell them everything honestly," he said.

I remembered an article I'd read about a photo studio in Musaffah near a large compound housing thousands of migrant workers. The photographers would take photos of the men and edit them into suits, behind fancy cars, in front of office towers so they could send them to family back home—a stilted image of the life they wanted to project, a curated white lie. I thought also about how limited an understanding my family and friends in America had about the region in general.

Marie said he told them it was easy to get a job, even as a bakla. "I just said I was a boy on all my forms and didn't act too girly when I went to get my ID here," he said simply, like that was the only hurdle. Perhaps, in some ways, it was that simple: learning when and how to fit in, to pass.

A moment of silence passed between us while he rifled through a plastic bin for some other tools. "They want to come because they can work in both salons like me," he said, winking. "I work in men's and ladies' salons." He explained that his Muslim boss owned both a men's and women's salon and that he offered Marie the opportunity to work and get paid in both after catching her leaving a shift having changed into a skirt. So convinced by Marie's appearance, he even permitted Marie to don women's attire and makeup at the women's salon.

I was stunned. He was not just viewed by his employer as cheap labor adept at beauty services, but had actually been sought out for his ability to subvert laws and disrupt the bifurcation of gendered spaces—and encouraged to do so. Marie's phone pinged again. I wondered who it was, if they would be able not just to pass across spaces but have the opportunity or recognition to do so.

Marie apologized for rambling, as though this were mundane conversation, and asked me about my job. I told him I was a writer.

"Maybe you can write my story," he said, giggling. I didn't know how to tell him that I wanted to. "But today, I have so many customers. Too bad you can't come to the ladies' salon to talk more."

He finished up with my nails and gently folded my arms into my chest. I told him I wanted to speak to him again.

"Would you like to come to a small party?" he asked. I smiled at him and handed him my phone. He entered in his number.

"This kind of party is where we put on the colored polish," he said. I walked back out into the full reception room. It was filled with men waiting for Marie.

▽▽▽

When Marie invited me to "a small party," I expected a few friends drinking wine around a coffee table, not a dozen bakla rifling through makeup kits and swigging straight from open handles of vodka. When I arrived at his third-floor apartment near Oud Metha, Marie ushered me into the apartment and offered to pour me a glass. Two bottles were already being passed my way from opposite directions. I chose the one with less lipstick on the rim and took a swig.

Despite their prominence on a foldup table, neither the booze nor the makeup was the centerpiece of the apartment. In the middle of the cramped living room, a mound of dresses sat bundled, some bursting out of an open suitcase, others spilling out of a thick black plastic bag, the discreet kind I recognized from my trips to African & Eastern, the alcohol shop near my apartment. Most of Marie's friends sat on the floor around the dresses in a roughshod circle like campers around a bonfire. Every couple of minutes, someone would rifle through the material and head to the hanging mirror in the corner to change and apply makeup.

I tried not to make a big show of my arrival, but Marie turned down the Filipino pop music and introduced me in front of everyone. Three were his roommates—like Shivani, four of them rented the illegal two-bedroom apartment—and all of them worked in salons. Even the two at the mirror turned around, mid-undressing, to smile at me and introduce themselves. I felt like I needed to explain why I was there. I mentioned *Paper Dolls* and told the room that I wanted to take notes and audio recordings if anyone wanted to talk to me. Marie turned the music back up, and everyone went back to laughing and singing. When I told him I thought they were all surprisingly easygoing about my request, he leaned over and said he had already told them, and that they were all enthusiastic. I thanked him, and he handed me a mirror so I could wash off the lipstick he had left on my cheek when he'd greeted me with a kiss.

"You can thank me for that," he said, laughing.

It was only after I scanned the group of people in the room—in various stages of makeup, dress, drunkenness—that I fully recognized the potential danger we were in. Police raids of queer events in the Middle East were infamous, including the Queen Boat raid in Cairo in 2001 that led to the arrest and subsequent sensational trial of nearly two dozen men, many of whom were handed multi-year prison sentences. But raids of private establishments and homes had also occurred in the UAE, including roundups in 2005 and 2012 in which dozens of people were arrested.

Marie stood up, grabbed a dress, and started stripping out of her oversized blue sweatshirt on his way over to a full-length mirror in the corner of the room, leaving me alone with a group of strangers. Most were deep in conversation with one another, but a few were looking at me expectantly, as though I should make a speech. I rifled through a makeup bag to offset their stares.

I politely motioned for the person nearest to me to hand me some makeup. He was already in a dark red minidress with lipstick to match and introduced himself as Crystal. I asked him about his name: I had noticed that some bakla used what sounded like their given Filipino names—many, like Sally's birth name, Catholic due to Spanish colonization—but many had adopted Western female names.

"I already knew one bakla named Diamond, but I still wanted to sound expensive," he cooed. He handed me some mascara.

"Ooh, you want to be a ladyboy, too?" she giggled and held another mirror up for me.

I cringed at the word. It seemed like such a derogatory term—a shorthand Westerners used, especially in Thailand, to place a diverse group of people into one category. It erased any nuance between intersex people, transgender people, crossdressers, gay men, and more. It seemed to both too easily group and inarticulately flatten.

But what did it mean for Crystal to use the term "ladyboy" for me? Was it a term she was reclaiming, a fraught process like the one I was engaging in trying to reclaim "queer?" Or was it just the case of a non-native English speaker adopting a derogatory term slung at them without fully comprehending the history and etymology of the word? Did it matter?

I started in with the mascara. I had worn makeup a few times for costume parties and theater, but this felt different. I tried to steady myself in the handheld mirror in the same way I did when Marie was digging under my nails at the salon. Tagalog music blared from a speaker next to my ear, and I watched in the mirror as several partygoers started singing. I thought about Reggie's performance and felt a sudden pang. We were all performing, but there was a weight, a consequence to their performance of gender that mine didn't have. My application of makeup was different from the others in the room: a sense of fun versus a need to pass or express femininity. I looked down at my recorder and wondered about my performance of journalism, about that responsibility, too.

I asked Crystal about his job. He explained that he worked at a salon only a few blocks from Marie. He had messaged Marie from his family home on the outskirts of the northern town of Baguio after seeing some of Marie's Dubai posts in a bakla Facebook group, drawn to the tantalizing opportunity to also work two jobs at two different salons across the gender divide. Not only could he double his potential salary—one that was already several times more lucrative than what he could earn in Philippines—but he would be doing it simply by being himself: a person who inherently broke categories. After three months of trying, he secured a visa to work in a men's salon and had arrived a few months earlier.

He proudly pulled out his residency card. His visa said he was a man, but he felt like he was between genders, he explained, though he didn't care much what other people defined him as. A week after he started working, he approached his boss at Marie's urging about working in a women's salon. I asked the group how many of them worked across both salons. Over half of them raised their hands, including one of Marie's roommates.

"It is easy, just put on eyelashes and push up your titties like this," one of them said, laughing. "I tape mine." He lowered his dress to demonstrate how he accentuated his bust. Like Marie, he had a nonchalance, almost a flippancy, about his flagrant breaking of several laws in a space where that kind of subversive act was embraced.

He introduced himself as Lino and explained that his visa was for a job working six days a week at the men's salon. He usually came in at 11 a.m. and stayed until 7 or 8 p.m., but four days a week, he walked three blocks to the women's salon owned by the same man and worked for the same pay from 8–11 p.m. At the men's salon, he mostly did manicures, pedicures, and some haircuts. At the women's spa, though, he had learned new skills, like waxing and henna.

I asked what else was different about the women's salons. The Filipino employees all knew about bakla and didn't care, they said. Other employees guessed, but they were mostly met with apathy. Lino spoke of a Sudanese woman who knew he was bakla and still helped train him in massage despite being a devout Muslim.

But what about customers and risk? I wondered. Usually, no one suspected anything, they agreed. But sometimes, it went awry. Crystal spoke about a bakla friend who was cited for using improper equipment by an undercover female health inspector at a woman's salon. Only when police responded to the report did they look at the beautician's ID and see that she was in the UAE on a male passport.

"She was so good at being a lady that she got sent back by the judge the first time because he didn't believe he was a man!" Lino shrieked. Everyone cackled.

The ability to command more income was an undeniable allure, it seemed. Some were able to study; one was taking online nursing courses. Almost all sent a large fraction of their paycheck home, often to siblings to further their own studies. And though most families understood and accepted bakla in the Philippines, it wasn't always the case.

Everyone had now returned to the circle wearing dresses, their T-shirts and jeans discarded in a pile behind me on the couch.

"I like being the man and the woman. I send money and I take care of them when I come home. Even if they don't like this," one of the group said, running her hands through her hair.

Working in a women's salon could lead to further opportunities. Two boasted of married female Arab clients regularly inviting them into their homes to perform beauty treatments specifically because their gender was perceived as unable to threaten a marriage: the woman couldn't be accused of inviting a man who wasn't a relative into her home, and her husband wouldn't be sexually tempted by a bakla. These kinds of informal gigs could be lucrative, one admitted.

Massage quickly became a hot topic as the bottles of vodka made one more circuit around the room. Some explained that they had wanted to learn the trade because they had heard they could get good tips, and others were encouraged to do it by colleagues to help generate business. I asked whether they ever felt pressured by employers, but no one explicitly did, though the pressure to make money—and veer into sex-based work—loomed.

"My boyfriend taught me to recite the Quran to myself if they start pushing my hands toward their cocks. Or sometimes I do the Bible," Crystal said, laughing. He explained how men often rub their knees against hers under the table during manicures. "But it's how I met my boyfriend. Julia Roberts did it!" He laughed. He later explained that he had flirted with his then-client over a series of manicures—"He was so handsome, I had to!"—and managed to extract increasingly large tips, until he asked for a massage. Later, they began meeting at his apartment, and he now considered him her boyfriend. It sounded like a familiar story of precarious queer people: employment that hinged on, or at least brushed up against, sex work—some engaging in it strictly for money, others for the prospect of a viable relationship, others for a kind of dignity and power over their lives to provide for their financially imperiled families, even in the face of their lack of acceptance.

Being a bakla in the UAE also provided another kind of mobility most couldn't get in the Philippines: further economic migration. There was a fluidity in terms of where they could make a living, and a life. Each knew people who worked across the Arabian Peninsula.

"We are everywhere: Kuwait, Qatar, Bahrain, Saudi, Oman," someone said proudly. Crystal explained that even jailing and deportation did not stop this mobility; many of the bakla they knew, including the one busted by the inspector, had already been deported from other Gulf countries and returned, including several friends who had been tried and convicted under a 2007 Kuwaiti law prohibiting "imitating the opposite sex." Deportation was not a deterrent—simply a minor speed bump.

I didn't want to bring the mood down, but I had to ask if any of them knew Sally. A quiet bakla who sat braiding his thick hair in the corner said he did. He introduced himself as Gizelle and said he had worked at the same salon as Sally.

"She was just going to the internet café for a few minutes, but I think she went outside with the wrong look: like, some makeup and no boobs, or boobs but no makeup. She didn't look right to somebody, and they killed her," he said simply, going back to braiding his hair.

I asked him if he knew whether Sally was working in a ladies' salon, but he said he didn't think she was. He was, however. I asked him the question I had wanted to ask all night.

"How did you know it would be okay asking your boss?" I was incredulous at the gustiness of asking such a bold question of a man who directly controlled his ability to be in the country.

"I knew I was beautiful enough to make him more money," Gizelle said, raising her eyebrows, defiant. "That was enough."

His phrasing made me uneasy. I recognized that they were in an aesthetic industry, but it seemed that their success, their very place in the country, was conditional at best, on beauty and capital. Sally's inability to go out into the street for only a few moments without looking like a standardized ideal of one gender reminded me of how people said to me growing up that they were okay with gay people as long as they didn't shove it in people's faces. We were accepted until we weren't anymore. Even if we were prized for our subversion, it was always conditional. I looked around at the booze and the karaoke machine, the dresses, the makeup. We had all placed ourselves in danger here, and yet it was also still an opportunity. It wasn't a binary; it could be more nuanced and complicated than that.

The night wound down. Everyone started dozing into each other's laps, though a few animated conversations carried on along the periphery. I was struck by how these salon workers were throwing their own kind of salon, in the early modern revolutionary France sense of the word: a gathering to circumvent government censorship and foster public debate in private, acts they continued in spite of witnessing harrowing consequences. Power may have been in someone else's hands, but perhaps this "small party" was a way to claw some of it back—and to move toward something, as dangerous as that may be.

An urgent wrapping on Marie's front door cut through my thoughts. Everyone sat motionless, staring at the entranceway. I realized that the cheap door didn't have a peephole, but I watched Marie confidently stride to it, swinging it wide. Another friend burst in, welcomed by a chorus of cheers, and the party started again.

▽▽▽

I started looking for the border between Abu Dhabi and Dubai: the color of the light, the shape of the lamps. I couldn't feel the difference in the pavement like Sunil could, but sometimes I thought I could see…something, until suddenly I wasn't sure, and the space between the two made them melt into one another again.

On the empty six-lane road between the two cities, Sunil would tell me about the projects he was working on. We'd often look in the direction of Palm Jebel Ali and search for any discernable changes, even though we knew they wouldn't be visible. Sometimes he'd give me updates about the lighting design he was managing for a bridge to a horse track just outside Dubai. But mostly, he talked about the new highway he was designing between Dubai and Abu Dhabi. It was almost perfectly parallel to the main highway we always drove, the E11, but instead of nearly hugging the coastline, it ran eight kilometers east through the desert.

I knew a bit about the road we were on—Sheikh Zayed Road, another major project named after the founder of the country, the main thoroughfare that bisected Dubai and became the E11 highway as it traveled north through the federation of seven emirates that made up the UAE. In the 1960s, before the UAE was a country, these emirates—Abu Dhabi, Dubai, Sharjah, Ajman, Umm Al Quwain, Ras Al Khaimah, and Fujairah—were a loose federation of tribes under British protection. Migrants of surprising diversity came to work between these lands where oil had only relatively recently been turned into industry, but many of them were from South Asia, and their anti-colonial sentiments helped foster the idea of nationhood in the UAE. In order to take advantage of the burgeoning national identity in the sheikhdoms, the Arab League attempted to leverage the situation, proposing a road to connect all seven sheikhdoms. The British fretted that they would lose the war of soft power, as they still hadn't delivered on previously promised road. Finally, the Brits made good, and the E11 was born.

Half a century later, this new road Sunil was helping to design would be an equally massive undertaking. I asked him how the aesthetics of the lights were chosen. My mind was still on the bakla and their eye for fashion and glamour.

"It's not aesthetics, it's safety," he said. I felt him let a little silence pass between us before he carried on. "You know, my uncle died on this highway."

Sunil didn't take his eyes off the road. He explained that his uncle moved from India to Dubai in the 1970s when the Emirates were still a British protectorate, driving lorries between cities for a living. It was tough work, driving back and forth between Abu Dhabi and Dubai when what would become the E11 was just compacted sand. His lorry was struck, and he was killed.

"There were no lamp posts like this," Sunil said, pointing out his window with a touch of gallows humor. He didn't know much else about the accident. "We don't really talk about my family in India," Sunil said. It was the same reason he didn't speak Hindi: his parents left India and wanted their children to be one hundred percent Australian: to go somewhere else and become someone new. To pass. But it underscored that these journeys—if the destination could even be reached—could be perilous.

We drove in silence. He had no more projects to point out. The infrastructure thinned until there were only occasional lampposts and the rolling black tarmac in front of us.

The story of the two roads felt like a kind of parable for the journeys of queer people and migrants as they quantify and appraise the alchemy of safety and peril between spaces: Sunil's uncle between Abu Dhabi and Dubai, bakla not just between salons but also between the Philippines and the Gulf. Sunil and I from casual to serious relationship. We were all going somewhere.

"I love working on these big projects," he said. He loved the scope and the scale and wanted to see them through, even this road that wouldn't be finished for years. Even the ones that were messy and imperfect. Perhaps those were the most rewarding ones to work on, I imagined. I suddenly realized this meant he was thinking of staying in the UAE for the foreseeable future.

"What are your dreams?" he asked. I noticed that this time, he briefly took his eyes off the road.

It was such a big question, the kind thrown out early in a relationship when the path forward is an endless dark road, when a bit of company from a like-minded traveler would be nice. I wasn't really prepared to answer it, but I reached out for his hand. I thought about what it would mean to stay here through the completion of this road project, about his projects and the impact he made—and where I might be, what I might be able to do in that same period of time.

I flipped my phone over in my hand like a worry stone, thinking about the interviews it contained. I was a writer; I could have an impact here too. I could have my own projects. My work could be a bridge between places. As we crossed the border between Dubai and Abu Dhabi, I thought about all the misconceptions of both. I could act as a kind of cultural translator for readers in Midwest America who didn't understand the Gulf. So many of the articles about the region mentioned fantastical images of gleaming skyscrapers rising out from the sand. But here we were in the in-between space when it was all still just underfoot, or just off in the distance.

Sunil turned down the volume and slowed as we went through a construction site. I asked him what the speed limit was. "You never can be too careful. You can travel this road a hundred times, but sometimes in a site like this, they'll just build a huge speed bump that'll tear out the whole undercarriage of your car with no warning."

I laughed and told him that sounded familiar, always needing to be on alert.

"Just wait until you try to drive in Oman next month," he said, referring to my upcoming trip. It would be the first time I was driving solo there, and I was suddenly a bit nervous. I tried not to think about his uncle. As we drove, I wondered if we were hurtling away from or closer to the exact site where he died. Sunil turned the music back up and we drove on.

6: A BORDER

(Bahla, Oman; Manama, Bahrain: Amir and Wasim)

THE FIRST TIME I TRIED TO CROSS from the UAE into Oman, I accidentally navigated onto a truck road. I desperately tried to keep my sorry Kia rental close to a pickup with four camels in its cargo bed, as a buffer from the fleet of articulated lorries around us that displayed no concern for the speed limit. On my second attempt a few months later—afraid I would end back up on this same stretch I learned was nicknamed the "Road of Death" for its high rate of traffic fatalities—I overshot my intended crossing, landing at the entirely wrong border post. I received a stamp in my passport from the UAE border guard and drove on through hundreds of meters of scrubland past wispy ghaf trees, but the twin border post on the Omani side never came. I U-turned and asked the guard how I had crossed into the UAE—from here to there—but hadn't officially entered Oman. Ala tul, he said, slicing his arm forward through the air. *Straight ahead.* The Omani crossing was nearly a mile away, he explained. I turned back around and crossed the extended stretch of no man's land, amused that I had left one place but had been too impatient to find myself fully in another.

When I returned again to Oman, I decided I should probably find another way. I could have taken the normal road through Al Ain, Abu Dhabi's second city, a border town with Oman that had a lush date palm oasis. But I decided on a detour, a more circuitous path across the emirates. My route would take me through the northern portion of the UAE, jutting out into the Gulf like a hitchhiker's thumb held aloft, where I could travel through six of the emirates strung together like charms on a bracelet along the E10. I breezed from Abu Dhabi in the south to the furthest northern emirate, Ras Al Khaimah—Arabic for "the top of the tent"—before turning east toward Oman.

I was driving to write a commissioned article that contended with Oman's fascinating history in the Gulf. Although it was only granted nationhood in 1970, a year before the UAE, Oman had more visible historical relics than nearly everywhere else in the region. The country had a rich history of Indian Ocean trade, and much of what was visible of its history illustrated this: sixteenth-century Portuguese forts, medieval ports for the once bustling frankincense trade, and even remnants of ancient wooden boats that traveled to East Africa, South India, China, and beyond, well before Oman had an Islamic civilization.

Like the rest of the Gulf, Oman was often written about through the lens of what modernity it had embraced and what antiquity it had preserved. Little was written about Oman in contemporary magazines besides the occasional and predictable "it's ancient but modern" travel stories. I wanted to pen something deeper, something perhaps less about travel and more about belief systems. I pitched to the editor an article about djinn, supernatural creatures that pervaded Muslim texts. But like the remnants of the ancient boats recovered along Oman's shores, many of these stories of djinn predated the arrival of Islam. The UAE's southwestern neighbor had an especially rich history of stories about djinn; I wanted to contend with how these stories got there, and how they were received by and their tensions with the population today. It felt like a unique opportunity both to explore the inherent power of storytelling and to engage in it myself.

▽▽▽

As I made my way through the sleepier, less wealthy northern emirates, I was tempted to continue on to the Musandam Peninsula, an Omani territory that lay even farther north than Ras Al Khaimah. I was fascinated by its geography and nomenclature; the Musandam Peninsula was an exclave, a piece of a country contained within the boundaries of another country. It jutted like a thumbnail from the UAE, separated from the rest of Oman by nearly sixty miles, a little piece of territory existing away from itself. The peninsula came under Omani control after a British-backed coup installed Oman's long-term ruler, Sultan Qaboos, in 1970, and its complicated mix of Persian, Hindi, and Arab influences was evidenced by the fact that it was still home to the only Indo-European language native to the Arabian Peninsula.

But instead, I was lured east by something else on the map, compelled by an even rarer geographic eccentricity further down the thumb, a few kilometers south, one of the few instances in the world of a counter-enclave: a part of a country completely surrounded by another country which is in turn surrounded by the first country. Nahwa, a five-square-kilometer town belonging to the UAE, sits entirely inside the seventy-five-square kilometer Omani enclave of Madha, which is itself surrounded by the greater UAE. It sat on the map like the hole in an inner tube cast off in a pool, and I wanted to climb inside.

I was fascinated by Nahwa's seeming improbability. After Musandam was declared, Madha also declared allegiance to the rulers of Oman. The Madhanis chose Oman in the 1930s based on the firm belief that Oman was wealthier, had a stronger government, and would be better placed to protect the village's water supply; the boundary was settled in 1969. But one town within Madha, Nahwa, stayed firm in its allegiance to Sharjah, creating a UAE counter-enclave.

As I neared the first border between the UAE and Madha, preparing my camera as I passed through the succession of signs, my phone rang. It was a man whom a friend from parkour had put me in touch with: Amir, a young Omani man from the town I was visiting, whose parents had him treated for djinn possession ostensibly because of his sexuality.

The call couldn't have been more than ten minutes; we made a plan to meet the following day just after an interview I had scheduled with a self-proclaimed shaman who purported to treat such possessions. We organized a time, a meeting place. I hung up, concentrating on the road again, and realized I had missed the signs for Nahwa and Madha entirely and was back in the greater UAE. In just under ten miles—the span of a ten-minute phone call—I had driven straight through like an arrow from one country, into another, back into the first, crossed another border, and then was out into the first country again. Nothing seemed to separate the two; I hadn't even noticed the difference.

▽▽▽

It felt tempting to regard modern Bahla as the kind of place that existed just because it was on the road to somewhere else. One hundred and fifty miles after crossing the UAE border, I circled yet another roundabout—their prevalence across the UAE and Oman a hangover from British influence—and turned toward Bahla along a wide road studded with the kind of boxy, anonymous commercial buildings that looked big enough to be wholesalers: carpet retailers, furniture stores, a wedding tent rental agency.

The town of Bahla, though, was once a destination in its own right: the Banu Nabhan tribe that dominated the central interior Oman region of Al-Dhakhaliyah from the twelfth to the seventeenth century made Bahla their capital, and it became the center of the branch of Islam, Ibadism, they practiced. Oman is now the only Arab country where it still remains the dominant sect. Proof of the town's place in history as a medieval stronghold still dotted the landscape, including twelve crumbling kilometers of mudbrick defensive walls and a mighty military fortress.

Though most who visited Bahla today did so to encounter these relics of antiquity, many preferred to keep driving for a very specific reason: the town was widely reputed as an epicenter of djinn activity, infamous not just in the Arabian Peninsula but across the Islamic world. The Quran relays the story of the birth of these supernatural creatures born of "smokeless fire," while further verses and Hadith—collections of quotes attributed to the prophet Muhammad that supplement the holy book of Islam—lay out further details of their principles. These texts present an unsettling picture: extremely powerful beings made in the eyes of Allah alongside humans but with a proclivity for following the evil lead of Iblis, a haughty djinn (later to be known as Satan) who refused to bow to the superiority of Adam and subsequently vowed to lead all humans astray.

I wanted to understand why Bahla was perceived as a hotbed of such unsettling activity. I was both troubled and oddly allured to the parallels between djinn and queerness; so often, they both seemed to be read solely through the lens of affliction.

I arrived as people were returning to their shops after the worst of the afternoon heat had abated. It was a difficult thing, trying to shoehorn djinn into casual conversation. As I puttered between shops—tailors, kitchen wares, groceries—I felt reserve from Bahlawis in speaking about the subject despite its infamy. I didn't know how I was going to conduct my interviews; the reticence to engage initially felt insurmountable.

But later that evening, meeting for a string of interviews I had arranged, it was a different story entirely. I sat with one family who told me how they woke each week to a low moaning outside the house and strange mounds of rock piled underneath the window of their infant son's room. A group of farmers described the sound they heard haunting the palm oases dotting town, preying on them after dusk by calling their names across the valley. Another man took me to the place behind his house where he witnessed green flames hovering above the sand.

More than the mere presence of djinn, it was the creatures' ability to possess a human that seemed especially disconcerting. "Many people allege that they acquire djinn when they start sentences and actions without first saying bismillah (in the name of God) or when giving a compliment without first saying mashallah (God has willed it)," explained one shopkeeper who reported djinn possession when he was young.

But it was the course of treatment after someone had been possessed by djinn that was perhaps the explicitly delicate topic. As one young resident told me, "With djinn, there is a fine line between Islam and something else. And exorcisms start to cross into that 'something else' territory." He paused, searching for the right word. "Something else even darker than djinn."

Bahla was a place to avoid because of its preponderance of djinn, and paradoxically to seek out as a place to be cured of afflictions. Here, an exorcism ritual known as zar was often practiced. In the academic journal *Mental Health, Religion & Culture*, Dr. Samir al-Adawi, a psychiatrist and researcher at Oman's Sultan Qaboos University, described the mechanics of a zar exorcism:

The essence of the ritual is to coerce the spirit to possess the medium so that it reveals why it has possessed that particular person. The shaman will lure his own zar spirit to possess him or her. The shaman is then used to lure the unknown zar spirit of the possessed person.... The client or "mobtala'a" (possessed or afflicted one) wears special dresses for the occasion and often fasts until the ceremony ends.... The shaman is sometimes also a trained singer, who knows the songs and rhythms of each particular spirit. As he or she sings each spirit's song and watches for a reaction, he or she is able to diagnose which type of spirit has taken possession of the person and how to "exorcize" it.

I had already been struck by how ritual healing in the UAE often seemed regarded as a distant and exotic force. In one story I had read months earlier, an African national arriving in Dubai was arrested for wearing twenty belts around his waist, which was deemed "black magic." "They are made up of animal skin, animal bones, papers with symbols written on them," a senior inspection officer at Dubai Customs reported in 2015. Around the same time, Dubai police announced a campaign against witchcraft, with Dubai Customs inspectors at Dubai International Airport announcing the seizure of 10,000 articles, weighing about 213 pounds, which they claimed to be associated with the practice of sorcery. The director of Dubai Customs at the time stated, "Practicing sorcery and witchcraft is a bad habit. It threatens the security of society by manipulating people's minds and taking advantage of their needs to deceive them."

It seemed clear that much of the concern about tackling spirits was focused on religion and notions of the safe and domestic. In Oman, concerns about zar, and people's reticence to talk about it, seemed to revolve around whether its ceremonies and rituals actually could be classified as Islamic exorcism, run somehow parallel to it, or—more worryingly—fall into "shirk," or beliefs that can't be reconciled within the monotheistic framework of Islam. Many of the stories I heard about goings-on in Bahla seemed to indeed fall well outside this framework: enchanted objects, ghost stories, people seeing their dead relatives walking. But these kinds of stories weren't limited to the present day, either; one story had ancient Bahlawi generals who were potent enough to stand atop the town's fort and command the djinn; another told how the now-ruined mosque just outside the town's walls flew in fully built during antiquity. The way these stories incorporated elements of pre-Islamic belief into Islamic frameworks seemed to parallel in meaningful ways how Christianity had incorporated elements of pagan beliefs and ritual into its own monotheistic framework. It made me ponder how we reconcile that which doesn't initially seem to square with our own value systems.

The next day, I met with the professed shaman, Muneer, at the Bahla Fort, an imposing mudbrick fortress at the foot of a valley which dated to the twelfth century and was undergoing a comprehensive renovation to preserve its delicate structures. Muneer had specified on the phone to meet him after the fort had closed; he had treated a guard afflicted with djinn and could get the key. We sat just inside the entryway, me propped against metal scaffolding, he in the guard's broken wheely chair.

I steeled myself, knowing I would need to walk a fine line talking to this self-proclaimed exorcist. I wanted to respect his beliefs, but I didn't want to enable someone who might be taking advantage of others.

I asked Muneer about his work. He stroked his close-cropped beard, explaining how he most often treated people: he listened to them and their families recount their affliction, prayed for them, and then performed a small ceremony. I watched him worry prayer beads in his right hand and asked him why religion made people seemingly hesitant to talk about zar.

"It's not just religion, it's where zar came from," Muneer said.

He explained that he had Zanzibari roots, and many people encountered him as black. It is a history I was ashamedly largely unaware of: Oman had colonized Zanzibar for over 250 years, from 1698 to 1968. When Sultan Qaboos made quick work modernizing the country after his ascension to power in 1970, many Zanzibaris were lured by the prospect of a broadened path to Omani citizenship. The decision to emigrate became an act of concerted appraisal: could the generous social welfare package Zanzibaris would receive in Oman outweigh new limitations on their individual political and social rights—from being discouraged from speaking Swahili in public to more conservative cultural expectations on gender mixing—as well as the potential hostility of still being "read" as foreign? For Muneer's parents, it did. For him, it was worth weighing the promise of greater opportunities against the power of ostracization as a perceived outsider.

Though zar is practiced in several Muslim majority countries from Egypt to Iran, it probably was brought to the Middle East by way of East African slaves. In Oman, zar was believed to have arrived with Zanzibari slaves during the mid-nineteenth century, when large territories of East Africa were controlled by Oman, and this tie to Zanzibar is problematic for some Omanis.

"Oman has its own problems with race, many unspoken," Muneer said.

It was a sentiment and reality I would hear again and again throughout my week, uttered quietly. Later, I would hear how it affected other aspects of Omani culture, right down to its music. "Society still doesn't address the traditional racism that's taken lightly," one Omani ethnomusicologist explained in an interview I later read about African influences in Omani culture. "Many people refer to black people as a slave or as the descendent of a slave."

I asked Muneer how many people he had treated. He estimated over five thousand patients had approached him during his two-decade-long practice, many from Bahla and the surrounding area. But some contact him from around the world. He said he was encouraging but firm in gently explaining to some people that he could not help them, no matter how desperate or dire their situation.

"Some say they see dead relatives walking around the market and then disappearing. This is not djinn, only ghost stories," he said.

Muneer seemed to have a clear line, or at least a personal belief system about what djinn weren't, and so it felt like the right time to ask him the question that had been rattling around inside my mind: whether he had ever treated someone for queerness. I watched him shuffle his feet in the near darkness, considering the question. After several moments, he said that he had not.

"But would you?" I pressed.

"I would consult with them if they asked," he said. "But that doesn't sound like djinn to me. That is something else inside."

I both wanted and didn't want to ask whether he thought that something was malignant or benign, inherent or foreign. Here was a man who himself was subjugated—not, as I thought, for his beliefs coming into tension with the predominant sect of religion in Oman, but for his own perceived racial difference.

We sat, him on the chair, me on the ground, a while longer. The sand underfoot still hadn't been compacted, and I felt the moisture, the weight, it carried. What he believed in his heart about queerness, I thought, was perhaps not as fundamental as what he did about it. In that vulnerable moment when someone came to him, he held the power, and it was a matter of how he exerted it. I watched him maintain his balance on the precarious chair, wondering if it would hold him.

▽▽▽

My phone pinged. Amir was ready to meet. Driving unaware through Nahwa, I had suggested a viewpoint on a winding road just outside of Bahla that I'd seen on Google Maps, one that overlooked the city. I arrived first and spent a moment staring out at the date palm oases that studded the landscape below me.

I heard Amir pull onto the dirt shoulder. He was out of his car and extending his hand in a flash. He pulled me in close with a surprisingly firm handshake.

"I hope a handshake is okay for you. I know the greeting in Oman looks a little gay," he joked, referring to the traditional custom of Omani men pushing the bridges of their nose together while maintaining eye contact. I laughed, relieved that he was affable. He pulled out a blanket and a thermos of coffee and fussed over me until I sat down.

He folded his starched gray dishdasha under his knees as he sat. I was relieved that he had brought tokens of hospitality that made our meeting look less suspicious. Over text, he had offered to meet me at a coffee shop, but I had wanted him to feel as open as possible to talk about his experience. Now that we were sitting together on the shoulder of a road, I felt even more conspicuous than if we were in town. I realized I had left my car idling like we were doing a quick drug deal. As in the UAE, homosexuality was also illegal in Oman, punishable by up to three years in prison. Though we weren't meeting for sex, the Omani government had recently sued an editor and threatened to shut down a weekly newspaper for writing a story about homosexuality in the country, so even our meeting felt risky. We talked for a bit about parkour, and he showed me some videos of himself practicing. I started to ask him about the djinn stories he was told in childhood, but he interjected and said he was okay to talk about being gay first if I wanted.

"I think it affects everything after it," he said.

Amir readjusted on the blanket and explained that he always knew he was different. At first, it was just that he wanted to play with girls longer than the age of six, the age that his father, a farm owner, insisted on separating him from playing with children of a different gender. But he also soon realized that he was curious about other boys' bodies in ways that his other friends weren't.

"You know what it is like?" he asked. He posed it as a question, but I knew it was more of an affirmation. I recognized myself in his words: an awareness of being somehow offset from everyone else before that difference can even be fully understood, let alone articulated.

He experimented sexually with some of the boys at secondary school, but he knew this fixation informed a larger part of him than it did them. As he grew up, he made friends with the men from Pakistan and Bangladesh who worked on his father's farm.

Some of them only worked for a few months, or their work was seasonal, but a few he knew well enough for years, greeting them with genuine well wishes and even the occasional hug when he was out helping his father. These men were away from their home, and he explained that he felt a kind of closeness to them for it. I pressed him to delve further, but he couldn't explain it—just that he also felt far from something.

"We were all far from something, maybe," he said, pointing to his chest and then the sky. I thought about the inherent difference he had felt so young, a difference I had acutely felt, too.

He developed a close relationship with one worker in particular: Wasim, a young man from the southwestern Pakistani province of Baluchistan. He would also occasionally walk with him through the date palms.

They began to fool around when no one was present, finding a spot off the walkway amid a plot of trees. But one day, a year after their relationship turned sexual, a family friend walked by them in the date palms as the two of them returned to the path. Amir greeted him, but the neighbor—usually a friendly man—was gruff and clipped. That night, Amir's father told him that he thought his son had a djinn.

"He didn't tell me exactly why, but he talked about my actions in a general way, like I was doing bad deeds, and that's when I knew that he knew," he said, downing his coffee and staring across the plane. "I was too ashamed to ask how he knew, but I knew that man had told him what he saw."

But Amir explained he was also surprised by his father's reaction. He had expected rage or some kind of wild fury, but instead his father seemed tender, almost supportive, in a way that took him aback. He was also surprised that his father told his mother. Later, she sat him down.

"She explained that my father just wanted me to be okay, to be normal," he said. "But I could tell that she wasn't sure of the situation—she said, again and again, 'He wants, he wants.'" Amir said he had always suspected that his mother had a sense he was different. She hadn't, for example, been subjecting him to the constant maternal harassment about marriage like his other friends' mothers were. He thought perhaps she knew that he was gay, or at least somehow set apart.

A few days later, his father took him to the house of a man who he said would do ruqya, a form of Islamic healing that involved prayer, remembrance, and supplication. But when the two of them arrived, the old man led him into a room with a clutch of amulets and stones. Amir was surprised his father was unfazed by the talismans. Since Amir wasn't religious, he wasn't especially concerned, but he was stunned that his pious father would deem acceptable these objects which blatantly stood in tension with his faith as a form of treatment. "People like my father call that stuff black magic. Simple," Amir said.

Amir wasn't sure if the shaman knew exactly why his father had brought him there. He was laid on the ground and told to close his eyes. He didn't see much—he fluttered his eyes a few times, he admitted—but he was alone in the room with the man for roughly ten minutes while his father waited outside. Amir treated the ceremony as he did the prayer he didn't believe in, staying silent and respectful while this man tried to fix him. After a few minutes, the man shook Amir's shoulder and coaxed him into a sitting position.

"Part of me wanted to give a big show—shaking on the ground and shouting, just to see if the man believed any of it," Amir said. "But then he was done. My father came inside, and he said I was better."

When I asked Amir if he had heard of conversion therapy, he grimaced and said he had. I explained that this felt the same to me: parents feeling that there was something fundamental that needed to—and even could—be fixed in a queer child.

"The thing that was most surprising was when we walked outside, my father didn't look relieved," Amir said. "I think he did it just so he could tell the neighbor who saw us that his son was better." He packed up the picnic stuff and told me he had a hope that his mother someday might try to convince his father that being gay is acceptable, or at least not detrimental.

"Some days I even think maybe they already know, but I'm not sure," he said.

He explained that there were longstanding rumors that Sultan Qaboos—the popular ruler of Oman who was also a lifelong bachelor save for a three-year marriage that ended in divorce at the age of thirty-six—was gay. Amir called it hypocrisy—that people could love and respect Qaboos but decry homosexuality in more abstract terms—but then admitted there was also hope, that perhaps minds could change through proximity. The real issue for Omanis, he said, was not born of concern over his actions or identity but based solely on worries about other people's perceptions. He hoped the same, someday, might be true for him: that any reticence people had about queerness might not be about the "unnatural" nature of the act or identity itself, but more generally on a vague social anxiety about respectability, which felt like an easier needle to move.

I had read the article about homosexuality in Oman before it was swiftly taken down, the writer deleted his Twitter account, and the newspaper was forced to issue a full-page apology. It was called "The Outsiders" and featured interviews with two migrants and an Omani, who detailed the struggles they faced but also how they succeeded in living in and operating within the country. It also interviewed an Indian psychologist who worked in the capital about his experience with queer people, whose words struck me as I considered my own djinn story, Amir and his father, and the limits of treatment and tolerance. "They buckle under societal, familial, and religious pressures," he explained. "Many of them come here looking for a cure. They think there is something wrong with their bodies, why they are feeling these things. They want so desperately to be like people they consider 'normal' that they cannot reconcile their own feelings with any sense of normality."

When I asked Amir what he would do next, he said he would finish university and get an MBA. He was hoping to go to the UAE because he had parkour friends there. I tried to delicately ask if his father might be worried that he would be improperly influenced by going abroad.

"He knows being gay isn't an imported thing. I think he knows it is from here, too. I think the bigger problem was that Wasim is Pakistani," he said. It was a statement that upended how I perceived his scandal: that its root may not lie entirely in sexuality, but in something even more nuanced and, perhaps, fraught—a worry about race and perception.

As we made our way back to our cars, he told me that someday he might want to move to Musandam, the enclave I had breezed past, and live with his friends. He liked rock climbing, and some of his parkour friends had started deep water soloing off the coast—climbing as high as your body would allow before letting go and falling back into the sea.

I had been out of university just long enough to recognize the idealized, slightly naïve notion of living with friends, surrounded entirely by those like you, without the sharp edges of the real world cutting in. But as he drove off down the road and back into the town, I was charmed by the queerness of the idea: living in an enclave, creating a chosen family in a place at just far enough a remove.

▽▽▽

I stood at the entrance to the oasis, wondering if I could go inside.

Amir had told me Wasim wouldn't have much time, but I was just grateful he had managed to arrange for us to meet in the first place. I was even more grateful that Wasim was willing to talk to me, though I was slowly coming to realize that other migrants frequently didn't share my own unease around speaking about queerness.

Amidst the clutch of date palms, we met along a falaj, a system of underground aqueducts constructed like a series of well-like vertical shafts, connected by gently sloping horizontal tunnels. They enabled large-scale agriculture to flourish in a dryland environment like much of Oman's interior. Some three thousand were still in use in Oman, I had read. Five representative examples of this irrigation system were so ingenious as to be inscribed as UNESCO World Heritage Sites. They stood as remarkable examples of how things could be sustained even in the unlikeliest of circumstances

Wasim was sitting on the ground, but I could tell even then that he was a short man, slighter than I would have expected for someone doing such intense physical labor. He was handsome and clean-shaven with a friendly smile, and he explained almost immediately in apology that he didn't see Amir much anymore—not so much out of shame but because Amir was now usually in Nizwa, a large city forty kilometers away, at university. As we walked past rows of palms, dates held aloft in rough nets until they were ready to be cut down, he told me in a mixture of Arabic and English about his job working on Amir's family farm.

Wasim had moved to Oman a decade earlier, he explained, when he was nineteen. University was not in the cards for him. "I wanted an adventure," he told me. "I had friends who talked about Dubai and Doha, but I knew Omanis were good people." Two men from his neighborhood, a few years older than he was, had moved to Muscat, the capital of Oman, and he knew the country had a large South Asian population. He came to work for Amir's father along with one other compatriot and developed a respectful relationship. He explained he was proud to still send much of his earnings back to his ailing father and younger siblings.

I asked if there was anyone else at home.

"I do not want a wife," he said, smiling.

Wasim explained that his relationship with Amir was one first of friendship. He was attracted to Amir but was afraid because of his precarity in being employed by Amir's father. He waited until Amir made a move one day when he was seventeen, brushing up against him in the field.

"I knew then," he said. He spoke of Amir in an almost paternalistic manner, though they were only separated by a decade. He never used the word "gay," but I could hear the affection he had for Amir. "Far away from family, it is easier sometimes," he said.

"But then that day here—" he said, a touch regretful, as though he wished he could do something differently. I wondered how much more discreet one could be than in a date palm oasis. I looked down at the falaj, thinking about the undercurrents that allowed all this to sprout and grow, but still required such cultivation to survive.

I wanted to ask delicately not about his queerness, but about something Amir had mentioned almost offhandedly: that he occasionally helped Pakistani compatriots who were smuggled into the country to beg during Ramadan.

I wasn't sure he would want to talk about it, but he opened up, proud—almost wily—about this subversive work. He explained that hundreds of Pakistanis from Gwadar, the port city and administrative capital of his home province of Baluchistan, smuggled themselves in on boats during the Islamic holy month.

"There are no jobs in Gwadar for men like me," he said. He explained that beggars sometimes went back after Ramadan with the equivalent of over a year's salary, all made on the streets in under a month. In addition to the higher wages and thus more expendable income in Oman, people were especially giving during Ramadan because zakat, or charity, was one of the tenets of the holiday. He said a few of the visiting men he had encountered slept with men too, despite the risks.

I asked him whether it was hard for Pakistanis to beg here because they were outsiders.

"They aren't outsiders," Wasim replied, a forcefulness in his response. He explained a history that I again didn't know: that Gwadar, like Zanzibar, used to be an Omani territory. Pakistani beggars coming in were a byproduct of its colonial history. Even if they were separated by a border that also included a body of water, they could cross that gulf and enter—dancing on a knife's edge, reckoned with even if not fully welcomed.

Before he left, I asked Wasim a question that had stayed with me since I met Amir. I wanted to know how he'd been dealt with after their relationship was revealed.

Wasim just looked at me and shrugged. "Nothing," he said. "Maybe you wonder why I did not get treated like Amir? I wonder, too."

I considered the avenues I'd seen people take when confronted with something they don't know how to contend with. Whether to consider it endemic, a threat, an outside force; to hope or action it away; pray for it to disappear; begrudge it as an undeniable reality. Perhaps the "treatment" had been a final desperate hope on the part of Amir's father. Or perhaps, as Amir suspected, it had indeed been pure theater: a convenient way to tidy up a young man's dalliance with someone who was perceived as an outsider yet also an undeniable part of the fabric of this place.

All Wasim knew was that he had stayed, continuing to work along the edge of the oasis. I asked him if he ever went back in again amidst the palms with Amir, and he just smiled.

▽▽▽

I was hoping for more of a ghost story? Can we amp up the spooky stuff? Give me a call.

I slumped back onto the couch and laid my head in Sunil's lap as I reread the dismissive three-line email aloud to him. I had written three thousand well-researched words that delved into the roots of zar and djinn in Oman, but my editor envisioned something else entirely. I gave him a quick call, and he outlined the trappings of a piece that seemed to parallel the kind of jump-scare paranormal programs I was beginning to see even on formerly reputable television stations like *The History Channel.*

Perhaps I'd made a stupid mistake, I told Sunil. It was my first time writing for a new kind of online travel magazine—the kind in search of what they were deeming "content," garnering clicks and advertising revenue with sensational headlines. My interviews and research had pushed the piece into one that contended with Omani colonial history and racial politics, and I thought a draft submitted with greater clarity and deeper considerations than my pitch would be welcomed. I scrolled through the recent article headlines of the new media outlet, all seemingly in competition with one another on locales more exotic, premises more astounding. I could find no articles that had even a surface consideration of race, and after another email exchange, it seemed to be a topic my editor was keen to avoid entirely. I realized this was also my fear in writing about homosexuality: that it would be stripped of any nuance.

After listening to me grumble as I laid in his lap, Sunil turned his computer sideways so I could see what was on his screen: a flight reservation on the final booking page before payment.

"There's a sale," he said, offering me a sly grin. We could fly to Bahrain, he suggested. The flight was in two days. The trip would be perfectly timed over a long holiday weekend, too.

Since I began studying the region, I had wanted to visit Bahrain, a small island five hundred kilometers northwest from the UAE with less than a million citizens. It was a fascinating place—a small archipelago made up of dozens of islands famed since antiquity for pearling before the commercial industry collapsed in the nineteenth century. But what had interested me the most was that Bahrain was the only country in the Gulf where homosexuality was not technically illegal. The country's penal code from its more than a century as a British protectorate was repealed in favor of an updated legal framework in 1976. The new Bahrain code post-independence did not prohibit non-commercial acts of homosexuality between consenting adults in private. I had read that the capital, Manama, was even home to a few de facto gay bars.

Though same-sex activity was legal in Bahrain, I knew the prevailing view was that acts of homosexuality and crossdressing sat together under an umbrella of general immorality. Laws designed to protect "public morality" and "public order" were vague, allowing police to arrest anyone deemed to be in violation of certain norms. I had read a year earlier about an Arab migrant who was sentenced to a month in prison for crossdressing in the Bahraini capital after a police patrol picked him up for walking "in a feminine way."

And yet, the gray area of a place where queerness stood outside the strict confines of absolute illegality was intriguing. Looking to get my mind off the disappointment of my editor's feedback, we decided to book the flight. We were giddy at our own impulsiveness, and even giddier when we arrived at the airport to a class upgrade. The whole trip seemed absurd—sitting alongside people in business class on legitimate work trips when we were going to hop gay bars. We ordered miniature bottles of champagne and watched the city unfurl beneath us after a short hour's flight, making jokes about spotting Michael Jackson's house.

I had first become aware of Bahrain as a teenager when Michael Jackson had chosen to live there—eleven months holed up in Manama after his acquittal of child sexual abuse charges in the US in 2005. Most of his previous four years had been spent flitting from one part of the globe to another, failing to put down permanent roots, but two weeks after the trial, reports emerged from Bahrain that he and his children had landed there on a private jet as the guests of Sheikh Abdulla Bin Hamad Al-Khalifa, the king's son and a friend of Jackson's brother, Jermaine, who had previously converted to Islam. The story fascinated me: a Black American superstar dogged by rumors of queerness escaping into self-imposed exile in a place where homosexuality was not illegal and yet was widely perceived to be. Even more beguiling were the reports that emerged of Jackson wearing women's abayas as a means to preserve his own anonymity. Crossdressing was against Bahraini norms, but it seemed Jackson was given a wider berth as an outsider.

In the taxi in Manama, we joked about keeping our champagne buzz going. Besides the distraction from my Oman story, the trip was also an impulsive celebration for Sunil's new job working for a government developer. He had invented and maintained a story that he was just perpetually single, pretending to be coy about dating girls, throughout the five years at his previous job. But now, he wasn't sure what he would do for a new charade with new colleagues, what new means he would need to devise to keep his sexuality a secret. Would it be best to keep up the act of being a singleton? Would it be too risky to explain he was in a relationship but just change some identifying details about me, like my gender? We delighted in the possibilities, laughing that my name was obscure enough that he could just tell everyone I was his beautiful Scandinavian girlfriend. We wondered if he might have the freedom to create any story he wanted to tell.

We arrived at the bar joking that it didn't know what story it wanted to tell either. The exterior featured a profusion of arches and pillars that look both Mughal and Andalusian, and yet neither at the same time, as well as a smattering of tile meant to look like brick. The interior was just as eclectic. Sunset clay portico tiles evoked the Mediterranean, but they were interrupted by deep red tiles that looked like they were pulled from the floor of my elementary school classroom. Both failed to match the color of the wood paneling, reminiscent of a Victorian drawing room. Heavy wooden frames with anonymous prints of people sitting in vaguely European-looking cafés lined the walls.

It wasn't clear *where* the place was trying to evoke, but it was immediately apparent to me that it operated as a gay bar. The pillars that framed the entrance were also present inside, cluttering the space and giving the impression of cloistered sections that might facilitate intimate conversations, although I watched diverse groups of men moving fluidly between them. Alcohol had always been banned for Muslims in the UAE, but a similar law in Bahrain had only been enacted three years earlier, and its enforcement seemed lax here. Men in dishdashas were drinking alongside South Asians and Filipinos, conspicuously raising glasses and toasting. Affable men approached us with drinks in hand as we made a slow lap around the bar, inviting us to join their groups to talk or dance. More than once, a man addressed Sunil with a Muslim greeting, assuming him to be Egyptian, only to laugh and genially slap us both on the back when I was the one to respond in Arabic. I was the only white man in the establishment.

Making our way around the bar, it became clear that many of its patrons hailed from Saudi Arabia. Bahrain was linked to Saudi's eastern shore by the King Fahd Causeway, a twenty-five-kilometer bridge, and though Bahrainis required a prearranged visa to cross into Saudi Arabia, Saudi citizens were free to enter Bahrain with a visa upon arrival. The only Gulf country where queerness was at least nominally legal welcomed citizens across a four-lane raised highway from a country where the death penalty was still on the books for same-sex acts and crossdressing. I pictured a bridge empty on one side and backed up for miles in the other direction, as if in an apocalypse film, but the first Bahraini man we sat next to boasted of his frequent trips to Saudi Arabia.

"I enjoy too much sex there," he said. All I could do was smile at him, thinking about how brazen I could be on the Corniche in a country that wasn't my own. "Sometimes it's simpler to be in a different place. You know this!" he said, clinking his beer with me as I watched a Saudi man reach across the bar with a brazen arm and stroke the face of the Filipino bartender. The bartender laughed and seemed at ease, but I could not discern whether there was deference or familiarity in his chuckling response. *What was simpler in an unfamiliar landscape?* I couldn't tell if the man sitting next to me meant it was simpler feeling at ease, forming a community, or just plain getting away with things.

Maybe they could be the same thing. I tried to replay the bartender's laugh, to read his face: deference or familiarity.

I ordered more Heinekens, their glass bottles free from condensation despite being pulled directly from the refrigerator. The bartender explained between pours that he was from Manila and had worked retail in Riyadh before he got a job behind a bar in Manama. "Every place is difficult, so we move sometimes," he said, shrugging. He spoke of the bar as an example: like the karaoke bars I had frequented with Sunil in Abu Dhabi, this bar had a Filipino house band several nights per week. But the owner was thinking about replacing them with Ethiopian female dancers, he explained. The bartender had heard he might be looking to lower the bar's profile as a gay hangout, if not change its identity entirely. "I lose my job, I find somewhere new," he said.

Later on, I found one of very few clues about the bar's short place in Bahrain's queer nightlife on a kind of message board: "This bar is [sp] best gay bar in Bahrain and you can [sp] sex even inside the bathroom of this bar but please take care of yourself." Fewer than four years later, this gleeful, brash post would have a disenchanted follow-up: "this bar is a bar for straight Saudis," the tone sounding almost thwarted, as though the poster longed for a previous time and place of evasion. The description and name of the bar were erroneously listed under another bar, the website an imperfect early open-sourced collaborative wiki map. The confusion was apparent: "where is this place can u sms me," one man posted. I wondered if it had already been gone by the time he posted his question. I would later text the number, years after its posting, out of sheer curiosity as to whether he'd found it. The number was disconnected.

I felt the buzz of my phone against my thigh. An email appeared on my screen, a solicitation for stories for another new online travel magazine—"a call for content," the subject line stated, my mind flashing to my editor and my stalled djinn story. The magazine was looking to center an upcoming issue around the theme of "borders." I considered what I could write about Nahwa and Madha but then remembered that I had driven straight through them; I hadn't even snapped a photo, let alone noticed the fine striations between the exclave and the counter-enclave. Perhaps I could write about Bahrain, how it seemed a bit like Nahwa, its own kind of counter-enclave for queerness: a legal outlier bordering countries hostile to queerness, which were themselves surrounded by a wider push for acceptance of LGBTQ+ rights. I thought about Wasim, his slight frame in the oasis, and how he imperiled himself helping men who were smuggling into Oman because it seemed their only option. The heavy but ill-defined corners of a question about necessity were pulling me in opposing directions: who was crossing which borders, with what degree of ease, how, and why.

I scanned the email once more, mulling over what I could write, what I had to say, and noticed a line I hadn't seen on first read. The call was for first-person reported stories; I would have to be a character in the piece. I deleted the email, telling myself I wouldn't have the time to write such an involved article. Maybe it wouldn't be too bad writing a cheap version of the djinn piece, I rationalized. It would certainly be easier than taking a hard look at what I had done, zipping through Nahwa for no real reason or buying an impulsive ticket to Bahrain, sitting next to this Saudi man with his hand on my leg. I took another sip of my beer, letting myself get pulled across the threshold from the bar to the dance floor.

7: ANOTHER CRUISE

(Jeddah, Saudi Arabia: Hameed & Naji)

It was called *Jazirat al-Saadiyat.* The Island of Happiness.

During my first few years in the UAE, I had mostly encountered Saadiyat in the form of a plastic model heralding what the island would one day be: here, a row of condominiums; there, a spate of beach villas; further afield, an idyllic sanctuary for the endangered hawksbill sea turtle. The island sat five hundred meters off the northeast corner of Abu Dhabi's main island and was touted as the future of the city; its development would eventually house 150,000 people, as well as outposts of world-class museums designed by leading celebrity architects, including Jean Novel's new iteration of the Louvre, as well as a Frank Gehry–designed Guggenheim. The model of Saadiyat sat alone in an isolated prefabricated art gallery on an otherwise undeveloped island—an obstinate sort of self-aggrandizing mythmaking—save for one fast-moving construction site: the future campus of New York University Abu Dhabi, my future home.

Three months before the campus was scheduled to open, I was handed a neon high-vis vest and hard hat and toured through the active construction site. I had been offered one of the new apartments in the staff and faculty housing on the expansive forty-acre campus. After four years on a temporary campus downtown, I walked through the university's first purpose-built facilities, including pristine science laboratories, an indoor pool, and dormitories for the eventual student population of four thousand students. But most relevant for me was the world-class arts center featuring three theater spaces. I had been producing theater for the university to keep my work visa while writing, commissioning regional artists for residencies and workshops with students and presenting public-facing performances. Finally, after four years of looking for space around the city to stage shows, we had our own.

But all the construction and new development of the campus came at a dire cost on a grand global stage. A month after my tour in 2014—two months before I was due to move in—the *New York Times* published a sensational investigative story: "Workers at NYU's Abu Dhabi Site Faced Harsh Conditions." The scathing piece headlined the newspaper's website for two days and generated an international outcry. It detailed grim living conditions for many of those who toiled on the site, including employers locking away workers' passports in violation of international law, fifteen men living per squalid bedroom, and physical assault in retaliation for a workers' strike, an action illegal in the UAE. NYU quickly responded by trotting out its detailed "Statement of Labor Values," which the university had enshrined before construction began. A spokesperson also noted that the university could not vouch for the treatment of individual construction workers since they were not employees of the university but rather of companies that worked as contractors or subcontractors for the government agency overseeing the project.

The photo on the cover of the *Times* showed seven adult men with chiseled faces crammed into double bunks lining the walls of a tiny room, the single beds intimating some ghastly distortion of a child's bedroom. Either side of the photo was hemmed in by the steel frame of yet more bunks—claustrophobic, prison-like, and sitting in uncomfortable tension with the prominence of haphazard laundry cords and piled suitcases. The grim composition of the photo felt like an indictment. I had self-righteously touted NYU's labor values as progress, a kind of blueprint for how any foreign entity setting up shop in the Gulf should operate. But the article felt like concrete proof that the entire endeavor was failing, and that my place within it was one of culpability. Perhaps it really was better to sit at a remove from all this and not to live here. If these men couldn't strike or organize, and I was delimited to writing "safe" stories that didn't shed light on their dire circumstances, then what kind of systems was I complicit in—or directly part of—upholding?

And yet I still held onto some shapeless hope that my affiliation with NYUAD could harness some subversive potential even amid the outcry. For one, it gave me the ability to live and work in the UAE while also writing. But even more: Sunil could live with me on the new campus. In addition to its statement of labor values, NYU had declared that its establishment in the UAE was contingent on total academic freedom as well as its adherence to US HR rules, meaning I could declare Sunil my partner. I would be part of creating a two-layered system: with the UAE government, I would obviously remain single, but according to NYU's records, I would have a same-sex partner.

We decided to move in together, though we took care to rent a two-bedroom to keep up appearances. Because we were ostensibly sheltered by NYU, we reasoned our domestic arrangement would probably be fine; it seemed unlikely that UAE authorities would invite further scrutiny and bad press by deeply investigating who was living with whom on the campus of an American school. But we wanted to cover our bases nonetheless. Working for a government developer, Sunil's HR was also inquiring why he was moving onto a campus. What had felt so promising in Bahrain—the surfeit opportunities for him to invent a story about his relationship status—had devolved quickly into Sunil giving the clichéd "roommate" excuse, one we recognized that gay people had been giving forever. And after abandoning the complicated piece on djinn in Oman, throwing myself into writing felt like a way to affect change. Even if I couldn't write about the men who had constructed the campus, or the queer men I encountered, I could at least write about topics that weren't being covered, I reasoned—and hopefully peel back some of the misconceptions surrounding the Gulf.

One of the stories I was actively researching and writing was on the Arabian leopard, one of the most endangered mammals on the planet. When I spoke of the story, people were consistently surprised that the Gulf had an ecosystem hospitable enough for a non-human apex predator. Over the course of a few decades, the animal's viable breeding habitat had indeed shrunk from its range across much of the Arabian Peninsula, Levant, and Sinai, but it still existed in a small area on the Yemen-Oman border. Fewer than two hundred leopards were probably left in the wild. I had written numerous articles about the animal's preservation, including time spent with a ragtag team of scientists in Yemen doing conservation work at the height of the country's civil war. I wanted to write about a promising conservation program funded by the Saudi government in the country's mountainous interior.

In the same way I was conflicted about my employment with NYU—feeling both oppressed by and able to profiteer from the UAE—I felt some ambivalence in writing about this project in Saudi Arabia. Even if the conservation project had merit, I couldn't shake my unease about composing an article that might position Saudi—a country where punishments for homosexuality and crossdressing could include public whipping, torture, chemical castration, and imprisonment for life—as a paragon of anything. Saudi was one of the few countries where queer people were still put to death. If I would be ignoring personal risks traveling there, perhaps I would also be pushing away another daunting risk—a kind of complicity.

As I began research for the article, we also began the rehearsal process for our first theatrical adaptation on the new campus. We had commissioned a Lebanese theater company to devise an adaptation of *Frankenstein*. It would be, as their director told me, "an investigation into monstrosity and brutality." I spent hours on the phone sourcing AstroTurf for a giant artificial mountain that would take center stage, actors running up and down its imposing height playing humans trying to build, trying to fix. Time felt suspended as I sat on hold, watching men beneath my window thread hoses through landscaping. At the height of summer, work was legally curtailed during the hottest afternoon hours, but that was still weeks away. I bought tickets to Saudi from the comfort of my office, watching the men below me sweating in the monstrous, brutal heat.

▽▽▽

I landed near the Red Sea. From the plane, the shore looked almost like a straight line, with the sea hugging the country's western coast on a nearly perfect north-south axis. But up close, near the seventh-century Old City, Jeddah's waterline was winding and serpentine, a profusion of bays, inlets, and havens. Many of its traditional buildings were built of coral, with green and brown wooden lattice balconies jutting into the sky like driftwood afloat at sea. The ocean felt part of the city itself.

I wanted to walk the city freely, but I was troubled by the idea of stumbling across members of the mutawa. The committee of Saudi men patrolled the streets and enforced the country's Islamic legal code, including how women dress, the separation of sexes, and the requisite closing of shops five times a day during prayer. Their official name sounded Orwellian—the Committee for the Promotion of Virtue and the Prevention of Vice—and they had the authority to stop, interrogate, and arrest people whose behavior appeared to violate the country's norms, values, and laws.

I was mildly frustrated with myself for not having lined up interviews in Jeddah, but I told myself that by puttering around its streets without a destination, I might get my bearings and a sense of the place. I would find that, like early Abu Dhabi, many of the city's roads often had no curb and no parking regulation, so walking meant weaving between cars. Sidewalks, if they existed at all, often ended abruptly, a path seemingly hospitable to pedestrians suddenly ending even where a parallel motorway continued. I wound circuitously from the hotel but felt myself being drawn to the waterfront. I was moving away from the city and toward the margins.

I knew both why I had not set up interviews and where I was headed. I was trying to find the city's Corniche.

I walked closer to the water's edge along streets with no other pedestrians and felt the specter of consequence as my only companion. In Saudi, I could face the gravest repercussions anywhere in the Gulf—anywhere in the world—for the kind of activity for which I was searching. A Saudi man my age had recently been sentenced to three years' detention and 450 lashes for meeting men online and "promoting the vice and practice of homosexuality." Punishments for homosexuality here also historically included execution. In the UAE, NYU seemed to provide some safeguard, perhaps both real and perceived. Here, I walked closer to the water aware that the safety net I relied on had not been cast before I dove in; instead, something just beneath the surface could entangle me and pull me into the depths.

I arrived late to the Corniche. Families and groups of friends had already finished their dinners and were packing up their picnics; discarded chicken shop boxes stacked with bones and gristle were scattered in the landscaping that edged the promenade. I sat in a grassy area between a few benches and a railing and felt the light dim. As I did on Abu Dhabi's Corniche, I watched as men who were eating or exercising or taking in the sunset were slowly replaced by others who were unconvincingly mimicking those same activities, preoccupied by other motives. I listened as one man ostensibly on his phone trailed off midway through a "conversation," turning and watching another man walk past, hoping he would turn back and acknowledge him. In Abu Dhabi, men had sex in the dark recesses of the shadowed walkway, but here everything seemed too well lit, cast in a yellow hue from the old bulbs overhead. I was unsure where else they might go.

I pulled out my phone and found a number stored as HA in my contacts. A few weeks before I left, I had been researching the pehlwani story when Mohammed divulged, to my surprise, that he was gay. When I mentioned that I was going to Saudi the next month, he gave me the phone number of his former lover, Hameed, a wrestler who used to live in Dubai.

I didn't think he would answer, but Hameed picked up right away. I asked him if Prashant had told him why I might call. He asked me where I was, and I said I was on the Corniche. He was silent for so long I thought the call might have dropped.

"I will finish work after one hour. I will meet you there," he said. "Don't go anywhere," he added, before I even had a chance to respond. I felt a pleading in his voice.

After only thirty minutes, my phone rang. Hameed said that he was already nearby. I leaned back against a landscaping retainer wall and waited until I spotted a man who walked with an urgency, who lacked the practiced, performed languor of the men who were cruising. I waved, and he spotted me, but still I watched his head turn to examine other men as he walked past them, hoping he might warrant a look.

His searching brown eyes held my gaze as he motioned for me to stand up, pulling a cloth out of his bag and laying it down for us to sit on, just as Amir had done in Oman. I noticed how close he sat next to me. I apologized, explaining that I knew very little about him, but thanked him for meeting me anyway. He patted my thigh. I couldn't tell if the gesture was simply friendly, but I wanted to know more about him, so I didn't discourage it. He explained that he worked as a tailor nearby and often came down to the Corniche in the evening. I offered him a knowing smile.

"Yes, I come here often to meet friends," he said, smiling.

I talked for a while about Abu Dhabi's Corniche like I might an old friend. I asked him if he had gone cruising in the UAE very often, but he said he hadn't. He hadn't actually lived in Dubai, but had resided in Sharjah, the more conservative emirate on Dubai's northeastern border, where even drinking was banned. I told him I often heard Sharjah jokingly referred to as the Saudi of the UAE.

"I moved to Sharjah because I thought it would be better for my mind," he said. When he was young, he explained, he felt like he could control his homosexual urges until he started drinking alcohol. Torn up by these impulses and hoping to make a fresh start abroad, he paid a recruiter roughly $800 USD and found a job as a tailor. He was grateful for the work and was paid regularly, well enough to live in a flat with four other men, which was better than many he knew.

For a time in Sharjah, he felt like he was able to ignore his attraction to men and busied himself by joining a mosque and making friends with a colleague who had carrom, a board game he loved from home. But soon, he developed a physical relationship with the colleague.

"It was the first time I felt something here and not just here," he said, pointing to his heart and then grabbing his dick through his pants, laughing.

But the relationship soured when another colleague grew suspicious of them. His lover panicked at the thought of being found out, cutting off all their socializing. He even grew terse with him in professional interactions in the shop. Hameed looked for another job as soon as his contract ended and jumped at the chance to move to Saudi Arabia, hoping an even more conservative environment would fix him. But unlike his move to Sharjah, this one had no celibate period at all.

"I started finding men on my first day," he said, lowering his eyes. He felt the gaze of a compatriot who worked on the same street right away and was propositioned during his first week by a Jordanian client while measuring his body.

"I was alone in the shop, and he suggested that I close for prayer with him inside," he said. He'd been nervous about engaging with a customer but could not resist, explaining—with what sounded like a glint of pride in his voice—that the man, Naji, then started coming to get new clothes from him every week.

"We meet all the time," he said. He pulled out his phone. I assumed he would show me the man's photo. Instead, I watched his fingers moved furiously for a few seconds in silence. A smile crossed his face.

"You will enjoy," he said. I asked him what he meant, and he said that Naji would pick the two of us up in half an hour.

I stared at him, not knowing what to say. This hadn't been at all what I was looking for. But then again, I thought: what exactly was I looking for, if not this?

We sat watching the last of the families pick up their things and leave. I knew I could follow, but I stayed, running my fingers along the blanket.

▽▽▽

I decided to climb into the backseat of Naji's black SUV only after Hameed sat squarely in the front. I had a moment's hesitation about where to sit—a window seat meant that I might be spotted from the outside, but the middle meant I couldn't quickly jump out of the car if I needed to. I decided on a compromise: I would sit in the middle but without my seat belt fastened, keeping my hands hovering at my sides above the upholstery, studying Naji in the rearview mirror. I considered all the competing scenarios that could unfold on the way to our destination: getting pulled over by the police, blackmailed by this man I had just met, whisked out to the desert before I could get my bearings. I thought about them, I realized, to distract me from the immediate peril we were embarking on: three men of different nationalities checking into a hotel room late at night.

Neither Hameed in the passenger seat nor Naji behind the steering wheel said anything as we drove, so I stayed silent. We made our way through the tightly knitted streets of Al-Ruwais, one of the oldest parts of the city, which had once housed fishermen and sailors but was now largely home to migrant residents who worked unskilled, low-income jobs. I had read a recent report that more than half of the migrant residents who lived in its cement buildings had lived there for decades. I thought about how much humans could withstand when they needed to.

I tried to peer into Naji's face, but it was obscured by the angle of the mirror. I was put slightly at ease by how he kept his hand on Hameed's lap, but then also unnerved when I saw him move it compulsively each time we crawled to a stop at an intersection. The act seemed to demonstrate both his willingness to push up against a boundary and also his acute awareness of everything that was at stake by doing so. He was risking everything. We were. I regarded us as a collective, safety as a unit, the three of us pulling into a dark parking lot.

Naji parked his car outside a cement building and got out without a word. Hameed explained that Naji could check only the two of them in. I watched Naji stand before a cramped reception just beyond the dirty glass door. When he pointed to his car in the parking lot, I instinctively ducked. There was no law specifically preventing men from renting one hotel room together like there was for unmarried straight people, but I had read stories of entrapment and arrest of gay men in Saudi hotels, and our late arrival felt like a beacon of wayward intentions.

While we waited for Naji to check in, I asked Hameed where the two of them usually met. He explained that sometimes they had sex in his car, but it was a last resort. And because Hameed lived with four other men, his cramped accommodation was out of the question. This hotel was both the cheapest and safest option, he said.

I asked why they couldn't go to Naji's house.

"It's not possible. He has a wife and three children," Hameed said simply. He looked at me like he was steeling himself for my judgment, but I offered none. I thought of all the times I had followed men with wedding bands into the woods of Wisconsin.

I asked Hameed if it bothered him that Naji had a wife, but he shook his head again. He explained that all the boys he had been with in Malabar also bragged about their girlfriends. He was given the nickname "Kundan" at school, a derogatory term for a man who has sex with men.

"But all of them wanted me," he said, with the same measure of pride I heard when he first spoke of Naji's affection for him. This boasting seemed to stand in direct tension with what he had said earlier about shame and trying to push away his urges, but I recognized the dissonance. In matters of lust, perhaps, this tension was unreconcilable: what one wanted as an ideal in their mind versus what they craved at the core of their body. Or more precisely, what one wanted versus what one needed.

"Do you trust him?" I asked. Hameed only nodded. I watched him stare at Naji in the lobby. I remembered all the men who hadn't just wanted to explore my body in a park but had tried to coax me into cars and back to houses, how I had mere seconds of appraisal to judge a quick display of body language and eye contact. All those times I had managed to extract myself from potential danger with a stranger's hand already on my thigh. This was how and where we were pushed—into the shadows, where we had to learn to operate in the dark.

I wanted to ask more, but Naji returned to the car with a hotel key in hand. He motioned for us to stay while he pulled out a cigarette. I watched him eye the entrance. I thought about the wrestlers I had just interviewed in Dubai—the urge I felt to preserve silence when they weren't speaking. I could see him mulling something over.

"We will wait for the shift change," he said. "A Filipina woman comes after."

"But you have wasta," Hameed teased.

I considered the term. It was an Arabic phrase reserved for people with clout, people who could make things happen. But the word also wielded a cutting edge of disparagement, suggesting nepotism, or at least an imbalance of power. After Hameed had dialed Naji's number on the Corniche, he told me with some pride that Naji was a businessman. But that certainly didn't offer enough wasta to circumvent Saudi morality laws, I thought. What he was waiting for instead was his chance to have and wield a different kind of power—to stand not in front of a Saudi man but a Filipina woman, a fellow migrant who was less likely to ask questions, to care, or to be able to do anything about it on the off chance she did.

Naji leaned out his window and threw his half-finished cigarette to the ground. It was time. This man who I had just met studied my face through the rearview mirror. It was not the stare of cruising, but one that seemed to assess my own proximity to power. Naji handed me the keys to his car and explained that he and Hameed were going to walk in together. I should wait a few minutes to go to their room. They only had a double, he explained, so it would be suspicious if all three of us walked in together.

Naji seemed unruffled by the situation. I wondered how many times he had done this—inviting men to his hotel room, imperiling everyone, himself included. I watched them walk inside and found myself turning the key in the ignition again and again in the minutes that passed. I had a clock on my phone, and yet I kept glancing at the dash each time it illuminated, perhaps not to know how many minutes had gone but to reassure myself that I was able to make a getaway if I needed. Even though I had never been in this exact scenario before, the secrecy—and the clear-headedness I needed to make my way unscathed through the peril I was barreling toward—felt familiar. I knew what I needed to do to get what I wanted.

I got out of the car and pushed my way through the glass door. A Filipina woman behind the beige desk nodded at me, and I offered a weak smile in return. I tried to affect a confident stride through the lobby, but I felt myself pushing the elevator button repeatedly, willing it to arrive before the woman spoke to me.

Naji greeted my light rap on the door and ushered me inside the tiny foyer. Our bodies were squeezed against a sink and chipped vanity shoehorned next to the entrance. I removed my shoes, and he feigned the action of Islamic ablutions, gesturing for me to wash before entering the room. In the mirror, I noticed an old, rumbling air conditioning unit set into the thick concrete of the wall, and a bed that took up most of the room. Only as I reached for a towel that wasn't there did I see that Naji was taking ropes from his briefcase while Hameed sat near the headboard. He began tying Hameed's wrists to the bed.

I froze. The room suddenly seemed too small. I wasn't sure if I was supposed to join them, realizing that we had never made clear what I would be doing. Hameed had said that Naji liked bringing men "inside," but I now didn't know if that meant as voyeur or fellow participant. I had been in rooms of heightened tension—of bondage and domination—before, but I had never seen the power dynamic laid so bare: a man in a suit tying up another man already half-stripped of the thin cotton clothes that so brazenly illustrated he belonged to a different class. Naji grinned at me and held my gaze. I noticed a metal chair sitting oddly in the surprisingly spacious bathroom, and I took it, sitting awkwardly, half in the room, half out. I felt myself grow hard through my jeans and felt the bulge of my notebook and pen through my backpack. What was I really doing here? With no answer, I pulled the utensils out of my bag.

I knew that any measure of credible objectivity was already gone. Even in sitting and witnessing, I was also participant. And in recording, I would be complicit—in what, I wasn't sure. What I was suddenly aware of was my own ungainly presence shifting the dynamic of the room fundamentally, even if I didn't make a move. I rubbed myself, unable to write. *Who is using, who is being used.* It was the only sentence that came to me, but I did not want to write it down.

Afterward, I watched Naji hand Hameed a cigarette as he untied him. He and Hameed would leave first, he explained, and I should again wait five minutes, just to be safe. Naji would return tomorrow to drop the key off to make it seem like they had used the room the whole night. I looked at my blank notebook. I wanted to ask so much more, but a post-coital silence pervaded the tiny room, and I knew so much had already been conveyed without words.

After they left, I washed again and pushed my way into the staircase, my hand leaving a wet mark on the door. I descended one flight, gathering pace, but was met on the second landing by an impasse. I registered it first as a static object before realizing that it was the Saudi receptionist, standing in the half dark. A cigarette dangled from the corner of his mouth, and I felt myself breathe in his smoke. I instinctively pulled out my phone and pretended to be deep into answering a message.

"Why you here?" he asked in broken English. I didn't know what to do except to carry on walking forward, pretending not to hear him. It felt absurd; we were the only people in the stairwell. Where was the Filipina woman to save me? I realized I was banking on the same power dynamic to get me out that Naji had used to get us in.

The man repeated the question more urgently, and I was forced, finally, to look at him.

"You with Jordan and Indian man?" he asked aggressively. Even beneath his billowing kandura, I could tell he was muscular. His arms were crossed as though he had been waiting for me. *Passport, passport,* he began to ask, over and over, in Arabic. He held out his hand like an accusation—like he wasn't just going to scrutinize it but see straight through the photo to my queerness inside. If I handed it over, I knew he would cross-check that I hadn't registered at the desk. And he would have my name; he would report me and hold onto my passport like the men who built the campus on Saadiyat Island. I would no longer have the power.

I decided to stare at him vacantly and keep walking. There was power in feigning ignorance, I decided. I tried to squeeze past him. It was a farcical tactic, trying to shuffle beyond his frame in a cramped emergency stairwell as though he wasn't even there. Even when he grabbed my forearm, I kept walking. For what seemed like minutes, we did what felt like a poorly choreographed dance, him holding my arm, me walking away.

I finally pulled free. Or he let go. I didn't register which it was—all I knew was I had emerged from the stairwell into the lobby. I felt myself trying not to walk too quickly toward the exit, as though my pace was the final shred of some fast-dissolving veneer of innocence. The Saudi receptionist was suddenly behind me, repeating shurta, shurta again and again in Arabic. I realized with a measure of relief that he probably did not have the language capability to say the word "police" in my native language, and his limitation was my saving grace. If he had been able to utter it in English, I might have stopped walking. By not being able to communicate with him—by pretending not to understand him—I could keep myself safe.

I made it through the dirty glass door and quickly looked left and right, devising the surest escape strategy. I expected the sound of footsteps running after me, but all I heard as the door closed was a string of insults I pretended not to comprehend.

The headlights of Naji's SUV shone a block away. He motioned me to keep walking when I approached but offered a nod and a wave of thanks. I nodded back, touched that he had waited. I thought about heading back to my hotel, but I found myself walking back to the Corniche instead. How many more people were stalking the shore, riding the edge of danger tonight, as we had done? I wanted, once more, to find out.

▽▽▽

In my Jeddah hotel, I scanned through photo after photo of dead leopards. The ones that had been poisoned almost looked like they were sleeping. But others had met more violent ends. In one photo, a leopard hung upside down, its legs akilter, a patch of skin missing from his otherwise majestic coat. The picture accompanied an article from a Saudi newspaper headlined "Killed Arabian leopard in Saudi found skinned." The article described how authorities had "retrieved only its legs and head after it was skinned." I didn't want to look, yet found myself unable to turn away, finding a kind of cathartic release in seeing something meet a violent death in Saudi Arabia that wasn't me.

As a writer, the story of the Arabian leopard felt both urgent and ignored, and I couldn't help feeling a kind of sanctimonious pride for pursuing it. It was an undeniably unusual tale that hadn't fully been told, and I knew this was part of what drew me to it: the story of a rare animal, its habitat lost, its survival threatened. It seemed worthwhile to tell the story even if the animals' long-term survival felt unlikely. Fearing the threat the leopards posed to their livestock, farmers had been known to kill them. Worse still were videos of poachers who tried to capture them alive, their legs tied to stakes, like a kind of rudimentary splint not for healing but to inhibit movement. The few photos from trail cameras of the last remaining leopards in the wild made the majestic creatures look ghostly. I knew I was picturing them in a sentimental light: stalking the landscape, aware of the dangers they faced, searching for others like them.

As I waited to confirm research meetings for the article, I pulled out the books I had brashly smuggled into my luggage, *Interzone* and a collection of letters from its author Williams S. Burroughs to Alan Ginsberg. The tone of both felt at once salacious and blasé. Many passages were shocking in their explicitness and lack of humanity. From Burroughs:

> *"Did I ever tell you about the time Marv and I paid two Arab kids sixty cents to watch them screw each other—we demanded semen too, no half-assed screwing. So I asked Marv: 'Do you think they will do it?' and he says: 'I think so. They are hungry.' They did it. Made me feel sorta like a dirty old man…"*

For some Beat Generation writers in the mid-twentieth century, the Middle East approached a kind of self-described utopia: fleeing the American framework they knew, they found themselves and a kind of libertarian autonomy in places like Tangier, Morocco, where they could enjoy the fruits found outside their cultural norms. Thus, Tangier, as Burroughs later writes, became a "sanctuary in which everyone is sheltered from all interference"—especially for gay American men of independent wealth who could afford the luxuries of international travel and leisure.

Burroughs is darkly aware, even bombastic in his cussedness, of the image of the Ugly American and those who derive their pleasure from a nearly interchangeable sexual labor force:

> *"I go to bed with an Arab in European clothes. Several days later in the rain … I meet an Arab in native dress, and we re-*

pair to a Turkish bath. Now I am almost (but not quite) sure it is the same Arab. In any case I have not seen No 1 again. When I walk down the street, Arabs I've never seen before greet me in a manner suggesting unspeakable familiarity (in past or future?). I told one of these Arabs, 'Look, I don't like you and I don't know you. Scram.' He just laughed and said: 'I see you later, Mister.' And I did in fact go to bed with him later, or at least I think it was the same one ... I really don't know for sure. Next time I'll notch one of his ears."

I felt something twinge in me as I read about a powerful white man dependent on a stream of subjugated brown bodies that he could barely differentiate to wring success and meaning out of his time, his work, his indulgence in the region. Burroughs's writing seemed to lay bare that there was a terrible power in the idle foreigner abroad entering into and disrupting the global marketplace and finding a queer freedom. The control could briefly swing to the subjugated one—"I see you later, Mister"—but the power always returned: "I'll notch one of his ears" *I will mark you. I can make you part of my story.*

I thought of the photos of splayed leopards, but the image of Hameed splayed on the bed supplanted them. I tried to write, to research, but my mind wandered back to the men stalking the Corniche. Was I here to write the story of the leopard, or was I here for something else; to investigate or experience pleasure? Could the two be parsed?

I knew that even if I wrote about queerness in Saudi Arabia, I might fall into the same trappings as the Beat Generation who had kicked around the Middle East more than half a century earlier. Already the stories I wanted to explore, of queerness and belonging, had been influenced by my own attraction. Any attempt at understanding Naji and Hameed's dynamic with each other and within the Gulf had been fundamentally shifted by the fact that I was now a part of their story as well.

Complicating matters further was that I knew Naji did not identify as gay; he was something else, perhaps an identity more nuanced than many would care to digest. It would certainly be easier to tell a more familiar story: that of a gay man living under abhorrent repression. I thought of the fiery denouncement of Joseph Massad, a prominent and controversial professor at Colombia University who coined the term "Gay International" to categorize the Western advocacy groups and media who worked to call attention to the perils of what they saw as queer people living in countries with anti-LGBTQ+ laws. "It is the very discourse of the Gay International, which both produces homosexuals, as well as gays and lesbians, where they do not exist, and represses same-sex desires and practices that refuse to be assimilated into its sexual epistemology," Massad wrote in his book *Desiring Arabs.*

Massad was pointing to a much longer and more complicated history of same-sex desire in the Arab world, one that challenged the neat categories and narratives espoused by writers and organizations who stumble into the region desperately waving their arms, trying to transform a state and culture they don't fully understand. For so long, I had heard the criticism and scorn about the queer community: an "alphabet soup" of inclusive letters, "LGBT" and "Q" and "I" and "A" and on and on. It was all too complicated, the complaints went. How, then, was I to engender sympathy for what might appear on the page like a straight Arab guy taking advantage of a working-class younger Indian man for sexual gratification? The easiest way was to flatten Hameed and Naji's story into one of gayness—of romance—but even if I were able to capture something truer, I would still be dragging them into a queer orbit whose pull they might have otherwise resisted entirely.

It was also a proximity to immediate and mortal danger that gave these stories their urgency, the kind of power I would rely on to get them published and in front of the eyes of a readership. And yet the reality was that the most perversely tantalizing element of the story—the death penalty—was enshrined in law in Saudi Arabia but not really implemented. Human Rights Watch, the kind of organization that Massad might place in the category of "the Gay International," had even produced recent reports that appeared to quickly gloss over the fact that executions for same-sex actions had not been documented for years, even as they banked on their possibility to generate urgency for their cause. I thought about my escape from the hotel and wondered what might have happened had I been caught.

Danger, pleasure, and purpose seemed to shift with each consideration, coming into view and then suddenly falling out of focus: Hameed in the bed, Naji in his car, me in the stairwell, me writing the story. Hameed had identified Naji as the one with wasta, but I had used my own perceived power to escape. I had come here to write about danger and peril perhaps because they had become inextricably linked to how I conceived of desire and power. I thought about the construction of my new home, the one I happily moved into after the publication of the Saadiyat story and the real danger and exploitation the men in the photo had faced. The story easiest to tell—that I had come to Saudi to tell a noble story of a rare leopard, that I was working at a noble institution—was not the most accurate: that in both my work and my leisure, I was coming into close proximity to, if not directly seeking out, exploitation.

I tried to return to the story at hand, the leopard, but as I wrote, it seemed to have too many caveats. Perhaps the Yemen-Oman border, the only place with what had been deemed "a viable breeding population," was indeed the only region left on Earth worth focusing conservation attention and resources. And yet I was drawn to this breeding program in Saudi, the kind of shifts its power might create, as well as the provocative claims that a few leopards may still exist further afield in Palestine, perhaps even in the Sinai, stalking the landscape alone. Three subspecies of Arabian leopard had once roamed the Gulf, but there was only one left, and I would need to account for a complicated history while refraining from trafficking in superlatives. I wanted to ignore that the qualities that drew me to Saudi to write about the leopard—rarity, mystique, the exotic—uncomfortably paralleled what drew me to the region itself, and also what pulled me to seek out these queer stories with which I still hadn't done anything.

I didn't really expect to get to see a leopard before I left. So few of them remained. But as I was ushered into a dark office where I would wait to interview a man who never arrived, we came face to face. I sat in front of the taxidermized specimen, its feet glued to a wooden board, its body misshapen, almost unrecognizable. Despite having been stuffed—perhaps overstuffed, one side of its belly almost distended—the animal still had the curious look of having been hollowed. I stared into its glass eyes and tried to write down every detail I could about its grotesque form in as unadorned and detached a tone as I could muster. But I couldn't seem to get it right, preoccupied by the thought of how it had met its end.

8: A STORM

(Abu Dhabi; Sydney, Australia: Gizelle)

The bookshelves of our apartment were filled with the flamboyant spines of travel guides. Row after row held the blue and white of Lonely Planet, the orange of Rough Guides, the gray and white of Bradt. Many were for writing articles while I was simultaneously working at NYUAD; I had three copies of Lonely Planet's *India*, updated for each subsequent writing trip I took to the country. But just as many guidebooks were for trips I was taking with Sunil as we attempted to navigate the world together as a queer couple.

I was fascinated by their attempts at curation: how travelers themselves, often white men, attempted to present, distill, and organize foreign places for other travelers. I highlighted errors in them as I found them, many egregious, like how one edition of a guidebook I bought for Ethiopia contained the entirely wrong dates for Timkat, an Orthodox Epiphany celebration.

Same-sex relations were illegal in many of the places I was traveling, and I would often flip to the thin LGBT Travelers section of the index first, most devoting one scant paragraph to the illegality of homosexuality but very little about how one should, or could, actually operate in the country as a queer arrival. Perhaps it was easiest to avoid describing such minutia out of fear of liability or political statement. But I knew also that the establishment of public queer spaces was inherently volatile: brick-and-mortar venues quickly and frequently moved or closed, and activities like cruising were so often entirely illegal. The books' meager offerings felt like a kind of passive suggestion, or perhaps a more explicit warning: avoid these countries altogether.

The oldest guidebook I owned was an especially tattered copy of the first edition of Bradt's travel guide to Yemen, one of the few publishers who had ever devoted a full guidebook to the country. Shortly before I left New York to study in Yemen, I received it as a gift in brown paper wrapping from a queer friend whose parents had emigrated from the Philippines. She had been one of the few friends who immediately understood why I felt the need to go to a place perceived as notoriously dangerous and who supported my decision to do so. A few years after my studies, by the time the book was ragged and dogeared, I emailed the author and was surprised to receive not just a reply but a commendation: he had followed the blog I maintained while I was in Yemen. Impressed by my writing and assertive message, he invited me to write the second edition with him, incorporating some additional historical research and reporting on Yemeni culture and the environment. I was thrilled. I would finally sit on my own bookshelf.

But a few months after the project began in early 2015, Saudi Arabia led a coalition of countries in a series of devastating air strikes against a rebel group in Yemen. Our plans to travel to the capital were halted, and the project was put on hold indefinitely as the violence escalated. Over dinner each night, as I scrolled through bleaker and bleaker news out of the capital, the bright colors of the guidebooks taunted my peripheral vision. I slowly resigned myself to the disappointment that I would never have a book among them.

I recognized that much of the research for guidebooks would have involved the basics of hospitality, like hotel names and restaurant opening hours, but I also knew Yemen had negligible tourism infrastructure. This book—the book that would no longer be—felt like my chance to articulate what it meant to navigate through a place altogether more complicated than an all-inclusive beachside resort; to push past basics and write about topics like the historical influence of East Africa and India in Yemen, of both the strength and effect of immigrants and migrants. I could have delved into how the perfunctory questions travelers faced—like "When should I visit?"—could become an especially fraught calculation for groups like migrants and queer people. Perhaps I could have even explained how finding a path through a country like this meant living within the tension between making one's own way and understanding how to operate within the confines of prescription. But suddenly, after what had begun to feel a little like gallivanting through whichever countries I wanted—in the Gulf and beyond—I could no longer travel to the place I wanted to most.

To take my mind off my disappointment, Shivani began inviting me on urban spelunking expeditions across Saadiyat Island with one of her gay TCK friends, Arjun. I had only heard of urban spelunking in relation to the exploration of abandoned manmade structures or ruins—intrepid adventurers breaking into old German sanitoriums or the catacombs of Paris—but in the UAE, the practice contained elements of the futuristic. Except for NYU's campus and some beachside housing, most of the structures that would service the island's eventual population of a quarter million residents were still a distant dream, but the massive infrastructure was often laid well in advance of any visible construction. Like Sunil's Palm Jebel Ali project, roads, streetlights, and substations often bloomed before any buildings at all. It was like a skeleton appearing somewhere all at once, instead of erecting each limb, one at a time, from bone to muscle to skin.

Accessing much of Saadiyat Island was illegal, but law enforcement was rarely present to enforce trespassing laws on a nearly empty island. We began first to explore the areas around the campus and its jumble of construction sites. Shivani's favorite was a ready-mix concrete batching plant with a guard outside who was always staring at his phone. But the site that transfixed me most was an underpass for an incomplete five-lane road. I looked out upon it each day from my apartment windows, sand half covering its unfinished roadworks. Each time, I wondered when the stoplights might appear, finally illuminating which direction to go.

We walked to the tunnel one afternoon beneath a bright morning sun, a few wispy clouds lazing offshore. As we trudged through the sand, Arjun shyly recounted why he had been absent from parkour for over two months. I knew he had been holding out for a job at a trampoline park due to open soon, so his absence at training—as well as his silence over text—had worried Shivani. She even wondered aloud to me if he might have gone to India, a place he hadn't lived since he was a child, without telling anyone. Instead, he explained how he had met a man cruising on the Corniche who wanted to take him back to his building. When they arrived, the man confessed that he had family in the apartment and wanted to have sex in the stairwell. The building's security guard caught them, called the police, and blocked them from exiting. In a panic, Arjun ran up to the second-floor window and jumped out, breaking his foot and fracturing a vertebra in the impact.

"I didn't go to the hospital until the next morning. I was in so much pain, but I didn't know what to tell the doctor," he said. "And then I couldn't stop thinking about how I'd never know what happened to that guy."

My mind flashed to what might have happened in Jeddah had the security guard held fast to my arm in the stairwell—or if he had caught Naji or Hameed instead of me.

Inside the tunnel, the three of us skirted a large, stagnant puddle that filled most of the road. The tunnel clearly had some kind of drainage issue; it had rained a bit recently, and the unfinished road dipped, but this much standing water shouldn't have gathered. To stay dry, we shimmied along the concrete barricade at the edge of the tunnel like a balance beam, daring each other not to fall in.

We emerged on the other side of the tunnel a half hour later under a low, dark sky. The swiftness of the weather change was extraordinary, but so was the very presence of gray skies. I had spent five years feeling like I didn't need to check the weather forecast because the danger of being caught beneath a thundercloud in the Gulf felt so astronomically low. But the storm quickly descended, and it arrived in a torrent. Shivani and Arjun sprinted to their cars, and I ran back to my apartment under heavy sheets of rain. I watched from my window as the tunnel in which we had been standing flooded completely. I thought of wadis, the low valleys in Oman that filled up fast—how I'd seen news reports about a few clouds in the sky morphing into deadly flash floods. You were safe until you suddenly weren't.

We largely escaped the deluge, but it had been a close call. That afternoon, news broke that the storm had been one of UAE's largest on record. Wind speeds had reached over 125 kilometers per hour, hurricane strength. In a country where fewer than four inches of annual precipitation fell each year, nearly four times that much—a foot of rain—had fallen over the course of the storm system.

When Sunil returned from work, we stared out together across the carnage. He pulled out a blueprint for one of his infrastructure projects he had been working on that day, a storm drainage system. As we sat on the balcony, he explained the detailed calculations they used in their planning, like industry-standard sizing that incorporated probability and statistics of local weather phenomena. These meteorological events were named after their own likelihood, ten- and twenty-year floods, he explained. But that day's storm had been the rarest and most catastrophic: a hundred-year flood. Sunil rolled the blueprint back up and said these simply weren't feasible to prepare for because of their exceptional improbability—the kind of event people might never see in their entire lifetime.

"Building a system large enough to account for the worst possible storm isn't seen as something that makes sense in planning," he said, tucking his work back into his bag. "For them, it's just better to expect some damage from a fluke when it does come." As we sat in silence, I wondered who "them" was and thought about my own encounters with danger, the risks I accepted spelunking, cruising, and living on this island of happiness in the first place.

I returned to the underpass with Shivani as soon as the waters receded. When we emerged on the other side, this time under clear skies, we could just catch a glimpse of the construction site for the Louvre. We had both read the developers' terse acknowledgment in local papers a few months earlier about the death of a twenty-eight-year-old Pakistani construction worker. The articles were quick to mention that his was the first recorded fatality on the site. A fluke, the flippancy seemed to suggest. I wondered how long he had lived in the UAE, whether it felt like home. As we turned our back on the site, I mentioned another press release I had seen about the island's other crown jewel museum, the soon-to-be-constructed Guggenheim Abu Dhabi. Its legendary architect, Frank Gehry, had called Saadiyat "a clean slate in a country full of resources." A few steps ahead of me in the compacted sand, I heard Shivani wonder aloud if Gehry meant that the migrants constructing the site were themselves the expendable, replaceable resources. Her question was buffeted by the wind, gone before I could decide whether I was meant to respond.

We kept walking toward two mammoth hotels under construction along the beach. We'd explored in the vicinity before, watching their progress, but had never dared enter the well-guarded main building site, wandering instead amid the shells of naked cement casts of holiday homes along its periphery. These hotel sites would be completed before most of the island's residences were even built. Tens of thousands of visitors would experience the island as a place of temporality and hospitality—a short-term welcome—before anyone had ever really lived here. Before, perhaps, the opportunity to really get to know a place. I wondered what I would write had I been asked to pen my guidebook here instead.

My phone buzzed as we picked our way through construction dust past a pair of discarded safety gloves, the reinforced fingertips already frayed. I had received a seven-second voice note from an unfamiliar number. I hit play, realizing I didn't even recognize the international code.

"Hello. I am now in the Philippines because I was deported. Because I am a ladyboy. Please call me."

I had set all my voice notes to play at two-times speed, and the distorted, artificially hastened voice bounced strangely through the empty carcass of the villa. When Shivani asked me to play it again, I realized she was staring at me and had abruptly stopped walking. Motioning her back toward the exit, I looked for the setting on my phone to slow the message down. I told her I'd play it again when we got back outside. I didn't want such urgency echoing all around me.

▽▽▽

It took a few minutes of back and forth to establish who was on the other end of the phone. The messages were so frenzied, a tumble of words—*arrested, jail, deported*—that the person hadn't actually offered their name. After a couple of back-and-forths, the caller finally stated their name: Gizelle, one of the bakla salon workers I had met two years earlier at Marie's party. I had a flash of a lone figure in the corner, braiding their own hair. Gizelle was the one who'd worked at the same salon as Sally, I remembered. I didn't even know I had given out my number. I sat down on a construction fence and asked him to start again from the beginning.

Gizelle explained that, two months earlier, he had gone to work at the salon like any normal, slow Tuesday. He began work at 10 a.m., completing a couple of pedicures and a few massages. Later, he got takeaway from a Lebanese restaurant and shared it with his colleagues while they sat around watching an Arabic film to pass the languid afternoon. He had concentrated hard on the film—he had a new Lebanese boyfriend and was trying to better learn Arabic for him. So he was slightly annoyed when an Emirati customer came in for a pedicure and kept asking questions in broken English about Gizelle's life in the UAE. An hour after the customer left, two police officers entered the salon and detained Gizelle. He wasn't told why, but when he got to the police car and saw two other bakla salon workers, he knew.

I asked if he thought one of his colleagues had ratted him out.

"No, I had a good relationship with them, even the serious Muslim one," he said with a strained laugh that betrayed his exasperation. He explained that all of his colleagues knew he was gay, and some of them were even genuinely curious in a good-natured manner about his love life. Sometimes they teased him, but it was in a fraternal way, he said; they also respected him for bringing in business and getting along well with their customers.

"I think it was a roundup," he said.

I remembered speaking with Marie, Gizelle, and the others about the UAE authorities' periodic anti-crossdressing campaigns. I'd also seen news stories about them: one report from 2010 even encouraged citizens to report crossdressing to an anonymous hotline. "A team from the Criminal Investigations Department will go to the location and detain these cross-dressers at once. The caller's details will remain confidential. They will not be called to the police station or the public prosecution at all for inquiries. Even if the crossdressers were not causing any problems, dressing up as women in public places is violating the laws here," the authority had announced.

Once at the police station, Gizelle was interrogated about his residency—he did not have his ID card on him, and for this was chastised—and told to take off his clothes for a strip search. His heart fell when he heard the demand because he knew he would be found wearing women's underwear under his work scrubs. Gizelle said the two police officers laughed as they took photos of him naked. Before he was given any information about going to court, he was forced to sign a paper in Arabic he didn't understand, which he later realized was a confession to crossdressing.

Gizelle said he was transported to a prison outside Abu Dhabi and put in a cell with three other men, none of whom spoke English or Tagalog. After Gizelle's court appearance several weeks later, he was deported back to the Philippines. He had just gotten credit on his phone and was calling people to let them know he was gone. He said he was troubled by the fact that he did not know the location of the other bakla he saw in the police car that day. I thought about Arjun, haunted by the same unknown fate of his cruising partner.

"It's not true, your honor, I am no crossdresser!" he said to me suddenly, like I was a judge on the other end of the phone. He was suddenly wry. "I am a full woman!"

I asked what he meant. He explained that he had been taking estrogen pills since a few months after the party. I asked if he was transgender, and he dodged my question with a joke: "It's to make my tittles more fabulous," he said. I had heard about a healthy trade among some bakla in the Gulf for these illegal pills. Because he was taking them, he said the charges were factually incorrect. "See, I'm not a gay now! I'm whatever you want, your honor!" Gizelle laughed.

I felt a kind of twisted relief that Gizelle could find the beguiling humor, a kind of impishness, in what felt to me like a bleak situation. But the truth was that being transgender wouldn't have helped in the UAE. A surprising Medical Liability Law had just been enacted in mid-2016 to allow gender reassignment surgery in the UAE, but the law defined the necessity of the surgical procedure "by which a transgender person's physical appearance and function of their existing sexual characteristics are altered to resemble that of their identified gender" strictly as "part of a treatment for gender dysphoria in transgender people, as advised by a medical commission to be set up for this purpose." Unfortunately for Gizelle, she would thus not be included. "Our laws are based on Sharia," an Emirati lawyer was quoted as saying when the surprising law was announced. "If a person has both organs and one is hidden, for example, they have a right to undergo a sex-change operation. But a complete woman with female organs wanting a sex-change operation is unacceptable."

In the eyes of the UAE legal system, any kind of queerness—gayness, transness, crossdressing—was conflated and punishable by law. A distinction didn't matter. But Gizelle also troubled LGBTQ+ community definitions that I understood as a Westerner; as she spoke, she slipped in and out of pronouns, called herself gay, straight, a man and a woman. In one breath, she said she was in a gay relationship; in another, she was adamant that she was only breaking the premarital sex law because she was a woman sleeping with a man.

"I am fucking my Arab boyfriend before marriage, your honor!" she said in mock histrionics, still roleplaying. "That's the real problem!"

I had noted this kind of fluid language and logic around queerness with other bakla in the UAE. I also saw it in an op-ed written in a Filipino newspaper entitled "Lessons learned of an OFW after facing deportation," written by a bakla resident who had been deported from Dubai. "I also used to take pills to minimize Adam's apple and the male muscles in the body. I can't explain my happiness every time [my boyfriend and I] are together and I live like a real woman...I am not ignorant of the law. Homosexuality is against Sharia law; that's clear to me. In case I really couldn't control my feelings then. But it is true that there is no forever." Queer, gay, transgender: the slippage felt both troubling and wily.

With Gizelle, it was difficult to parse what was a joke, what was second language, and what he really believed. Perhaps that was real queerness: in speaking and defining herself with shifting identifiers, she was subverting not just UAE laws but my own attempts at trying to classify and categorize him by my expectations in the LGBTQ+ community. I realized I was unsettled by his continued courtroom playacting; the skit no longer felt like a skit. I did suddenly feel like his judge, making value judgments about a situation that I didn't, and perhaps couldn't, fully understand.

Our voice notes grew shorter throughout the afternoon. When I thought they were wrapping up, he asked if I could do him a favor: go to his flat, which still held most of his belongings, and ship some essentials back to him in Manila. He was apologetic but explained that he didn't want to risk getting his remaining bakla friends in the UAE into any trouble. I asked what he needed, and he said he just wanted a few things, a mix of the practical and the sentimental: some photos, his electronics, a few documents he didn't have scanned.

But there was one more thing, he said, his voice growing sheepish and quiet for the first time. He admitted he had started sex work a few months earlier. He was giving purposefully erotic massages to extract tips from customers and had also been meeting some men outside of work. He kept a wad of cash in a drawer and wanted me to send it to him through Western Union, ashamed even to tell his friends, though he had suspicions that several had also dabbled in sex work. Even in the queer community, I realized, there could be the desire to appear perfect, the attempt to seem like the exemplary resident. I remembered a story I had seen two years earlier about two Pakistani men sentenced for having sex in a waste disposal room, the only place they could find privacy. They'd been caught by a Nigerian security guard and had turned on each other, one accusing the other of forcing himself on him in what read like an obvious case of self-preservation.

"What about the rest of your stuff?" I asked.

"I will be back," he said.

The statement seemed absurd, yet I recognized the determination in his voice to live in this place that could be read as outwardly hostile to him. He explained that he hoped to be able to obtain a fake passport. Even with the gender reassignment surgery he wanted (he called it "my sex change"), it was illegal even in the Philippines to change one's gender on their passport, so this was out of the question as a means of return to the UAE. If a fake passport didn't work, he explained, he would try again on his own with his assigned birth name in a few months. He had heard of other bakla who had succeeded this way; either the authorities didn't care, or their systems weren't good enough to keep track of deportations. Otherwise, if the UAE didn't work, he would look further afield in the Gulf.

I gently asked what he was going to do in the meantime. He lamented that he would have to go back to being a cam girl again to make a living and raise enough money to return to the UAE. I remembered at the party how he described the hours he'd spent each day cooped up in his bedroom masturbating online for American clients until his penis was sore, enacting East Asian tropes of subservience so he would get more tips.

Later that night, I went back to my notes and recordings from the party and found his voice above the melee. "Sometimes it was fun," he had said about his cam work, his voice seeming then to have more brightness, more effervescence. I remembered how when he told me these stories, it had all seemed so empowering and subversive: a sissy boy in the Philippines taking money from rich American businessmen to fund his way to the Gulf. Suddenly, four years later, I could only see the other, darker side: how he was dependent on a systemic objectification of his race and gender expression to pay his bills. I thought about his scant choices other than reengaging in this system, one of egregiously unbalanced power, in order to earn money to return to a country that might not even welcome him back.

Part of me wanted to tell him not to return. Why put himself through this? But then, what about me, I thought? Why did I feel the authority to declare what was right for someone else? Wasn't that in dangerous proximity to the people who told me I shouldn't be queer because it was wrong or hard—or that email from my former teacher so long ago, accosting me for my own decision to engage with the Middle East at all?

When Shivani met me the next day for another expedition, I told her I was compelled to write and publish a story about Gizelle's plight. I had been kept up all night, turning the idea over in my head. It felt so important, I tried to explain. I might affect some change here: question the nature of her detention, obtain information on whether a roundup of bakla really had occurred. Human Rights Watch and other organizations had amplified stories of court cases in the Gulf involving queer people before. Maybe this was the kind of story that would garner an international outcry.

And yet, the risk of deportation or serious consequences in the UAE seemed so small; I had witnessed so many balka who had thrived. I could already hear an editor pushing to frame the piece as people thriving "against all odds," but the very phrasing failed. It was possible—probable even—to succeed. Gizelle himself wanted to return.

I asked Shivani if she thought my writing the piece would do more harm than good, as we walked through a sparse area of Saadiyat where I'd read Neolithic pottery shards had recently been uncovered, potentially pushing the history of human civilization on this island back thousands of years earlier than previously known. It felt suddenly urgent to find and identify something ancient and visible and true. I tried to conceive of what might happen to the bakla community and others if the piece garnered an international outcry or campaign from a queer or migrant human rights organization. I told her to keep her eyes on the sand, and she told me what she had learned about the nomadic Rumaithat Tribe frequenting this island in the eighteenth century, collecting fish and wood from dense mangroves. I half-listened, wondering how I might frame the edges of Gizelle's story. The law was the law: Gizelle had broken it. Was it really the place of a queer migrant to come here, brash and defiant, and lobby a change in its norms? And was I worried about Gizelle, or myself?

I had briefly toyed with writing a story about Marie two years earlier, when I was just beginning to freelance, and I'd learned in my research that bakla had a long history of acceptance in the Philippines as a third gender. But their trajectory into subjugation and occasional persecution had shifted with the arrival of Spanish Catholic missionaries. Arriving colonizers had brought and spread their own beliefs about how sexuality should be defined. About how things should be in this place they weren't from.

I looked over at Shivani, wondering if she were even the right person to be discussing this with. Months after meeting her, I learned that she'd attended an American international school in Abu Dhabi. When I'd asked about the student body, she told me there had been a surprising diversity, even amidst the many American classmates—a diversity not unlike the kind I witnessed among the parkour athletes who frequented the Corniche each week. And yet, her teachers were largely American, as was the very basis of her curriculum. Maybe TCKs like Shivani were pushing against dominant culture and forming something new, as I had first thought while I watched her jumping over a city's infrastructure. But perhaps that force of domination was still exerting itself upon her—a kind of imperceptible power that defied detection or reckoning. In writing about bakla, or any queer migrant subcommunity, with the explicit aim of drawing attention to it, was I potentially wielding something similar that neither of us could see the beginning or end of?

I wondered what queerness had once looked like on this island—before the Louvre, before an American university campus filled with students from all over the world. Surely men had lain together in this very sand—during the times of the Rumaithat Tribe, yes, but also before that. I looked around at discarded plastic bags and construction flotsam. *A clean slate*, Frank Gehry had said. But this island that had been marketed as new and pristine for visitors had already been marked, history upon layered history complicated by cultures and belief systems and identities coming into tension with one another.

I watched my own feet combing through the sand, Shivani leading the way. I wasn't sure what to look for and yet was holding out hope that we might spot it—perhaps a shard of something, half-obscured yet still familiar enough in shape or pattern to be identified. I wondered what I would do if I actually found something. Leave it? Move it? Claim it as my own?

▽▽▽

A few weeks after Gizelle's belongings were safely on their way to Manila, I caught a flight with Sunil to Australia. Buckling our seatbelts, he encouraged me to shut my brain off and sleep as much as possible during the fifteen-hour flight. We would have family commitments on my actual birthday, he explained, so he'd planned a full itinerary of early surprises the day after our arrival. *I'm making up for it*, he apologized as we taxied down the runway, but I wasn't bothered; I couldn't really conceive of a birthday celebration in Australia. And life seemed to require these kinds of concessions anyway, sometimes without even fully grasping what an alternative might have looked like.

Sunil roused me soon after dawn the next morning in Sydney and drove us to the Taronga Zoo. The name was an Aboriginal word meaning "beautiful place," he said, a fitting title for a spot that looked out upon the multitude of coves and bays in the Sydney Harbor that had first enticed British colonial explorers centuries earlier. But we were going to have the best view of all, he said, smirking and coy as he pulled into the parking lot. I only understood what he meant after we walked inside: we would be scaling a ropes course high above the zoo. We traversed wooden suspension bridges and ziplines whose views encompassed both the harbor and the jagged city skyline. I found myself instead staring down at the enclosures of the native species beneath us: koalas, wombats, kangaroos, animals whose images in picture books and encyclopedia diagrams had offered a first window into Australia, a child's understanding of a foreign landscape.

The truth was, I still had no real connection to or grasp of this place even after four years with Sunil. The closest I had come to an encounter with the country before I met him was when a letter embossed in black and gold arrived in my mailbox one spring afternoon when I was twelve: I had been invited to take part in a program called People to People, a student ambassador exchange program founded by a public diplomacy agency of the US government in 1956 to, as the letter said, "bridge cultural and political borders through education and exchange, creating global citizens and making the world a better place for future generations." As I read the letter, I daydreamed vaguely about a trip to a strange land on the other side of the world until the multi-thousand-dollar price tag put the whole notion out of reach. The path I had dreamt of—a month-long sojourn traversing a foreign continent—suddenly no longer existed, and since I had scarcely begun to conceive of what the trip would even look like, I quickly felt like it had never been a real prospect at all.

Surprise begot surprise after the ropes course: a motorcycle ride across the Sydney Harbor bridge became lunch at the Opera House became a sunset sail through the harbor, a romantic whistle-stop tour of some of the city's highlights. The increasingly elaborate gestures should have betrayed that Sunil's birthday story was a ruse, but it wasn't until I returned to the deck of the sailboat from the bathroom and saw the captain motoring away into the sunset like some Bond villain that I realized what was happening. Sunil pulled a ring box from his pocket. Though he must have said the words, I can only remember the shapes his mouth made as he asked the question I hadn't ever thought I'd be allowed to hear.

As he stood before me waiting for an answer, I cycled through the events of the day as if watching them on a projector and wondered: if same-sex marriage had been within the realm of any possible imagined future during my childhood, might I not have been so oblivious to the now-recognizable signs of his impending proposal? For so long, marriage never felt like a tangible prospect for me. Even as I witnessed the possibility of men marrying men gain legal momentum across a broad swath of countries, Sunil had never been able to make a true public romantic gesture to me in the Gulf, and so my very perception of what was quotidian and what might be grand was scrambled. I had no point of reference for what all this—an extravagant proposal, a queer future together—could even look like.

I said yes.

We embraced. Sunil pulled some champagne from a mini fridge beneath the sail rigging, explaining that we were going to spend the night on the boat in celebration—a final surprise in a day stuffed with them. I sat on the gunwale of the boat and considered all the signs I had missed, cracking a joke about whether Sunil had the captain's number on speed dial in case, in shock, I'd said no.

Looking out across the great expanse of water, I noticed the clouds beginning to gather in the northeast. I let Sunil lead me by the hand below deck to escape the rain. I thought of the storm that had pelted Abu Dhabi, my close escape from a hundred-year event, and looked over at the man I had just agreed to marry. Suddenly aware of all the things I had missed, I watched him attempt to appear casual while opening each cupboard and drawer on the boat as the wind whipped closed the companionway door leading to the upper deck. I gently asked Sunil what he was doing, and he grimaced, leading me to the boat's barebones bedroom with nothing more than an empty mattress atop a wooden bedframe. For all his meticulous planning to arrange the day's event—months of secret phone calls and spreadsheets when I was out of our apartment—he had forgotten that the boat operator asked if he needed bedding. We laughed and polished off the champagne, balling up our clothes for pillows and huddling for warmth.

I tried to sleep atop the naked mattress, but I could feel a violence in the churn of the waves. Sunil had curated a full day around the safety of the harbor, but now that the storm was out on the open water, I wondered whether the refuge of this vessel would be enough. Could we wake the next morning having drifted far off course, out into the Pacific, never to be heard from again? I tossed in bed, suddenly anxious about not understanding the mechanics of precisely how—and by what—we were anchored in place. My whole childhood, where my deepest desires were met with an abhorrence intended to make me feel unwelcome in the place I called home, had been consumed with the notion of escape, even when I couldn't conceptualize what an alternative place or state might look like. It was certainly not a city in the Gulf, let alone a marriage to a man. I wondered, as the waves tossed the boat and I felt my stomach churn, what it would be like to live here, to shift my life to Australia, this place I had no ties to except through this man to whom I had just agreed to legally bind myself.

We were affixed in a harbor just around the bend from where James Cook first landed and deemed its waters safe, charting the way for British settlement. None of this history or space felt like mine, but perhaps it now would be, bestowed upon me through marriage. Or perhaps I should have always felt the burden of this history, and I had just been oblivious.

Whenever I traveled somewhere new, I was always fascinated by the flicker of time—sometimes just a day, or perhaps even a few hours just after I arrived—when I could still remember with perfect clarity my earlier perceptions of that place, unchallenged by the reality of actually being there. It was as though during that small window I could see unincumbered down two paths: a time when I thought I understood a place through whatever signifiers I had learned of it, and the future when all that was swiftly blown away by experience and veracity. After the clamor of the day, I could barely remember what I had thought Australia would be like from the scraps of depictions I had seen throughout my life.

I thought again about People to People, the program had seemed so noble until I later learned the organization was in fact a for-profit company employing dubious marketing tactics for their expensive de-facto vacations, including using the forged signature of a Virginia state senator in an attempt to suggest a government affiliation that no longer existed. I once showed Sunil the letter I had kept all those years, and he noticed that it still used the colonial term "Ayer's Rock" for Uluru, the sandstone monolith of spiritual significance to the local Aboriginal population, despite a government decree over a decade before my letter was sent giving the shrine back its original name. I wondered what my perceptions of Australia would have been had I first traveled there all those years ago. Surely, a morally questionable travel company wouldn't have prioritized encounters with the reality of the country, including swaths of diverse people—immigrants, migrants, those like Sunil's family ("the only brown people in town," he would always say)—who had helped build and shape the place.

As we swayed precariously in the middle of the harbor, I was confronted by the tightness of the day's events across a few square kilometers: nothing too far or arduous for my first day in Australia, despite the monumental occasion. I wondered what I hadn't, or wouldn't, see with Sunil. What, then, of engagement, of marriage?

I looked over at Sunil, peaceful in his slumber despite the awkward sleeping arrangement. The love I felt for this man who had bunched his shorts into mine because he knew I slept with two pillows was already obscuring the ambiguity I had harbored, only hours earlier, about queer nuptials. I had always felt like my place as a queer man was out on land, stalking the shore in the night for other men, but here I was sequestered out on the open sea. The mirth of the day had already begun to plaster over the skepticism I'd had whenever I saw a viral video of a queer person's ostentatious proposal. I'd felt that the grandiosity of the gesture was rooted unconsciously in an attempt to counteract others' perceptions; that the very act of marriage was playing into someone else's hand.

Maybe entering into an agreement to build a life with someone, and the gestures and ceremony surrounding it all, was a bit like trying to discover and understand a new place. Profit, inequity, and privilege were undeniable. Even in queerness and migration, even in trying to start a life outside of the frameworks one had once known, these forces were still here, too, waiting.

When the captain came to pick us up the next morning, he confessed that he had almost pulled the plug on our overnight stay due to the storm. I was heartened that we had weathered it. Maybe it had actually been an auspicious sign after all: if we could endure that, maybe the equivocal feelings I had about marriage had been misplaced. We spent another week in Australia, and I felt these worries dim. I began to look forward to the prospect of having our relationship legally recognized. We would be joining something; we could enter into an institution that would afford us rights and offer us a seat at the table.

As we celebrated, I let voice notes from Gizelle pile up. For all the compassion I had for his situation, I suddenly felt like he wasn't the right person around whom to structure one of the first ever magazine articles about the queer community in the Gulf: a sex worker, brash and loud, someone who troubled the categories for the LGBTQ+ community that seemed to finally be gaining the foothold of acceptance. I realized what I wanted was to write a piece about a more model queer—someone who was doing a slightly better job of fitting in. After all, didn't Gizelle admit that his own ostentatiousness had likely drawn the attention of the authorities, ultimately leading to his deportation? Perhaps writing instead about someone with a little more restraint, I decided—the kind I was demonstrating by settling down—was a better choice. Or maybe just not writing the article, not rocking the boat at all, would be the most prudent of all.

As I closed my laptop with boarding complete on our return flight, I realized that the tabs and folders I had created for Gizelle's story, the ones I kept perpetually open on my laptop, had been replaced that week by pages on marriage laws and wedding planners over two continents. Waiting for takeoff, Sunil seemed especially quiet as he absently spun the globe on the electronic flight map, following coastlines and flight paths. I watched him zoom in and out on countries as if trying them on for size.

"I think I'm ready to leave," he said.

It felt like we had been stuck on the tarmac for some time, but it was always difficult for me to tell when we were in motion. I always needed to look out my own window for points of reference. I told him it had been a dream of a trip, two weeks in this place I'd barely known, but that I was ready to get back home to the UAE, too. I reached out to hold his hand, still surprised by the band of metal around my finger.

"No, I mean, I think I'm ready to *leave* leave," he said. It was futile to be married in a country where it was illegal, he said. He was doing what he had done four years earlier on our early drives back and forth to Dubai, I realized: he was telling me about his dreams for the future. But, in doing so, he was imagining a somewhere else.

I was suddenly reminded of James testing me about returning

to New York, and how the very question made it feel like my world was shrinking. I let Sunil keep talking, turning his words—an alternative future—over in my head like a stone. We could still make it work in the Gulf despite the danger, I thought; we had done it so far. I didn't really believe what had happened to Gizelle would happen to us. The chances were so low. And anyway, we were doing our best not to attract attention, I rationalized. We could carry on.

The pilot came on and announced turbulence as soon as we took off. We would be passing through another storm. I tightened my seatbelt. I had flown so many times, but storms still unsettled me. I was embarrassed that they could still catch me so off guard.

I looked over at Sunil. He had not declared where he wanted to be, just a desire for departure. But with him, in this new calculation of our relationship—of all relationships, a same-sex marriage—I now had a new potential port of arrival and settlement in my future, perhaps a constellation of them.

I thought about those settlers in Sydney Harbor, what their arrival had wrought. I willed the turbulence to abate, but it was relentless. Sunil gripped my hand. I fixed my gaze out my tiny window as we skipped over dark clouds, unsure which was more distressing: the distance between our plane and the ground or the chasm between our imagined futures.

PART III:

BETWEEN

9: A JOURNEY

(Door County, Wisconsin; Djibouti City, Djibouti; Abu Dhabi: Ahmed and Noor)

THERE WAS A LINE SOMEWHERE, but I wasn't yet sure if I'd crossed it.

I paged through my passport as I waited for two mimosas at the Abu Dhabi International Airport, flipping past recent stamps from Saudi Arabia, Kuwait, Bahrain, Yemen, Australia. Even though I was still in the UAE, it felt like I should already have a stamp for the US as well: moments earlier, a US Customs and Border Protection agent with a thick Texas drawl had cleared me to enter the United States. Seventeen hours later, I would breeze through O'Hare International Airport in Chicago without any security screening—the privilege of a domestic traveler despite the fact that my plane had taken off half a world away.

The United States government established this unusual program, US Customs and Border Preclearance, in 2014 in Abu Dhabi to, according to the congressional authorization act, "prevent inadmissible persons from entering the United States." Though preclearance had a history that dated back to 1952, the UAE was the first country outside of North America to receive a site besides Ireland, and the decision to establish one in the Middle East raised more than a few eyebrows. But it was the legality after clearance that confounded me. In Ireland, though US officials were primarily stationed to facilitate ease of entry into the United States, they could also detain someone whom they reasonably suspected to have committed an indictable offense under Irish law. In a country like the United Arab Emirates, with stricter morality laws, the space felt even more fraught: any traveler who passed through preclearance facilities technically remained in the legal jurisdiction of the host country, but US authorities also retained the right to arrest or detain travelers. I felt the strange reach of two authorities, two legalities, at once as I sat back down next to Sunil.

Across from us, I watched a woman place two American passports on the same table before resting her head on her male traveling companion's broad shoulder, slotting her hand through the open button of his shirt, and closing her eyes. I wondered if anyone would dare arrest us if I tried the same thing with Sunil, or if we were comparatively safer in the lounge than outside at one of the gates, in view of roving authorities. I let my thighs spread open, touching my knee to Sunil's, but he moved his leg away. There seemed to be no information, no model, for what might happen to us in this liminal space; we would be the example court case setting legal precedent. I shifted in my chair, noticing that Sunil had chosen the ungainly single seats, too low for the table, instead of the two-person, loveseat-style sofa the straight couple now occupied.

"Are you ready?" he asked.

I wasn't, but I didn't want to say it aloud. We were returning to the United States to look at wedding venues. We had chosen the US because of my family, but also because it felt like the only option: same-sex relationships—let alone marriage—remained illegal in the Gulf, and only civil partnerships were recognized in Australia. We had briefly considered a low-key unofficial party in the UAE, but it felt too risky: in 2005, authorities detained over two dozen men in a Dubai hotel chalet after a raid on what they described as a mass homosexual wedding. Officials declared that the men could face lashings, hormone treatment, or imprisonment for five years. Even in Australia, known for its socially liberal citizenry, twenty-two bills to legalize same-sex marriage were proposed and resoundingly rejected in parliament between 2004 and 2017. So

America it was.

I watched Sunil cycling between Excel spreadsheets, his mimosa going untouched as he fine-tuned our schedule: which wedding vendors we were meeting, when, where. He was so organized, so prepared for all this, it seemed. But I also spotted another tab open: a job application in London. He had seen an internal posting at his company a few weeks earlier and gingerly shown it to me.

Sunil had been dancing around moving to the UK since our flight back from Australia. I could hear him trying to get me to be, if not enamored with the idea, then at least curious about it. He peppered London into our conversations and spoke nostalgically about visiting his older siblings there on unaccompanied overseas trips when he was younger, sneaking out to gay bars and enjoying the city as a naïve visitor. The mental through-line as to why he was talking about all this now was easy for me to follow: London was the place where his brother had married and where his sister had moved after her own wedding. Our moving there made sense to him in a lot of ways. He'd bring it up while casually cooking dinner, watching TV, driving through the city, trying to gauge my reaction. He had been working for a government developer in the UAE, but that was where he was seconded; the company that actually employed him was British. "Why not try the mothership?" he'd asked me repeatedly.

I was struck by his use of the word "mothership," picturing us on an alien craft, spending our life hurtling through space on some futile mission until we were called back home. He meant "mothership" in regard to the headquarters of his employer, but it seemed to be how he regarded the UK in general; he had an attachment to the Commonwealth as an Australian that I, as an American, couldn't understand, a kind of inarticulable, untranslatable connection with the place. The muddling of the US and UAE I felt in Preclearance, the ill-defined space between them, evoked the same unease I felt contending with the invisible, alien British orbit that exerted itself on Sunil.

I tried to rub the outside of his knee again but felt his eyes squarely on the straight couple.

"We're almost there," he said, pulling away. Through his gritted teeth, I couldn't tell if he was annoyed or relieved. I also wasn't sure whether "there" meant our arrival in the US or our flight out of the UAE, whether on this particular holiday or in terms of some tangible, definite departure that felt near to him. "We can be a normal couple soon," he said, leaning in to take a swig of his drink, his voice low.

I responded by holding out my right hand toward him with great ceremony. He lowered his eyes as if to question me, but I knew he knew what was coming, and I watched a little smile cross his lips. He grasped my hand with his, and I declared, with much purposefully overwrought and affected stiffness and formality, "Good business meeting," looking over at the straight couple. As I vigorously shook his hand, pretending to be a grateful client, I rubbed the inside of his palm with my index finger. Even as he rolled his eyes at me, he smiled and rubbed my palm back. It had been our secret way of showing affection in public for years—a joking, knowing artifice. We instinctively knew when to employ it, rolling it out especially when one of us needed a bit of encouragement, solace, or an apology and we weren't able to provide it in public. I used it in that moment to provide a bit of levity, but I had never regarded it as a coping mechanism or substitution. It was an alternative language we had developed and that we loved. We didn't need someone else's metric for normality.

▽▽▽

She shifted her weight from leg to leg, looking uncomfortable no matter how she positioned herself in front of us. Before we had a chance to shake off jet lag, we stood in a midcentury Midwestern resort in northern Wisconsin in front of a wedding venue manager flipping her blonde hair every time she moved her feet. It seemed like an anxious tick, and the way she laughed too much after each sentence we uttered betrayed the fact that we were the ones making her nervous.

"Wedding dress trains look stunning coming down this staircase," she said. "I mean—" she countered, before cutting herself off awkwardly. She walked backward through the venue, from the hallway to the receiving room and out into the garden. I was sure she was going to trip, but it was like she didn't want to turn her back on us, as if, if she turned around, we might descend upon her like a pair of gay wolves. The nervous woman handed Sunil a pamphlet, and I watched a dawning recognition on her face as he thumbed through page after page of women and men, a perfectly bound, glossy sales pitch for legally recognized, heterosexual coupledom.

It seemed like she had never led a same-sex couple on a tour of her venue. To alleviate the awkwardness, she asked why we were considering this place. "It's the only place where it's legal," I replied, before Sunil gave me a little kick, and I realized she was asking specifically about her venue.

I tried to smile and play along. I reached out for Sunil's hand, but I felt him tense up. It was a reflex I recognized—I had done it in Australia, too, on the day he proposed. Even in places where LGBTQ+ rights were more enshrined, it would still take us days before we began to publicly express any affection. To refrain from doing so was the reality we lived and knew.

"What's your vision?" she asked suddenly as we stood at the threshold between the hall and the garden. Sunil and I stared at each other. "For the wedding," she clarified. This time, I felt myself shifting my weight, suddenly uncomfortable with the prospect of having to account for all our decisions.

I realized we didn't really have a vision. We had planned on getting married in the US because it was our only viable option, but we didn't actually know what the event itself would look like. Perhaps this inability to envision an ideal was informed by our inability to ever be a couple in public. I thought again about our little handshakes; it seemed like queer people had always charted their own way forward like this through hostile waters. It didn't feel endemic to the Gulf. Hadn't queer people always made our own maps?

We talked through our limited wedding venue options in a Wisconsin dive bar beneath a television blaring a FOX News report on President Trump tweeting about the barring of transgender people from the US military. It was an environment that felt familiar to me even after so many years away, and we instinctively kept our voices down without needing to remind one another. It felt like another kind of handshake. We made a list—a historic church, a resort lodge, a yacht club—and then promptly crossed them all off: too religious, too touristy, too stuffy. We had toured multiple venues, and each felt deflating. Wasn't there something else, a different way, a nod to queerness itself?

Sunil reopened his laptop and pulled up his tabs again, but I was busy looking through my own: speeches by and interviews with American queer rights activists lamenting the national push for what they felt was a demand for acceptance into an inherently straight, subjugating, and assimilationist institution. He wanted me to help brainstorm, but my mind was elsewhere. Stumped for ideas, I downed my beer and went to the bathroom.

At the urinal, I sensed the familiar weight of eyes on my body. The figure beside me was taking me in, I could feel it. But when I tried to make eye contact, the burly man was staring not toward my groin but at the top of my head. His eyes were glassy, and he fumbled for his zipper, swaying, drunk in the middle of the afternoon.

"What does that say?" he asked, pointing toward my head. I was suddenly conscious that I was wearing a cap, neon green, with Arabic script.

"Oh, it says 'cool' in Arabic. But it's kind of an ironic joke," I said, moving hurriedly to the sink.

"Why are you wearing that? You think you're funny?" he asked. I felt the sudden bite of malice in his questions. "You bring Arabic here, man?" He came up behind me. I moved toward the hand dryer to put space between our bodies. He was suddenly venomous, staggering at me. I sized him up—a full head taller than me, and more built. But he was also drunk, I reasoned, so perhaps I could take him if it came to blows. It was the kind of quick calculation of perceived and real danger that I'd been doing all my life, not just in the UAE, but also here, since I was young, in this place that was supposed to be home.

I pushed out the door. "And who's that towelhead you're with?" he asked.

I made my way to our barstool, telling Sunil to down his beer so we could leave. What could have been the start of a cruising encounter had ended with me being accosted for wearing a cap perceived as foreign. I had taken risks cruising for so many years, not sure whether the man next to me was interested or disgusted. As we drove away, I thought about the words—both hateful and imprecise—he had aimed at Sunil, confounded by how life in the US, with a president spouting off anti-trans tweets and signing executive orders to begin constructing border walls, was idealized as a home for both queer people and migrants.

Sunil made a dark joke about how he was surprised the man didn't pull a gun—"This being America and all"—and I instinctively checked the rearview mirror. Four years earlier, a skinhead fatally shot six people in a Wisconsin Sikh temple in what was reportedly mistaken anti-Muslim terrorism. I had left for Yemen in 2009, all those years ago, specifically to remove myself from this environment of both blind ignorance and xenophobia, and yet now the call to affirm our relationship in the eyes of dominant cultural forces had pulled me right back—and pulled this man I loved into palpable danger.

My knuckles grew white gripping the steering wheel. I chastised myself for wearing the hat. Of course it would stick out; hadn't I known that? Had I been asking for trouble? I thought of all the times I had to police myself as a queer person—*say this, don't say that; act like this, not like that*—and wondered about all the times Sunil had to do the same, not only because of his sexuality but also because of his race. Moments I hadn't even registered. Maybe our future nuptials, what we couldn't envision at the wedding venue, were easiest—or best—as an act of purposeful, concerted assimilation. Maybe the goal should always be to make as few waves as possible.

When we got back to the hotel, one of the sites where we could get married, we sat on a porch swing on a peninsula jutting out into a lake. We leafed through the wedding packet of the first lodge, past all the photos of white brides and grooms, men and women making a vow. We'd decided the only vision we had for our wedding was a celebration centered around food—the kind of Arabic hospitality we had witnessed—where we could bring together through cuisine the places we were from: a hodgepodge of Midwestern bratwurst, Middle Eastern fattoush, Australian lamingtons. We looked at the food options in the packet: beef, fish, chicken.

"This peninsula feels like the Corniche," I said to Sunil, looking out upon the large rocks acting as breakwater. The wood of the swing we sat on, the one where we could sit for wedding photos if we chose this venue, reminded me of the recessed benches where men came to join their bodies together each night in a different kind of commitment. The Wisconsin summer night was nowhere near as humid as Abu Dhabi, but it suddenly felt all the more stifling.

Maybe getting married, relocating to a place where we could be legally out, and stopping cruising so we could be the perfect little gay couple was the right move, I tried to rationalize. We could reflect back the image the world wanted to see: assimilating queers playing by the rules of a place where we should be grateful for being recognized by law. But it nagged at me. Actions like cruising, like our handshake, didn't seem strictly improvisatory; they seemed like means of surmounting staid ways of operating. Couldn't a freer way of being—a different way to live—exist?

I thought about whether Gizelle, Sunil, and I could be considered "model minorities," the term coined in the 1960s by American sociologist William Petersen to reckon with how Asian immigrants, despite their marginalization, had achieved "success" in the United States. But who was measuring this success, I thought, and by what metrics? I wondered whether choosing cruising, or even just choosing not to marry, not to assimilate, would look like the opposite of success. I stood up with Sunil, and we headed inside. It was the exact reverse of the path we could take down the aisle at this venue, one we would soon follow unless we decided to do something different.

We brushed our teeth in silence in his and hers sinks and listened to the porch swing creak in the breeze. Even decades from now, I reasoned, nothing could stop us from sitting on that swing together if we didn't marry and our relationship remained outside the confines of a heteronormative legal and moral framework. I pictured us squeezing together to fit a third—or fourth—alongside us, though articulating these scenarios practically, or even conceptually, to so many people in our lives would surely prove exhausting, if not entirely unsuccessful.

Perhaps it would always remain beyond the capacity of some people's imagination to understand why others operate the way they do: move to a foreign country, make a life in a way that comes into tension with prescribed norms. It seemed entirely likely that the man at the bar, or someone like him, would be anywhere, incoherent yet paradoxically demanding an explanation for what was perceived as deviance. Maybe pursuing safety above all else really was folly, just as trying to marry was asking for an acceptance we would never actually receive. I just wasn't sure whether endeavoring to operate as a beacon of queerness and reject institutions altogether was any less fanciful. Was this even possible in the Gulf? I could sense a loose patchwork of assimilation, risk, belonging, and privilege before me, but perhaps I could never make my way to the other side.

I spat and watched the toothpaste drain down the sink. Through the window, I could just make out in the darkness that we had left the wedding catalog sitting on the bench. I climbed into bed next to Sunil, deciding to let the nighttime dew claim it. I would relish paging through it in the morning, each warped photo unrecognizable.

▽▽▽

An impending wedding, a potential move, a queer future with Sunil: instead of contending with any of it directly, I bought a flight to Djibouti with no return ticket. I had stories that needed to be written, and I didn't know how long they would take me. My remaining time in the region felt truncated, and with the Yemen guidebook indefinitely shelved, I found myself turning to a project I'd wanted to pursue on the shape and nature of asylum, whether this protection was achieved through a process of claiming or bestowal, and whether the distinction mattered. It was not a status I needed—though, looking at the political landscape of our respective countries, it wasn't inconceivable that we one day would—but it felt urgently linked not only to my own questions of peril but to how I understood assimilation.

The ongoing war in Yemen precluded my travel to the country. Freelance journalists were almost always liable for their own safety and accountable for their own cover—a daunting litany that could include travel, medical, medevac, kidnapping, ransom, and body repatriation insurances—and despite the risks I exposed myself to in the Gulf, this all seemed a bridge too far. Instead, I decided I could write about the country from a wider angle, a kind of sequel to one of my first major stories about living with Yemen's activist rock band during the height of the Arab Spring protests, the story whose publication prompted Sunil to surprise me with our first celebratory trip to Dubai. I could pen a kind of follow-up on one of the band members, Omar, five years later. We had stayed in touch via periodic texts and social media, and I knew he had fled Yemen and was stuck in Djibouti. His escape, and his relationship to the very notion of mobility, might inform my own.

Since studying in Yemen, I had been intrigued by Djibouti, a small country sitting just across the Bab Al Mandeb strait, the perilous "Gate of Tears." There, the Arabian Gulf pinched into the Gulf of Aden and then the Red Sea, with trade flowing from Asia, through the Suez Canal, and on into Europe. I was captivated by how a seemingly insignificant country roughly the size of New Jersey had such a surprisingly long history of strategic trade and military importance.

But Djibouti also had a parallel history in the role of human migration: it was the place where migrants from East and Sub-Saharan Africa reached a critical point in a daunting voyage to the wealthy Gulf, journeys that were usually illegal and often life-threatening. A risky boat journey from Djibouti into Yemen began a perilous 1,200-mile trek across the land border into Saudi Arabia. The end goal: employment in a country where asylum was near impossible and undocumented workers were routinely exploited, jailed, or deported—often in succession.

But since the start of the Saudi-led bombing campaign in Yemen, the migration route had suddenly reversed, with Yemenis fleeing their own country for Djibouti. A place that had been the point of embarkation for one group had now become a destination for another. Many Yemenis ended up in Markazi, a scorching UN refugee camp in the Djiboutian desert, but I made a plan to meet

Omar in the capital, Djibouti City, where some Yemenis with the economic means were able to rent long-term hotel rooms or negotiate apartments off the books.

We met not in his apartment but in a ramshackle café off a commercial side street. Though it was only May, the place sweltered, and we greedily sipped Coca-Colas, dabbing our foreheads with cheap tissues. Omar explained that he lived in a windowless room with no air conditioning. I had lived with him in the band's house in Sana'a, which had its own drawbacks—temperamental plumbing, threadbare furniture—but his current living situation sounded dire. He felt ambivalence about living in Djibouti, and when I tried to tease out the root of this unsureness, he confessed something I hadn't known.

"I am half Djiboutian," he said.

Despite having lived with him, written about him, and communicated with him for years, this was a part of his story he had not divulged. Taking into account the two countries' proximity, I knew a child being born of a Yemeni father and a Djiboutian mother wasn't an unusual occurrence. But its regularity did not necessarily make the identity accepted in either place: I had heard, in the streets of Sana'a, Yemenis with African heritage called "muwaladeen," a derogatory term roughly translating to "half-caste." Omar explained he felt in a kind of limbo between these two worlds, not sure of the permanence of his time in Djibouti, this place that was both familiar and foreign, his and yet not his. His first home, Yemen, the place he grew up, was now a war zone; his other, of both limited economic and social prospects, was a place he had never even visited before he arrived, let alone lived in.

"People say 'belonging,' but doesn't it have kind of two sides?" he said, finishing his Coke. "There's belonging where you're accepted. Then there's belonging where you feel right." The situation was exacerbated, he explained, because of his Djiboutian heritage, which made his status as a refugee administratively ambiguous, despite having had to flee his home and country. I was struck by how he technically had two places, two homes, and yet neither was sufficient. He seemed to have a kind of privilege—of identity, of rights, of movement—and yet it deceived.

Later, I was introduced to a Yemeni refugee, Ahmed, a young, closeted gay man. There were few instances of publicly out LGBTQ+ Yemenis, a situation so remarkable that the BBC had published a major article in 2013 about the plight of a man named Alaa Jarban, whom it titled "One of Yemen's first openly gay men." We met on the other side of the city along a street strewn with plastic bags that tumbled through the wind. He offered a light handshake and a warm smile, thanking me for meeting him outside and apologizing for not sitting down with me. He was one of the fortunate Yemenis who could afford to pay to live in a hotel, but he explained he did not want to risk being heard talking about his sexuality or bringing someone into his room. I was nagged by the uncomfortable feeling that his having a place outside a refugee camp made him less representative of what the model for asylum "should" look like, as though this privilege pushed him too far up some intangible ladder of subjugation to warrant an interview

As we walked, he explained that he was still in a decade-long relationship with his childhood best friend when he left Yemen a few months earlier, a migration precipitated not by his sexuality or any imminent threat it directly posed, but by the political situation in the country. He sketched a story whose edges felt familiar to me, as many queer stories have: a dim sense as a boy of harboring a secret with a friend about the nature of their relationship, one that wouldn't fully be reckoned with until they were older. For nearly two decades, Ahmed and his self-described "best friend" were fraternal in public, only able to speak or express their feelings for each other when they were alone. The sexual and romantic nature of their relationship needed to stay hidden or the consequences could include death, Ahmed explained. As in Saudi Arabia, I knew this severest of punishments likely hadn't been handed down by a Yemeni court in over a decade, but with power vacuums in the country forming, reports had emerged of extrajudicial killings of queer people by al Qaeda and other extremist groups. The possibility of danger felt both distant and immediate.

I asked what his plan was, and he said he was at a loss. Initially, he had thought about trying for asylum in the UK because of how Britain's long colonial history in the country had created another history, one of Yemeni migration to the UK. But after researching the contemporary asylum process, he was doubtful that using his sexuality would work.

"I read everywhere about cases where the judge asks you to prove it," he said.

It was true. I had read about several incidents of men being forced to prove their sexuality for asylum purposes in court. According to a report by the UK Lesbian and Gay Immigration Group, a worryingly high proportion of LGBTQ+ asylum claims were refused because the Home Office did not believe that the claimant had "proved" their sexual orientation. The UKLGIG report referred to several astonishing statements in refusal letters. Some recurring threads appeared, including doubt about those who couldn't claim sexual promiscuity (especially for gay men), an unforgiving methodology for any trivial inconsistency in stories, and an expectation that gay people would immediately offer deeply personal details to officers. One claimant was rejected because he had not visited "gay websites" or clubs. In another, a gay woman from Uganda who hadn't disclosed her sexual orientation on a previous student visa application was said to have lied. In yet another, the fact that the claimant and his partner said a Valentine's card was two different colors was held against him.

"What can I give them to prove who I am?" Ahmed scoffed, holding out his hands. He compared the impracticality—not to mention the danger—of keeping meticulous notes about his relationship with a film where the hero goes on a self-righteous monologue only to give the bad guy just enough time to escape.

"They think we should have all these records, all this proof, but I cannot. But that doesn't mean the relationship doesn't exist," he spat.

I thought again about the term "model minority," and how that metric for success could not account for all the steps and hurdles it took for one to fit in, let alone for how to stay true to oneself.

I felt the strange pull of objection in hearing Ahmed consider "using" sexuality for asylum when it wasn't, by his own admission, a direct factor in his departure. And yet, perhaps there was no clear-cut singular reason for migration. Identifiers like "asylum seeker" and "refugee" might allow admittance into the Global North, but to attain the latter signifier, Ahmed would likely have to play by the rules of dominant cultural and legal understandings of queerness, a perverse reversal of expectation and decorum where, instead of hiding, he would dutifully offer up exacting proof of an identifiable monogamous relationship. The formidable consideration of where one was from, passed through, and hoped to end up was a daunting triangulation with which to contend. For Ahmed, I felt these considerations pushing uncomfortably against how he was perceived—by himself, by others, by the law. I wasn't sure if it was possible to push beyond this geometry, whether there was a formlessness—an ever-moving shapelessness he could inhabit in his destination, means of arrival, and identity. Maybe proverbially ticking a box or flattening his story so he could gain entry somewhere else was the right way forward, a concerted *fuck you* to an exasperating system.

I asked Ahmed if he had ever dreamed of the United States. He just pointed to a tangle of razor wires and blast walls in the near distance, the barricaded entrance to Camp Lemonnier, a United States Naval Expeditionary Base home to the Combined Joint

Task Force, the linchpin of the US drone and surveillance program across the region.

"All of your countries and their borders…" he said, gesturing in each direction. We were surrounded by national military structures in Djibouti. I saw the signs everywhere: bases and camps not only for the US but also for the Brits, the Italians, the French—the country's former colonizers.

I waited for Ahmed to continue before I realized he didn't need to utter another word.

"Did you know all this was here?" he asked me, not without a hint of accusation.

The truth was, I didn't. I was only dimly aware of the vast reach of these apparatuses of enforcement, and their encroachment not just into this one small East African country but beyond, because I didn't really need such knowledge. My lack of familiarity with foreign military presence in Djibouti felt the same as my unawareness that Bahrain's legal code punishing queer acts was a holdover from the reach of the British empire. It did not feel like mine to carry, even if it was. I wondered what I had been producing—or reproducing—as a queer American migrant in the UAE; what we might be producing as a queer couple in this space that was not our own. We could not have biological children, so perhaps we were propagating a kind of ignorance instead. I didn't want to linger on Ahmed's statement, so I asked him where he might want to go after Djibouti, if not to the UK or US.

"What a question!" He laughed, with a touch of scorn. "Help me understand where I *can* go. Like I have all these options!"

I didn't know that either—where this hemmed-in man was allowed, where he might thrive. What I did know was that, in the same way he likely would never make it to the US, Ahmed would probably never make it to the Gulf. The UAE, part of the coalition of countries bombing Yemen, was handing out humanitarian aid but was not accepting refugees. Even though it did not yet exist, I felt the weight of my return ticket. I was free to book it whenever I wanted. We stood for a while longer in silence along a metal gate, watching plastic bags roll and then abruptly stop, tumbleweed against razor wire.

▽▽▽

I stood behind Sunil, hands on his shoulders like a fretting parent, as he pressed send on his London job application from our apartment on Saadiyat. I was torn between cheering on his professional advancement and hoping the opportunity might somehow fall through—wishing not that he would struggle in the process, but that the choice wouldn't materialize. It felt too binary, even though the options—stay or leave—seemed like the only absolute ones.

I made Sunil walk me once more through the visa process as I made lists of all the nonperishable foods lying in the back of our cupboards. He would enter the UK on a Tier 2 Intracompany Visa, a specific immigration category for those who belonged to a multinational organization and were being transferred to a job in a UK-based office. Both the employer and potential employee had to satisfy a set of conditions that seemed to circumvent many of the UK's stringent visa regulations, fast-tracking "skilled workers" into the country. I, however, wouldn't have to prove anything: the doors were held open for me as Sunil's dependent.

My ability to reside in a country to which I had no attachment nor offered any discernable use was a benefit of marriage I hadn't even considered, and yet the power dynamic inherent in the designation "dependent" made me cringe. I thought about Ahmed and the impasses he faced trying to enter nearly anywhere, and here I was on the precipice of moving to a foreign place solely due to my relationship with a man who felt a connection to it through hundreds of years of colonial history.

Later that afternoon, I met with a man who conducted research in Djibouti. He wanted to hear about my time with Omar, but when I told him about my encounter with Ahmed, he expressed skepticism about his homosexual love story. He cited instances of asylum seekers feigning religious conversion or sexual minority status in hopes of heightening their chances of resettlement, even though initial decisions on these kinds of asylum applications lodged in the UK had less than a fifty percent chance of being granted. I couldn't tell if he also disbelieved the notion of Ahmed's sexuality more generally, but I didn't care to delve into what he believed. I wondered if part of the reason I didn't doubt Ahmed's story was because he had delivered it to me personally; I had been there, I had heard him. But a wily part of me faintly hoped he had indeed been lying just to upend this obstructing system as a whole. Even though he hadn't used queerness in an application, I felt a little thrill that it might offer a migrant some kind of ascendency, even if for a fully contrived story.

I left the meeting brusquely and headed off to commune with Imran. He'd gotten better at curtailing his rapid-fire messages since the day he left his number on my bag, but lately he'd been insistent that I meet his Emirati friend Noor, even though he hadn't explained why.

"She's new to town," was all he'd messaged a few days earlier, after an extended silence in our communication. I'd already experienced how a friendship like ours could seemingly lay dormant through months of transience—his work travel, my busyness—only to bloom once again. "Well, she's a little new," he added a few minutes later, his ambiguity both cryptic and intriguing.

The three of us met at a pizza place inside the skating rink where Imran had given me his number, where those photos of the founder of the country had scrambled my sense of direction all those years earlier. Noor, a slender woman decked in a graphic T-shirt and a loose abaya, told me about her work in the humanitarian sector and how she had recently returned from working in Europe, a place where she had also spent part of her childhood. We bonded quickly when I told her I had studied in Yemen; she had Yemeni heritage, she explained, and her tone became fiery as she spoke about how distressed she was by what she described as the wholesale destruction of Yemen that the UAE was complicit in supporting. I told her about Ahmed's plight in Djibouti, and we lamented the systems that prevented him from entering either of our countries. But I suddenly found myself lamenting my own situation as well: my ambivalence toward departure, but my love for the man who felt ready to leave.

"If I've learned one thing, it's that you can't understand anyone else's connection to a place. Maybe they've had it since birth, or maybe it's developed because they lived there for two months or two decades, but I think you can't judge its merits from outside of it," she said.

I set my ice skates down and felt myself staring at her boxing gloves.

"Boxing helps me process," she laughed. "It also helps when I'm pissed off. As a queer woman, I'm pissed off about a lot."

Imran smiled at me. "See, I knew you'd want to meet her."

Noor explained that while she was in secondary school in Europe in the late 2000s, the UAE police had launched a joint campaign with a government authority to "combat" what they understood to be a phenomenon called "boyat," Emirati girls who were rebelling by dressing like boys. The government messaging surrounding these people—not to mention their general misunderstanding and mischaracterization—was excruciating, she said. The Dubai police had called on the government to carry out research on the phenomenon, and the chief of police at the time blamed co-educational schools. It was another history I had never heard.

"It was crazy, like a moral panic. No one knew anything," she said. The campaign was conflating practices and identities—

crossdressing, tomboys, lesbians, some transgender people, she explained—none of which were new phenomena, and she had felt a kinship with these compatriot young women experimenting with their identity and expression, especially as she was trying to do the same while thinking about her own assimilation abroad. Hearing the discourse while out of the country was painful, but broaching the topic with Europeans was even harder, she said.

"I tried to explain it to people in [the country she was living in Europe] and they all said, 'That is so backwards,'" she fumed. People told her to forget about her homeland because it was a hopeless kind of place that would never fully welcome her because of her gender, her time away, and—as she began to talk openly about it as a teenager—her sexuality. "I wanted to tell them what was backwards was that kind of thinking, the thinking where taking my headscarf off or whatever was 'saving' me. But saying that wasn't seen as my place, either."

After we finished our pizza, we stood together outside her boxing gym. The photo of Sheikh Zayed watched us from above, and I was reminded again of everyone from my own home who had said the UAE and the Gulf in general were too problematic to engage with.

"You have to remember that there can be a difference between a nation and its people," she said.

I asked her whether that just made us apologists, complacent in the face of abhorrent policies.

"Sometimes you defend a place to one group of people, and sometimes you have to renounce parts of it with others," she said. "It's not simple." I thought about all the times I felt the whiplash of needing to correct assumptions about the region while still pushing back against aspects of it.

I asked her if she thought institutions could be changed from the inside, and by outsiders. She hesitated.

"Yes, but keep your head down some of the time, stick your

neck out other times," she grinned, feigning a quick-step bob and weave with her arms raised. I thought about marriage, too: how the dubious institution had only recently been opened to my community, and yet I was already set to benefit from it, much like my sudden relationship with Australia and the notion of the Commonwealth.

"The time will come to do something bigger," she said, as though reading my thoughts and movements like a sparring partner. I asked her if she knew what her "something bigger" might be, but she said she wasn't sure.

I wondered if this push and pull, this delicate weighing of assimilation and agitation—when to defend and when to reject particular aspects of one's home, adopted or otherwise—was just an issue of timing. Perhaps sitting and waiting at the nexus of privilege and subjugation could curdle into an act of complicity.

"I also think it's okay just to leave," she said, laughing. She knew several lesbian women, Emirati and otherwise, who had left their homes, their countries, migrating somewhere else. She felt like she had done it twice at different stages: giving up on both her home in Europe and her homeland in the UAE.

I asked her if she felt settled here.

"Honestly, I don't know what that means to me," she said. "Maybe it doesn't really matter where I am. Maybe I am between places forever." She hugged me like we were old friends. I thought about all those I had befriended here as quickly as her, the queerness of how most of them were migrants, and how she was one, too.

She walked inside, slowly disappearing into shadow until I was watching myself wave at my own reflection in the glass door.

10: A HAVEN

(Abu Dhabi: Ajay)

THE HEAT OF THE DAY still hung in the air, threatening to paste my gray button-down to my body. I trudged through the sand trying not to think about Sunil, handsome in his white formal shirt a few paces behind me. If I thought too much about him, about the nature of the moment, I knew I would begin sweating from more than the humidity in the air.

We had devised a rough plan to meet a friend who would snap a few photos for our wedding invitation. We made the decision after searching through six years of photos of us together. In one: Sunil and I stand atop a Portuguese fort in Bahrain, just before some local boys asked if we were in a band because of our instinctively rigid poses, a flagpole between us to keep our bodies at a distance in public. In another: we sit with beers discussing wedding venue options at the Wisconsin dive bar, the Arabic cap casting my eyes in shadow, my chest puffed out, a giveaway that I'm aware of how my mannerisms might be perceived as feminine in such a male-dominated space. (Much later, in the background of the photo, I would spot the Iron Maiden shirt of the man who'd accosted me in the bathroom. His face was blurred, but I imagine him already eyeing us as we pose.) In a third photo, from four years earlier, I've missed most of Sunil's face, misaiming the lens atop a Christmas fair ride high above Hyde Park during a trip to London together. The gray sky fills most of the frame, but I look like I'm tentatively surveying everything beneath me. The tight corners of my mouth were likely me tensing up due to the movement of the ride, though I can project onto them the unease I'll feel knowing the unfamiliar city will one day become my new home.

Through all the hundreds of photos, we didn't have a single one of us looking affectionate in the UAE, this place that brought us together. I thought of Ahmed and his lack of evidence about having been in a decade-long relationship, so we decided to snap a photo together somewhere private that still showed the city—future posterity, so that we might one day be able to point to it and say, "Once, long ago, we were queer together here."

Above all, I tried not to think about getting caught. We chose a weekday afternoon at the beach, just after working hours so fewer people would be out, but it was busier than I'd expected. I walked through the sand first, Sunil four steps behind so as not to attract suspicion, our friend tailing, ready with a discreet verbal signal if we had any lingering stares or a security guard on our tail. I rushed to a spot studded with dunes and pricked with tall grasses—enough cover for two nervous men to sit in the sand together away from prying eyes, I hoped. I tried to put my arm around Sunil's waist, but I felt like a cardboard cutout of a human.

We were just visible to a group of brawny men sitting in loungers a few hundred meters away, I realized with rising panic. I quickly stood up to scan the dunes again for a more sheltered spot.

"Not quite Provincetown, eh?" Sunil joked, tossing a handful of sand at my legs. I needed his dark humor. I wondered if I would hear as much of it once we were in London or if, like our little handshake, he thought of it more as a coping mechanism, something situational and substitutional. I wondered how we would shift, individually and jointly.

A few months later, just after we'd packed up our belongings, got married in Wisconsin, and prepared to move to London all in one fell swoop, we would visit Provincetown for a quick honeymoon. We'd never been to the famous queer vacation seaside town, a haven for the LGBTQ+ community since an artists' colony developed there at the start of the twentieth century. We'd never been to any recognized gay haven together, really—not Provincetown, Palm Springs, Mykonos—so we didn't know quite what we were missing. We would arrive too late for Pride by a few weeks, but we didn't mind; Sunil had once walked past a Pride parade before he came out, but I had still never even seen one. We perused all the listings for drag shows and gay bars in the tiny resort town, overwhelmed by the profusion of visible queer culture that I had only seen briefly in New York. I was fascinated that a town of transience—once described by Cape Code historian Henry Crocker Kittredge as home to a motley crew of "fishermen, smugglers, outlaws, escaped indentured servants, and heavy drinkers"—could morph into a queer haven. But I was drawn also to its sandy dunes, where these lawless men had cruised for over a century.

We had finally found a place to get married in Wisconsin: an old barn adjacent to a sloped cornfield near the edge of a beautiful peninsula, where both the sunrise and sunset were visible over two separate bodies of water each day, the tranquil Green Bay in the west and the steely Lake Michigan in the east. A hundred kilometers away, on the lake's other shore, dunes also provided historic shelter in another queer resort town I had only recently discovered: Saugatuck, Michigan, often given the moniker "the Provincetown of the Midwest." Newspaper articles referenced nineteenth-century men laying out in the nude on its sandy dunes, and its reputation as a gay cruising and meeting place gained more traction after the Art Institute of Chicago opened up a summer program in Saugatuck in 1910, drawing in crowds from across the United States. By the 1960s, it was the premier American getaway for gay men not on a seacoast. I hadn't known of its existence growing up, and I wondered what would have happened if I had. Without an answer, I was comforted by the idea that we could look out across the bay on our wedding day and know other members of our community were there causing trouble—and had been even when we didn't know they existed.

We were getting married in an area that became known as Porte Des Morts—Death's Door—by early French colonial explorers for its treacherous strait between the two bodies of water. This was the name bestowed by settlers who undertook the perilous journey of migration—outsiders with power to come in and make such declarations, just as they would later do with thoughts surrounding what we call queerness as well. And yet before that, the Potawatomi, the Native American people violently displaced from the land, had a specific name for this queerness: M'netokwe. We were accepted.

I thought about the divergent paths these arrivals had created, about what might have been. But I wondered also about what could still be. Perhaps batches of "fishermen, smugglers, outlaws, escaped indentured servants, and heavy drinkers" demonstrate that this place of transience and arrivals was fertile enough land to sow a queer haven.

Loosen up, our friend said, *shake it off*. She was trying to bring me back to the present, back into my body; she could see I was tense, thinking about being between the past and future, between here and there. I tried putting my arm around Sunil again. We were playing by the rules in so many ways: taking an engagement photo, sending out save-the-dates. I wondered how the institution of marriage might change as it was infused with a queerness like ours, if only we could figure out how to shake it up. Our friend quickly showed us the picture on the camera's screen: Sunil laughing, looking out into the middle distance, his practical brain keyed in on the here and now; me, eyes down, staring at the sand, wondering what was and what could be. I was buoyed looking at the photo, this future archival evidence. We were captured sitting closer than I thought we had been, our affection and love visible in the frame.

Back at the apartment, we spent our final evenings looking not out across the dunes of Saadiyat but at our computers, Sunil designing a wedding website while I trawled more photos for representations of us as a couple. The website wasn't just an archive of us as a pair, we realized; we also needed to compile practical information for travelers. Over one hundred people were coming to celebrate with us from across the world. Some of Sunil's family from India were attending, as were friends from the Middle East, none of whom had ever been to the US. I looked through hotel websites for hours, trying to find the right places to suggest. Did I want to reflect back at them an image of the America they thought they knew, or did I want to challenge them?

Sunil worked on arranging wedding tables and how we would match people together. How did these connections happen, what created those sparks? He wanted to push people, to create unexpected community like we had experienced here. Sunil had been a natural at it. So many of our friends had developed friendships with each other through him, through his relentless pushing together of seemingly incongruous people—"the great gay connector," several had called him. I thought about how his parents had started over in Australia, what skills that imbued Sunil with, how people like him learned to move through the world.

As I worked, I tried to stay offline. I could be so easily distracted by the news: anti-LGBTQ rhetoric each day from the American presidential administration, children in migrant detention facilities, breathless talking heads devoted to "migrant caravans" and the creation of a debate around who a place really was for. But we were moving to London, and it also felt—as perhaps it always should have—my responsibility to begin to understand how xenophobic principles were detaching an already-isolated island like the UK from the European Union, an economic and cultural body vilified in large part because of the freedom of movement its capaciousness espoused.

Our role as long-term guests in the Gulf suddenly felt inextricably linked to our role as short-term hosts in the US and soon-to-be arrivals in the UK. What lenses did we have, and which ones would we provide to others, to understand and operate within these places? I wondered if I had done enough: on the website, in my writing, in my living.

Distracted, I picked up *The Stopping Places,* a book I was reading to learn more about the UK and its Roma community, people who lived their lives in a way that was perceived as being between places by those with the power to declare what those structures were. I had circled a passage its author, Damian Le Bas, a Roma writer and journalist, had written with the kind of dexterity with which I hoped to live:

> *The core belief of the culture is that it is possible to live in a different way: in your own way, part of the world, but not imprisoned by the rules. That you can know the ropes and yet not be hemmed in by them. That you can dwell alongside the mainstream, whilst not being part of it. Otter-like, you can live in the bank of the river and swim and hunt there when you need to, and then climb back out with equal ease and alacrity.*

I felt like I needed to account for so much: why we were marrying in America, why we were marrying at all, why we had lived in the Gulf, why we were moving to the UK, yet another place neither of us has lived. Maybe I didn't need to explain all this; maybe I really could climb in and out of the river as needed. But I was bothered by the seemingly inherent inequity of the act of marriage: that disengagement from it, even if it felt like a possibility, was a kind of privilege, too.

I could feel myself floating far off from the wedding admin tasks at hand. I was growing distracted in the way I'd be when I wanted to write another story. I had so little time, and so much to get done, but maybe this story wouldn't be a distraction; maybe it could be a kind of illumination. I went to the window and looked out over the dunes, just visible in the distance.

▽▽▽

I had first seen the phenomenon a few years earlier, in Abu Dhabi, as I descended a stairwell into a tiled underpass. A group of men lurking in a dingy underground walkway looking jumpy as soon as I turned the corner would have been notable on its own. But it was all the more intriguing because I walked closer and saw the men crowded around a fold-out ironing board.

I started recognizing the same scene in various places around the city: a group of South Asian men standing around an ironing board in furtive commotion. It had an element of queerness to it, the lurking, the quiet, the jumpiness. I wanted to know what it was, this hiding, secretive behavior.

I tried to make mental notes of the standard building blocks of the scene whenever I happened to walk past. The commotion always seemed to have three elements: an ironing board, a screw-driver, and a belt. I couldn't figure out the purpose, the mechanics, the etiquette of the event; I noticed a sort of jostle for what seemed like a queue, but I couldn't figure out its purpose. Men seemed to pull at a belt on the board and either jump in jubilation or shout and mutter in lament. Once, I saw an irate man standing before the board slap another across the face. There was a freewheeling carnival air about it all, but the scene always unfolded in Urdu or Malayalam, so I could never be exactly sure what was occurring. It was yet another reminder that, though I was living in a country where Arabic was the official language, studying something in addition to the linga franca would have done me well.

With only a few weeks left in the UAE, I focused on one location where the event with the ironing board always seemed to be occurring: a sprawling market in the shadow of a Musaffah labor camp housing thousands of migrants working in construction. It was these labor camps—indeed, these men—that were the lens through which so many regarded the Gulf: the image of the lone male, trapped far from home, victim of poor safety regulations and human rights abuses.

The very existence of the teeming market was notable. Each Friday, blankets and fabric were gathered by the corners and suspended aloft by ropes to create a bright, makeshift canopy that shaded row after row of tarps piled high with wares, utensils, gadgets, and the men who perused the busy aisles. All commercial ventures in the UAE were required to have a license, so this kind of sprawling, unregulated enterprise was illegal. I'd read of several unsuccessful attempts by the UAE authorities to shut it down. The municipality had even opened up a nearby official market, the Musaffah Bazaar, to curb the unlawful street hawking. Yet still the phenomenon persisted, vendors coming together to sell clothes, food, and electronics under no central authority. More than one of the "shops" sold items pillaged from condemned buildings—old telephones, mattresses, furniture—before they were dismantled for new construction. Men shouting, "Balance! Balance!" orbited around its periphery, peddling phone credit by the individual unit, circumventing the official prepaid top-up minimum for those who couldn't afford its twenty-five-dirham fee. It was an ingenious informal economy flying in the face of tight regulation.

I registered that my presence was a curiosity, if not a cause for outright trepidation, for those engaging in this ecosystem, especially as I drew nearer to the scattered ironing boards. Men cast nervous glances as I approached. I probably wouldn't want me around either, if I were them, I realized. They projected the same nervous suspicion I knew LGBTQ+ people could feel witnessing straight people entering queer spaces. The breach raised a question of intentions: was the purpose a kind of novelty, like poverty tourism, or was it something else? I thought again of the "fishermen, smugglers, outlaws, escaped indentured servants" demographics of early Provincetown. I wanted to put these men at ease—to convey that I, too, felt a belonging in the underbelly.

Since we did not share a first language, I tested the non-verbal communication I knew through queerness, making eye contact as I walked through the market, cruising. I watched some men understand my presence immediately, a few making overt and explicit passes—gazes held, hands adjusting groins—despite the glare of the sun and the lack of privacy. A few also laughed, not in scorn but in recognition, that I wasn't in their presence as a figure of authority or enforcement but that we were all creating something of our own here. Illegality and informal economies brushed up against and layered on top of each other, a patchwork of humans doing whatever they could to navigate a place.

I caught the eye of one man who stood around the board nearest the entrance to the labor camp. He seemed like a carnival barker of sorts, shouting in Hindi, grabbing men by the shoulders as they walked past. I was drawn to how cavalier he seemed, setting up shop closest to the camp's security outpost, bellowing and gesticulating, daring to get in the face of anyone who walked near him. I made a circuit as on the Corniche, and he smiled each time I walked past. On my third pass, I brushed my hand along my inner thigh, and he waved me over.

In English, he asked me my name. He flashed a smile that exposed a chipped front tooth and said I could call him Ajay. *How many years here*, he asked—a now-familiar question wrapped up not in its normal perfunctory acknowledgment that we were all from somewhere else but tinged with a deeper question, a challenge: *How well have you done to make your way here?* He looked about my age, closing in on or just past the milestone of thirty, and had an attractive, slender face and a wide mustache that twitched through his fast talking. He conveyed interest, looking me up and down and lingering on my body, but each time I thought I had his full attention, he caught the shoulder of another passerby, waving him over to the ironing board. When he finally coaxed a hesitant man by the small of his back to a group of six or so others already standing around the board, I followed.

After what looked like some haranguing, the hesitant man pulled a twenty-dirham note from a faded pleather wallet and slowly handed it over. Ajay grew somber, even grateful, as he received the crumpled bill with great ceremony, holding his right palm aloft while clutching his wrist with his left hand. He placed the bill under a can of tomatoes on the table and handed a screwdriver to the man who stared at a belt coiled like a snake atop the ironing board. The audience leaned in closer until the man stabbed the screwdriver down in the center of the coil in one swift motion, as though he were slaying a beast. The man at the other side of the table grabbed the end of the belt and pulled it free. The screwdriver sat suspended as if on an upturned dartboard, and the man let out a groan before walking off. Ajay took the bill from beneath the can of tomatoes and pocketed it, raising his eyebrows at me.

I watched the scene repeat a few more times with different men before I finally had a moment alone to speak to Ajay. His English was shaky, and I had no translator, but we cobbled together English, some Arabic, and the language of cruising. I hoped our perilous language bridge would hold. With one hand still on my thigh, I held eye contact with him and asked him about the ironing board. It was a betting game, he said. *Gambling.* I told him I wanted to know the rules. He nodded his head to the entrance of the labor camp and motioned for me to follow him.

It was illegal for me to enter the camp. At the very least, I would be trespassing, but I could also be nabbed for conducting an interview without the proper press credentials. Journalists had been arrested and deported before for attempting it, but I knew this might be one of my last chances to enter this kind of dwelling that was the center of so much attention: a deplorable, inadequate space given to men in a place that was not their own. I thought about my first iftar with Imran near the police station, and how nervous I had been, but I had met him anyway: drawn by some unknown calculus of opportunity, risk, assimilation, and subversion. All forces that affected my trajectory as a migrant and queer person, from that first meeting with Imran, to the Gulf, to my life with Sunil, and—once more—into the camp.

I followed Ajay to a set of creaking metal turnstiles at the camp's entrance. We got into one metal turnstile together as it swung around like a carnival ride, his body pressed against mine. I was ready with a cover story if the security guard asked anything, but he didn't look up. It didn't slip my notice that I was banking on my ability to convince a South Asian guard I was a construction company executive while wearing shorts and sandals. This was the privilege I wielded.

Inside, Ajay led me through tiled halls, pushing open a cheap clapboard door into a large, windowless bedroom. Pointing to a sleeping figure in the corner with one hand and grabbing his dick with the other, he grimaced and shrugged apologetically: whatever he hoped might have happened in that bedroom between us could not happen right now. I pointed to the ground; we could sit and talk quietly, I motioned. He shrugged again, hesitant, before pouring us two cups of flat Pepsi from a two-liter bottle underneath his bed, no doubt having envisioned another kind of encounter. I thought about Tahsan, how our roles had been reversed then—the eager hedonist and the measured conversationalist—and wondered where he was now.

I counted eight double bunks in total. Sixteen people slept here, Ajay told me quietly. He explained he had left India nearly a decade earlier and was now working construction on a Saadiyat Island site. I thought of the men in the *New York Times* photos, the ones who had constructed the place I called home. Settling into our interaction, Ajay began on a laundry list of complaints in hushed, broken English while his roommate slept, getting a little louder with each grievance. The room had no ventilation. *Bad air,* he said. The lights were always on in the room because everyone worked different shifts. There weren't enough keys for the door, so it stayed open all the time. I asked where he kept important items, and he pointed to a small, rusted locker under another bunk that looked like it could be carried away under the arm of a child. Three of his friends in the room shared it, he explained. I asked him if he felt comfortable storing his passport there.

"Arbab," he said, using the Arabic word for boss. He didn't have his passport; it was with his company. It was a human rights violation he seemed nonplussed about. I asked him if he would rather be in India. He shrugged once more, ambivalence coloring every gesture. "It's difficult here, it's difficult there," he said.

I wondered if we were able to speak more eloquently in a shared language what else he might say. Perhaps it would be the same if we spoke about queerness—a tacit, hesitant acknowledgment that nowhere was quite right. But there was a simple profundity in his singular sentence, though I also noted the ease I felt not being able to dig much further. I wanted this queer migrant to be able to make his way here, if not with complete ease, then at least with the clarity of perspective. I watched Ajay mop his brow; his room really didn't have any ventilation. The worst of the summer heat hadn't yet arrived, but it wasn't far off.

After some silence, I asked him about the game.

He explained the convoluted scheme as best he could, pulling off his own belt to demonstrate. The belt was folded in half and then loosely coiled, making a ying-yang shape in the middle. Players got to choose if they put the screwdriver in the middle or outside of it, placing bets as to whether the screwdriver would catch when it was unfurled. It was an easy betting game and seemed like a sure way to make money to an impressionable passerby, he explained: if you could follow the coil to its very center, good fortune felt like it was in your hands.

But the game was rigged, he said. I watched a wily smile cross his lips, his mustache twitching again. Depending on which of the two positions the contestant chose, the man running the board could unfurl the belt in either direction with a bit of sleight of hand, determining the outcome. The house would always win. Ajay's job was indeed to act as a kind of carnival barker, keeping the crowd enthused and encouraging passersby to place bets. To drum up excitement, he also facilitated the occasional "winner"—a friend who was in on the scam and would only look like he walked away pocketing earnings. The fake prize money had already been collected earlier from the hopeful, the gullible, or the desperate, depending on how one looked at it.

I had thought there might be a real chance at winning the game; I'd held out hope that everyone had the same shot. I felt the hot flush of embarrassment. Of course power dynamics had always been at play: between the organizers and the bettors, between the oppressors and the oppressed. But it had taken me too long to reckon with just how layered, how thorny it all was, the slippages between each neat category, to know at which point who was on which side of the board. Today, in terms of our dynamic, I could access Ajay's camp—a name that absurdly connoted both impermanence and a kind of hedonistic summer indulgence—but he could only access my Saadiyat to build structures, not a whole life.

I finished my Pepsi. I felt Ajay grow restless in his small room. I didn't harbor any illusions that he'd made his way to the Gulf without any peril, in the same way I knew cruising him to hear the story behind the ironing board wasn't necessarily the ideal way to connect. But I had seen how both migrating to this place where queerness was illegal and yet living a life of queerness there were viable modes of operating.

Sitting on the floor in front of our Styrofoam cups of Pepsi trading personal stories felt like the only real way to bridge wider misconceptions about prosperity, pleasure, and personal motivation. It was a flawed process, I knew: I found I always struggled to articulate the allure and potentiality of this home in the same way I still struggled to convey queerness to anyone who wasn't queer. And I still had difficulty fully comprehending the magnetism that drew the person I love—an English-speaking, Australian man of Indian heritage with a Portuguese last name—back to the Commonwealth. Forces that were colonial, personal, and mimetic pulled so hard and from such varied directions. I was nothing like Ajay, and Sunil was nothing like me, and yet in operating in the Gulf as queer outsiders, I wanted us to be alike: in some facets of our lives as the organizers of the game, in others, those who struggled to play it.

Perhaps the deepest source of discomfort in learning the truth of the rigged board was in contending with Ajay as someone capable of taking advantage of another migrant. Even after all these years, I wanted a clear, clean image of him, as the subjugated queer or exemplar of industrious migrant work ethic. Because if that wasn't him, it certainly wasn't me either, and in acknowledging a fuller picture of Ajay, I had to acknowledge it in myself, too. He was collecting their money, I their stories. I suddenly wanted to leave the room, wanted us to be out in the world together, operating the same, the very paradox of queerness.

We exchanged numbers outside. As he handed me his number, his hand lingering on mine, I thought about Noor's comments, about what subversion and change could look like, and what it might someday bring. Maybe that change could include just quietly breaking the law: setting up a flea market, gambling, cruising. We should not have to be the model minority to be recognized; our humanity should be enough. But even if we weren't accepted—in the Gulf, in the US, in the UK—we'd still keep arriving, keep trying. Maybe my collecting stories of movement and quiet defiance for all those years was my protest; maybe it was my way forward. I waved goodbye to Ajay as he walked back to the board, thinking about how I might get this all down on the page, and hoping that writing it just as I was leaving wouldn't be too late.

▽▽▽

We watched a team of movers put most of our worldly possessions into boxes and tape them shut. I put some of my most sentimental items into my carry-on bag, along with the wedding rings we would exchange in a couple weeks and the passports that would facilitate us breezing through security on our way to a wedding that would be illegal in this country. I stared at our little blue passports, tattered and worn from a decade of use, but still safe in our possession, before closing up the bag. Sunil came up to me and whispered in my ear.

"Where the hell is Richard?" I didn't understand why he was whispering in our own apartment until I processed his question.

I felt my eyes grow wide. Richard was a giant dildo. Or, less a dildo and more a giant silicone flapping penis. Sunil and I had improbably found it during a boat trip to an island just off Abu Dhabi a few years earlier. He had spotted it hermetically sealed in a plastic bag, lapping in the waves of an otherwise pristine beach. We had no idea how or why it got there, but the story, and Richard itself, became infamous with our friends, so we kept it on our desk as a kind of tribute to subversion itself—even after it had split in half when a friend swung it around too wildly, narrowly averting shattering a mirror.

I ran into the office to discreetly retrieve it, but a Filipino mover with long hair had already set to work clearing my desk accessories into a bag. I watched him grab both parts of Richard and put them into a little box with paper clips, staplers, and sticky notes like they were any old stationery.

"Here, let me just, um, grab this from you quick," I said, carefully pulling the broken head and then the testicle section out of the box like they were family heirlooms. The mover was stone-faced and seemed completely unfazed. I couldn't help but chuckle: in case the movers suspected our relationship, Sunil and I had devised an elaborate story about how I was the only one living in the apartment, and he was just visiting. But if the mover didn't care about a broken dildo, they probably wouldn't care about our living arrangement.

I had worried for so long that someone would discover me or turn me in to the authorities, but over eighty percent of the population was like me—not in the queerness of their sexuality, but in the queerness of cobbling together a home in a place that wasn't theirs. Perhaps there was more similarity in these two categories than I had ever realized. It was yet another example of how outsiders could shift a place in ways both subtle and profound.

Without stopping his packing, the mover told me he recognized me. I scanned his face and wondered if we been together long ago on the Corniche.

"I was in the band!" he said.

It was Manuel! Six years had passed, and he had cut off a few inches from his long hair, but he was the same guitarist in the bar where Sunil and I had first sung karaoke—the one who I was surprised to discover Reggie was dating.

"I recognized both of you straight away," he said, winking.

I asked him what he was doing now. He explained that the band had split up when the two backing singers returned to the Philippines to marry. Reggie had moved to Qatar to keep singing in a new band, but Manuel had been sending money back to his parents to build a house, and he hadn't wanted to leave the UAE. So he got a job for a moving and logistics company.

He waved me off when I asked if he was still with Reggie. "It's complicated," he said. "So much movement." All I could do was smile at him and nod, understanding and empathizing as best I could.

He and his team of movers made quick work. As they dismantled our sofa, I sat on a cardboard box while Sunil showed me the website where we could track our belongings once they were in a shipping container. They would pass Yemen and Djibouti on their way through Bab El Mendeb before heading into the Mediterranean Sea, on into the Atlantic and the Celtic Sea, and then through the English Channel to a dock somewhere in the south of England. I tried to imagine the migrants who might have already taken this route. I wondered how many had been nervous about starting a new life, how many had fashioned a life of not-quite-assimilation, a kind of queerness in itself. I kissed Sunil as they kept working. It didn't feel like much of an act of defiance, but it did feel right.

I grabbed my swim trunks from out of an untaped box and packed one last bag. I was meeting skating friends for a birthday party on a boat in Dubai that night, a final trip out into the sea. Imran had connected us all—my first queer friend here, though he had abruptly taken a temporary position in Canada. He had left so quickly we didn't even have time for a final skate. But he would return; he wasn't sure if the new position would lead to anything, or if he wanted it to. We had emailed a few times, and he said he loved Toronto but missed Abu Dhabi. Both could be true, and that gave me hope. Maybe soon I'd understand a bit more clearly what exactly he missed here, and what a pull from somewhere else felt like.

The sun had already begun to set when I parked in Dubai. The marina was quieter than I expected for a surprisingly dry early summer night. I made my way to the dock. The rented boat was large but simple, and there were just over a dozen people on board. I recognized several familiar faces, but some were new, a rotating cast of familiarity and transience like the Gulf itself.

I already knew from WhatsApp that everyone on the boat would be queer, even the attendees I didn't know. We sat in the dock and talked as we waited to unmoor, some of the newbies more awkwardly, some more openly. Sailing out into the water, someone made a dark joke about how we were more obvious than the *Queen Mary*, the infamous boat that had been raided in Egypt.

I watched this loud, boisterous mass of queers and thought again about whether the Gulf was a fertile enough place to be a haven. I thought back to P-Town as it was before, filled with troublemakers. Maybe I hadn't done enough here; maybe I was leaving at just the wrong time. Maybe we really were in the process of forming a nascent queer haven. Or maybe I was just idealizing the place because I was leaving it.

I spotted a few stars out on the water, away from the lights of the city. I could feel myself growing wistful, but was brought back to the present by two young men offering me a glass of warm white wine. They were a relatively new couple—one Jordanian, one Omani. One was studying in Dubai and had lived here his whole life, and the other was from Musandam. I thought of Amir and wondered where he was, whether he might ever reach, or build, his queer Musandam dream.

They were younger than me—much younger, I suddenly realized—in their early twenties, about the same age I had been when I first arrived. I suddenly felt the weight of my time here, some of my most formative years. I still wasn't quite sure what it had done to me, or if I had done anything to it.

The Jordanian asked me about myself. I told them I was getting married in a few weeks. I expected congratulations, but he just raised his eyebrow. "Married, masha'allah. But isn't that for the heteros?" He laughed.

His question, a playful dig, delighted me. Why did I need to get married? Why did I need to buy into an institution that had historically excluded me? I still wasn't sure about marriage, but I knew I wanted to be with Sunil; we would take the rights we deserved and trouble the rest. And likewise, couldn't migrants enjoy the same privileges of being in a place without having to integrate? I felt a twinge of hope at the prospect of a young queer kid, a third-culture migrant, reimagining countries, institutions, and the very nature of assimilation. I wondered how they both might carry those radical ideas with them across continents, across time.

We returned to shore just past midnight. Disembarking, I realized I hadn't told anyone that it was one of my last nights in the Gulf. As we disbanded, I considered mentioning it to the group, but I decided I didn't need to say anything aloud. I knew, and these people all knew, that words weren't always necessary. And that farewells could be both vital and temporary.

11: ANOTHER RING

(London, United Kingdom; Abu Dhabi: Anonymous)

THE INVITATION ARRIVES in my inbox on a gray day in early October. I'm sitting in our newly rented flat in South London using a cardboard box as our table, just as I did while Manuel packed up our Abu Dhabi apartment. Our belongings are taking longer to ship than we had anticipated; there is some kind of holdup in customs whose source and resolution both remain elusive. We arrived during a late summer heat wave, the city's cobbled streets and sturdy brick façades all cast in a golden hue. But after only eight weeks, the weather is already starting to turn toward autumn, and I'm suddenly conscious that we don't have much in the way of protection from the British cold.

I feel another kind of chill as I quickly flick off a news program about Brexit and "soaring" numbers of migrants trying to cross into the UK via the English Channel. I curse our mistake of buying a television right away, allowing the hyperbolic and incendiary British media into our home before the space feels like ours. I remember my first day in Abu Dhabi—the ice rink, Imran, my anxiety—and wonder if I ought to grab my skates and go out into the city, away from the half-unpacked suitcases and wedding gifts.

We married on a day of unseasonable warmth for a place hemmed in on both sides by lake breezes. Much of Sunil's family made the trip, arriving from India and Australia, including his stalwartly Catholic, octogenarian parents, who took four flights over the course of twenty-six hours to meet my own and witness our wedding. On the night before the ceremony, Sunil's mother pulled me aside as we walked the shore of Lake Michigan and asked if I would take care of her son wherever I went. I was struck as much by the candor of the question as the geographic qualifier. *Wherever you go.* Perhaps only a woman who had uprooted her family in one place for life in another would know to include it in the framing of the question.

The attendance of Sunil's parents made me consider the potential for minds to change, for previous assertions and avowals to shift beneath one's feet even while mid-stride. Sunil's sister, an early and ferocious ally who counseled Sunil on coming out to his parents soon after we began dating, stood at the front of the barn to deliver a speech and Mangalasutra ceremony. It was a ritual usually reserved for Indian brides, but she enlisted my new niece and nephews to bestow us with necklaces of gold and black beads and made it queer as hell. It felt like a ceremony not just for us, but for her children as well—teaching them what it means not only to exist in a world connected to more than one place, but also how to reconsider and reshape institutions and traditions across these divides. If only the boys from the boat could have seen it. Maybe they would have declared it too performative, but afterward, I sure did feel part of a wider family who knew a thing or two about building ties in new places.

In her speech, she also joked how the expectation in a family of immigrants was always to message "Reached" at the end of a journey, just to declare one's safe arrival. Now that I was part of the family, I would need to do it, too, she said. Wanting to be the good son- and brother-in-law, I had seemingly been firing off "Reached" messages in rapid succession for the two months since—Provincetown, Heathrow Airport, our new flat—though I wasn't sure if these counted as separate journeys.

I'll have to send another "Reached" soon, I realize: the message in my inbox is an invitation to return to the NYUAD Arts Center where I once worked, but this time as a performer. I've been invited to read in a public event called Hekayah, meaning "story," in celebration of the UAE's National Day. It will feature multidisciplinary performers from across the UAE—an Emirati pianist, a Filipino poet, a Pakistani theater-maker—in an artistic rumination on home and the stories we tell about it, the ways in which we make it.

I don't realize how excited I am to return until the plane tickets arrive in my inbox a few days later. I'm already looking forward to seeing Noor again, maybe even watching her box. We can talk about anger and ambivalence, though I know she'll be happy when I report that Ahmed declared asylum in Northern Europe. I hold my breath when I read about the increasing incidences of far-right, anti-immigrant rallies in the liberal city where he's settled, but so far I'm pleased to say I've only heard him complain about the food. We chose a flat near Brixton because we wanted to be part of the diversity and energy of an immigrant community, though it's surreal to hear people express concern for us based on the neighborhood's history as a flashpoint in race riots that occurred over a quarter century earlier. My worries instead lie in this explicit racism and also how our arrival moves the needle of gentrification.

Each day I pass a plaque for a Brazilian man killed by police officers after he was mistakenly identified as a suspect in a failed bombing attempt. Jean Charles de Menezes's appearance—dark hair and eyes, the latter of which were described as "Mongolian" by one of the officers who followed him onto the tube where he was shot seven times in the head—were listed as reasons why he was mistaken for a terrorist of Middle Eastern heritage. I can't help but think of Sally, and also Gizelle, navigating the perils of being misread. He never did make it back to the UAE, but he did find a job in a salon in Bahrain, and I'm heartened by his resolve and subversion every time I start to worry that I don't have a place here.

He wasn't able to make it to the gay bar before it closed—another causality of precarious queer nightlife and place-making—but I like to think that if anyone could open and run a queer venue in Manama, it would be him.

We also settled close to Clapham, a neighborhood frequently derided for being packed with young Australians. When I mention to Sunil that it's actually our nearest Tube stop, he gets agitated and says it's not technically where we live. "I don't want to be a cliché!" he says one day as we pass a group of loud Australians. I think for the whole walk back to our new home about how our identity is constructed by others' perceptions of us.

I'm also studying in Glasgow. I'm doing that annoying American thing where I claim Scottish heritage even though my ancestors left five generations earlier. Still, I ask my father to send me the genealogical research of our paternal line, even as I recognize how it perpetuates a kind of heteronormative fixation on lineage that my queerness precludes me from biologically maintaining. But I'm happy to be carving out a place for myself away from London, a place that feels my own in this country where I followed someone else. I'm reading about Edwin Morgan and the histories of cruising on the Glasgow Green and feel like I'm catching up somehow on where and how to claim public space as queer.

We're trying to claim space in other ways, too. Just before we left, we discovered a caveat to Sunil's visa, the one that allowed us both to avoid more stringent residency regulations and enter the UK quickly because of the long arms of his British company reaching into the UAE: we cannot be granted permanent residency or citizenship. The double-edged sword of the Commonwealth allowed us ease of access to the country, but after five years, we must leave—on the dot, no exceptions. In order to bypass this barrier, we devised a convoluted plan for me to enter the country on a student visa for my doctorate in the hopes that I might one day be granted a "skilled worker" visa and then be able to shift Sunil under my visa in turn. Though I followed him here, he would then become my dependent, a destabilization of the strict categorization and power of UK immigration. I take a small measure of delight in subverting this arcane bureaucracy with the kind of novel workaround that both queer people and migrants have always needed to use, though I recognize our privilege which allows this particular ploy. It feels too early to be worrying about where or even who we will be in five years, but I made a commitment to take that journey with Sunil, and I remember vividly how both of us arrived in the UAE nearly a decade earlier with only a two-year contract and a dim sense that this place was not, and could never, be ours.

For Hekayah, I decide to read an excerpt from my essay in an anthology about the hidden corners of Dubai, published just before I left. The book features artists, scholars, writers, and intellectuals investigating and celebrating things hidden in the corners of this misunderstood place: Soviet architecture, lush mangroves, a subspecies of red fox. It's the kind of thoughtful meditation on place that most enamors me, and I was heartened by the energy of the young Emirati female editor whose daring work inspired me that I might write not about queerness explicitly, but about barbershops, a space where I recognized queerness reflecting back at me.

I refamiliarize myself with my essay while I walk down to my new barber in Tooting, a nearby South Asian neighborhood that sells jaggery and embroidery just like the backstreets behind Sama Tower. I pass a shop that stocks the same tassels Imran bought that first week. I stare at the display for a while, struck by how I keep finding myself thinking about places as they relate to somewhere else.

▽▽▽

It feels strange to arrive back in Abu Dhabi so soon after my departure. More than ever, I think not about its transience, but about how stable I felt here, how I carved out space. As a guest of the Arts Center, I'm entitled to a chauffeur back to my old home, but I head to a car rental agency instead. I want the freedom of movement. I instinctively flip through my passport to pull up my visa page at immigration before I remember it was canceled. I pass through security as a tourist would, no evidence of my decade making a home here.

Fewer than six months have passed, but I glimpse a spate of new commercial construction on my drive to the campus despite night already having fallen. One construction site looks like a twenty-four-hour operation, shifts of men clocking in and out even in the darkness. I spot a new hotel sprouting near my guest accommodation and second-guess whether it began after I departed or if I just hadn't noticed it in the busy weeks before I left. There are no windows, or even discernable rooms, just elevator cores and scaffolding. I consider calling Shivani and seeing if she's been on the site yet or if she deems it too dangerous, but I look at my watch and remember it's late for her now—she got a job teaching and goes to bed much earlier than she likes to. "I'm like a boring old woman now!" I heard her joke on more than one occasion, but I know her ability to stay in the only country she's ever called home, despite no likely path to citizenship, matters more to her than a few lost parkour practices. I try to peer out at the new hotel, and I wonder if I'll be back to see it welcome guests. Perhaps Sunil and I might even get to rent a room there as a couple; maybe we could even share a door with Shivani and Yasmine.

When I arrive on campus, I stay up late making edits to the essay. I want to read the whole piece, but each performer has a time limit, and though I'm tempted to run a little long, I want to give space and listen to everyone else's story. Crossing out lines, then paragraphs, I try to get the flow just right so that people might understand, so that I might be able to articulate what these spaces have meant not just to me but also to others who have inhabited and passed through them. After a couple hours of editing, too much time for such a short piece, I check the alarm clock. After midnight. I do the math, knowing down to the minute how much time it would take for me to arrive on the Corniche.

I want to go back to the Corniche for the thrill, the joy, the unabashed hedonism, and the expressly political act of it all. But I also want to return in order to search for community, both new people to seek out as well as familiar faces—and bodies—to reencounter where language wouldn't be necessary. I dream of seeing Hameed and Naji there and how they would navigate this space simultaneously similar and so disparate from the hotels of Jeddah. But I lost touch with both a few years after our encounter. After a few months of silence, I went to message Hameed, but his WhatsApp profile photo had changed. I meant to message Naji, but by the time I remembered a few weeks later, his photo had changed, too. I alternated between dreaming that they ran off together somewhere—the BDSM clubs of Berlin, or perhaps even a wedding aisle (or both!)—and hoping that they both remained in Saudi, continuing to find other partners, their relationship nothing but ephemeral, ecstatic, unapologetic physicality. I could reach out to Prashant or Mohammed for Hameed's number, I knew, but what did I really need to say to them? And anyway, maybe I would encounter them again more organically—and what a queer delight that would be.

I walk on stage the next day in front of projections of photos I took inside barbershops and feel the weight of responsibility to get everything just right. When I worked here, I produced the work of other storytellers, but now I am conveying my own even while I'm telling others' stories. I begin: *The story of Hor Al-Anz is a familiar one: an elegant neighborhood once reserved for the privileged, then neglected to the point of disrepair, but ultimately reinvigorated by an influx of outsiders.* I continue, not mentioning queerness overtly, but speaking in coded ways of the male comradery among diverse migrants I witnessed and partook in within those barbershops. When I finish, I exit the stage and listen to storyteller after migrant storyteller articulate their own version of the UAE as home. I am reminded of Amir and Wasim: that "outsider" is a term of positionality and flux, one, like queer, of both scorn and reclamation.

I feel a tap on my shoulder as I prepare to leave. A young South Asian man who looks like he might be in college thanks me for my reading. He is shifting in place and looks up at me expectantly, but then begins to speak.

"I recognized everything you said," he says.

I'm heartened that a young man might find fellowship in the same spaces I did. "Oh, thank you, which barbershops—"

"Everything," he says, cutting me off. He raises his eyebrows and offers me a knowing smirk.

Performers and audience members mill on all sides of us. He seems too young to know any peril or illegality at all, but then I remember the way I learned to navigate Midwest America as a lost queer boy. He, like I, might actually feel more adept at and comfortable within acts of subversion than anywhere else because of our strange familiarity with forging paths by running afoul of laws. I want to ask him why he is here, how long he might stay. But he just nods and melts into the crowd. All I can do is hold his gaze as long as he'll allow it.

▽▽▽

I have an important errand to run before I get back on the plane to London. I have to replace Sunil's wedding ring. Two days after our ceremony, on the third and final day of our marriage festivities, my parents invited to my childhood home all the travelers who attended the wedding from furthest away, a final sendoff. At some point while swimming, the ring I gave to him just days earlier slipped off his finger and sank to the bottom of a murky pond.

"Just get me an onion ring," he'd said in the leadup to the wedding, not entirely kidding about his aversion to jewelry. Why were we getting rings anyway, we both wondered. Or, more precisely: what might we be unquestioningly perpetuating in wearing them? Still, he was shaken by the inauspiciousness of losing the symbol of our commitment to each other only forty-eight hours after we'd made it. But I got him to see a kind of subversive joy—how losing a ring that stands as an outward symbol to others is a small queering of an institution that we're entering into dubiously.

I married not for its conventions or traditions but for the rights and freedoms it offers, still holding close an ambivalence about the institutions that have and continue to sustain me—same-sex marriage, the Gulf and the profits I reaped there, the laws around queerness and migration in all the countries I get to call home—yet there is precarity both in defending and rejecting them. I consider the migrants around the world who are dismissed as ungrateful when they critique, criticize, and demand more of institutions. Losing a ring didn't change any laws or minds, but it did help guide us, that we are not beholden to accepting anything wholesale. But I knew that there was also privilege in the loss: that even unseen, the ring remains in a place I get to call home—through all my escape, through all my transience—as fraught as that place may feel. And like our pivot to a new country, I have the ability to get another one.

Already I've had to retell the story of the ring dozens of times. Like the queer people and migrants I've met and befriended over the past decade who are endlessly expected to justify their choices and account for their lives, I know I will be required to rehash the story again and again for those who don't understand it. Why didn't you just find a ring that was a better fit? they ask. I wonder how they'll retell it: a futile journey, a recklessness, a story exoticized and distorted.

Sunil had found an Egyptian jeweler for our rings, the first woman to train in Cairo's famed Khan El Khalili jewelry quarter. We liked the idea of supporting a regional female artist, and it didn't hurt that she crafted stunning calligraphy with each piece she made. For Sunil, I chose a silver ring featuring a line from one of my favorite Arabic poets, Ibn Zaydun, an eleventh-century Andalusian. I was drawn to include in our marriage the words of a poet who had engaged in a homosexual romance before going into self-imposed exile. If we were doing the marriage thing, I joked to Sunil when we bought it, we needed to explicitly bring some queerness into it.

Engraved in the ring is a line in Arabic that translates literally to, "And if you attended, then all the people attended." On first read, the line appears a touch overwrought, but translation is a funny, imperfect thing, and the less literal translation evokes the idea: "When you're here, the whole world is with me." The temptation is to imbue the line with the sentiment of coupledom insularity, as in, "You're all I need in the world." Instead, I think about how this man, and our queerness, has created, strengthened, and enlarged my sense of community, including as I follow him to a new place in the world that isn't, and perhaps won't ever fully feel, mine.

With the replacement ring safely in my pocket, I decide to spend my final evening at the first barbershop I ever went to, the one where the barber pointed to me and ushered me inside. When I walk over, I half expect him to be gone, but he's still at his same chair. I hadn't told him I was leaving in the same way I hadn't told many people, partially because I didn't quite believe it myself.

I sit in his familiar corner spot, and he smiles at me like no time has passed. He asks me the normal questions about cut and shape, and I point to a new footballer on the wall and decide to get a drastic haircut like I used to, something severe that will make me stand out. I request a shave too—anything so I can stay longer.

He turns off the television during one bout of intense chatter to focus on our conversation, and I realize we are the last people left in the shop. There is silence, too, moments when words aren't necessary. When we do speak, we do it across second and third languages as we did for years, translating and retranslating story after story. He asks me about family, though I don't quite know how to convey that it's all over the world now, how it's gotten bigger and more scattered at the same time. How it's here, too. He doesn't ask about abroad, about home. I think we've stopped using those words. I think we know the perilously thin line between them.

Na'iman, he says. He's suddenly finished. I know I have an early flight in the morning, but I take my time standing from the chair. Perhaps I could stay just a while longer.

ACKNOWLEDGMENTS

THIS BOOK SIMPLY WOULD NOT EXIST without the individuals who spoke with, befriended, and guided me, as well as the communities that welcomed and challenged me in equal measure throughout—and beyond—my life in the Gulf.

We built relationships in fits and starts or all at once, and I'm thankful to each of you for entrusting me not only with your words and stories but also for reifying new paths forward and other modes of being. Because of each of you, I reconsidered what it meant to be a journalist, a resident, a community member, a queer person, and more—both on and off the page. I extend my gratitude to those who led me to interviews with friends and lovers, everyone whose stories found their way into the book, and even more people who reverberate beyond its margins.

Special thanks to the irrepressible Gulf bakla community, especially C and F for their deep well of hospitality and life advice (as well as diplomatic yet firm guidance on flattering nail colors). And to all the people I encountered, convened with, or simply walked past in the precarious queer public spaces like the Corniche we continue to make: thank you for meeting my gaze, even if you didn't stop. *Sida, sida.*

My utmost appreciation also to K and H who read drafts and sections of writing and offered thoughts, feedback, and counsel across an ocean when the book was at its most unmoored (and when I was, too).

I would be remiss not to acknowledge how grateful I am for the support and friendship of queer Khaleejis. This book is one of queer migrants, but I know that even more kaleidoscopic stories—including those from citizens, Bidoon, Muhamasheen, and more—will continue to emerge from the region across artistic forms on account of remarkable fortitude, subversion, and joy. Deepest thanks to A for his direction and for, when I told him about this book in 2014, reiterating the same thing he told me upon my arrival: "Migrant: it's not a perfect word, but you are one, too." Shukran, *ya akhi*.

I am indebted to countless writers, scholars and artists—many of them queer, many of them (im)migrants—as frequently for their work as for leading lives that made me examine how I operate in the world. My writing drew me primarily to four fields of research, though there is slippage and imperfection simply in attempting to delineate and ascribe neat categories. In the spirit of queerness, I offer below a selection of further reading that informed my writing without a delineation between personal narrative, critical theory, or other forms:

On the Gulf:

Mahdavi, Pardis. *Crossing the Gulf: Love and Family in Migrant Lives*. Stanford University Press, 2016.

Peterson, J. E. (ed.). *The Emergence of the Gulf States: Studies in Modern History*. Bloomsbury Academic, 2016.

Reisz, Todd. *Showpiece City: How Architecture Made Dubai*. Stanford University Press, 2020.

Zahlan, R. Said and Roger Owen. *The Making of the Modern Gulf States: Kuwait, Bahrain, Qatar, the United Arab Emirates and*

Oman. Ithaca Press, 1998.

Vora, Neha. *Impossible Citizens: Dubai's Indian Diaspora.* Duke University Press, 2013.

On Migration, Exclusion, and Belonging:

Mehta, Suketu. *Maximum City.* Knopf, 2004.

Capildeo, Vahni. *Measures of Expatriation.* Carcanet Press, 2016.

Naffis-Sahely, André. *The Promised Land: Poems from Itinerant Life.* Penguin, 2017.

Unnikrishnan, Deepak. *Temporary People.* Restless Books, 2017.

DeParle, Jason. *A Good Provider Is One Who Leaves: One Family and Migration in the 21st Century.* Viking, 2019.

Balance, Christine Bacareza. *Tropical Renditions: Making Musical Scenes in Filipino America.* Duke University Press, 2016.

On Queerness and Sexuality:

Ahmed, Sara. *Queer Phenomenology: Orientations, Objects, Others.* Duke University Press, 2007.

Aldrich, Robert. *Colonialism and Homosexuality.* Routledge, 2003.

Atshan, Sa'ed. *Queer Palestine and the Empire of Critique.* Stanford University Press, 2020.

Boone, Joseph Allen. *The Homoerotics of Orientalism.* Columbia University Press, 2015.

Chisholm, Dianne. *Queer Constellations: Subcultural Space in the Wake of the City.* University of Minnesota Press, 2004.

Chitty, Christopher. *Sexual Hegemony: Statecraft, Sodomy, and Capital in the Rise of the World System.* Duke University Press, 2020.

Edelman, Lee. *No Future: Queer Theory and the Death Drive.* Duke University Press, 2004.

Espinoza, Alex. *Cruising: An Intimate History of a Radical Pastime.* The Unnamed Press, 2019.

Garcia, J. Neil C. *Philippine Gay Culture: Binabae to Bakla, Silahis to MSM.* Hong Kong University Press, 2009.

Gevisser, Mark. *The Pink Line: The World's Queer Frontiers.* Farrar, Straus and Giroux, 2021.

Ghaziani, Amin. *Sex Cultures.* Polity Press, 2016.

Habib, Samra. *We Have Always Been Here: A Queer Muslim Memoir.* Viking, 2019.

Massad, Joseph A. *Desiring Arabs.* University of Chicago Press, 2008.

Muñoz, José E. *Cruising Utopia: The Then and There of Queer Futurity.* New York University Press, 2009.

On Queer Diaspora and the Interplay Between Queerness and Migration:

Carbajal, Alberto Fernández. *Queer Muslim Diasporas in Contemporary Literature and Film.* Manchester University Press, 2019.

Hayes, Jarrod. *Queer Roots for the Diaspora: Ghosts in the Family*

Tree. University of Michigan Press, 2016.

Gopinath, Gayatri. *Unruly Visions: The Aesthetic Practices of Queer Diaspora.* Duke University Press, 2018.

Manalansan, Martin F. *Global Divas: Filipino Gay Men in the Diaspora.* Duke University Press, 2007.

Luibhéid, Eithne, and Cantú, Lionel. *Queer Migrations: Sexuality, U.S. Citizenship, and Border Crossings.* University of Minnesota Press, 2007.

In trying to ease myself into the waters of book publishing, I quickly found myself battling two opposing currents in the form of divergent advice: this book should either be a coming-of-age memoir or a work of strictly reported nonfiction. I have boundless gratitude for my agent, Amelia Atlas, for taking me on and believing not only in the shape of my manuscript as narrative nonfiction but in my career as a writer. Thank you for your steadfast navigation on this journey. My heartfelt thanks also to my UK agent, Sophie Lambert. You're both the dream team.

From our first call, my editor, Michelle Dotter, has believed in both the form and narratives that comprise this book. But more than that: you've demonstrated profound thoughtfulness and respect for the people, communities, and stories I wanted to bring to the page. You've given this book, and me, a profound gift: the assurance that we belong. Thanks also to Chelsea Gibbons and the whole Dzanc team for their enthusiasm, belief, and sheer will.

A big thanks also to my UK editor, Ellie Steel, and publisher, Harvill.

I wrote the majority of this book after arriving in yet another unfamiliar landscape—and most of that while negotiating the isolation of a global pandemic. I'm immensely grateful for the support and community I found through several institutions and remarkable people during this period, especially in the UK.

Thank you to the London Library and the London Library Emerging Writers Programme, the Penguin Random House WriteNow Programme, and the Bothy Project Creative Practitioner Writing Residency for their support. Thanks also to the Society of Authors and the Authors' Foundation, without whose grant this book wouldn't have been possible. And my utmost thanks to my community at the University of Glasgow.

A special thanks to Catherine Cho for early encouragement and professional guidance. Thanks also to my Tin House Summer Workshop and Bread Loaf Writers' Conference workshop groups for their thoughtful feedback, and to both conferences for providing community, camaraderie, and inspiration.

A final word on gratitude for institutions: I'm writing these acknowledgments where I've researched, written, and edited many words in this book: the Brixton Tate Library in London, UK. Public libraries are invaluable community spaces—as well as one of the first places where young people can learn about and imagine themselves into others' ways of living—and this book and I wouldn't be where or who we are today without them.

I'm immensely grateful for the mentors and educators over the years who catalyzed or deepened my interest in storytelling; narrative; the Middle East, North Africa, and South Asia; and language and linguistics. Thanks especially to Susan Orlean, Olivia Birdsall, Nicole Callihan, Pat Hoy, Nader Uthman, Nabil Awadh, Najeeb Aldaghashi, and Zachary Lockman.

My profound gratitude to the people who have solidified and expanded my understanding of what a family can and should be. Moths. Adams. D'Souza. Gloster. McCarthy. Cruver. Owens. Ronan. Wells. Harris. *Thalatha*. "Family and Friends." And everyone who gathered that day in a field in Wisconsin in person or in spirit. Birth, legal, chosen: I love you all.

And then there's Sunil. For your support, faith, humor, patience, direction (I mean in life but you'll assume in wayfinding, which is also often true), and your love. For all this and more: eleven nuances, one for each year that's deepened my understanding of who we can be together. B'luv you always.